An Introduction to Philosophy of Education, 4th Edition

'*Well written, accessible to students with no previous background in philosophy...
an excellent introduction.*'
The Times Higher Education Supplement (on an earlier edition)

What does it mean to be well educated?

In the fourth edition of this best-selling textbook, the authors introduce students to the business of philosophizing, thereby inducting them into the art of reasoning and analysing key concepts in education.

This introductory text is a classic in its field. It shows, first and foremost, the importance of philosophy in educational debate and as a background to any practical activity such as teaching. What is involved in the idea of educating a person or the idea of educational success? What, if anything, can be known and how should we organize what we know for curriculum purposes? What are the criteria for establishing the optimum balance between formal and informal teaching techniques? How trustworthy is educational research? In addition to these questions, which strike to the heart of the rationale for the educative process as a whole, the authors explore such concepts as culture, creativity, autonomy, indoctrination, needs, interests, and learning by discovery.

In this new updated edition, the authors draw on the latest research in genetics to argue that education is uniquely human and is essentially what develops us as humans. Resisting modern tendencies to equate knowledge with opinion, and value judgements with taste, this book leads the reader into the business of philosophizing and champions the cause of reason in education.

Robin Barrow was previously Reader in Philosophy of Education at the University of Leicester, UK; he is currently Professor of Philosophy of Education at Simon Fraser University, British Columbia, Canada where for ten years he was also Dean of Education.

Ronald Woods was until recently Senior Lecturer in Philosophy of Education at the University of Leicester, UK.

Related titles

Philosophy and Educational Policy
A critical introduction
John Gingell and Christopher Winch

Making Sense of Education
An introduction to the philosophy and theory of
education and teaching
David Carr

Spirituality, Philosophy and Education
David Carr and John Haldane

The authors are grateful to *Educational Philosophy and Theory* for permission to make use of some material originally published in that journal.

An Introduction to Philosophy of Education, 4th Edition

Robin Barrow and Ronald Woods

4th edition revised by Robin Barrow

Routledge
Taylor & Francis Group

LONDON AND NEW YORK

First published in 1975 by Methuen & Co.
Second edition 1982
Third edition in 1988 by Routledge

Fourth edition published 2006
by Routledge
2 Park Square, Milton Park, Abingdon, Oxon OX14 4RN

Simultaneously published in the USA and Canada
by Routledge
270 Madison Ave, New York, NY 10016

Reprinted 2006, 2007

Routledge is an imprint of the Taylor & Francis Group, an informa business

© 1975, 1982, 1988, 2006 Robin Barrow and Ronald Woods

Typeset in Times New Roman by
Newgen Imaging Systems (P) Ltd, Chennai, India

British Library Cataloguing in Publication Data
A catalogue record for this book is available from the British Library

Library of Congress Cataloging in Publication Data
A catalog record for this book has been requested

ISBN10: 0–415–38127–4 (hbk)
ISBN10: 0–415–38126–6 (pbk)
ISBN10: 0–203–96995–2 (ebk)

ISBN13: 978–0–415–38127–7 (hbk)
ISBN13: 978–0–415–38126–0 (pbk)
ISBN13: 978–0–203–96995–3 (ebk)

Contents

Preface

Philosophers sometimes refer to a ship that needs repairs over the course of a long voyage, in order to illustrate certain problems or questions about identity. The wooden ship leaves harbour and, while at sea, certain planks have to be replaced. A short time later some others have to be replaced; a few days after that, some more; and so on, until by the journey's end all the planks that went to make up the original ship have been replaced. Is this the ship that was originally put to sea or an entirely different one? Whatever the answer to that question, this book is beginning to resemble that ship.

Since the launching of the first edition in 1975 five completely new chapters have been added, one has been thrown overboard, and the remaining text has been subjected to repeated overhaul. Nonetheless, I hope it can be said that the book remains recognizably the same one that Ron Woods and I set out to write thirty years ago. That is to say, I hope that it still provides a helpful introduction to the business of philosophizing in the sense of engaging in conceptual analysis and coherent reasoning about education, while providing a plausible answer to some specific educational questions and establishing at any rate the groundwork of an argument for a particular view of what education is all about and what it therefore demands of us.

In this revision, three new chapters entitled, respectively, 'Thinking about Education', 'What is it to be Human?' and 'The Postmodern Challenge' have been added. 'Thinking about Education' attempts to set the stage by briefly examining the context in which philosophical thought about education operates, stressing in particular the rational tradition in Western thought to which philosophical analysis belongs, and the wider concerns of schooling of which education is merely a part, albeit, it will be argued, the major part. It seems important also to address the question 'What is it to be Human?' in view of much recent research, particularly in genetics, and in order to locate education as a peculiarly human activity. It seemed necessary to add the brief chapter on 'The Postmodern Challenge' not in order to address any theses associated with any particular individuals, but to combat the stultifying effect of certain propositions, such as that there is no truth or that nothing can be known, which, rightly or wrongly, are often classified as postmodern in tenor and which, if accepted, would undermine the key foundations not only of the positive educational argument of this book but also of the philosophical activity that it is concerned with. The chapter on 'Understanding' of previous editions has been dropped, not because we do not continue to believe that education is primarily and essentially about understanding, but because a great deal of the overall text is concerned directly and indirectly with issues to do with understanding and knowledge, and, given a need to cut something at the publishers' behest, it was felt that a direct examination of what 'understanding' means could be foregone. Beyond these major changes, the bibliography has been brought up to date and the remaining text has been subjected to various fairly minor revisions and one or two paragraph length additions.

I should like to conclude with a comment on the updating of references and examples. I have, by and large, attempted to bring specific examples of, for example, films up to date, so that the 'Straw Dogs' of 1975, which became 'The Texas Chainsaw Massacre' of 1988, now becomes 'Crash'. This is simply to help the majority of readers recognize the reference! And though, for example, a few references to the game of Bingo are retained, because as a matter of fact for a period educational philosophers used it as an iconic example and argued about its specifically educational potential, most of them have been replaced by reference to, for example, video-games, since clearly it is the latter that represent a potential challenge to education today rather than Bingo. But, and this is important, by and large the philosophical references – the author cited, the arguments explored – have not been changed.

A very minor reason for this is that after discussion with the publisher it was agreed to produce a new edition of this work rather than a new introduction to philosophy of education altogether, since, strange as it may be, this book has proven itself capable of weathering changes of fashion and focus over time. If all the topics and the arguments relating to them had been brought up to date, drawing on new material written exclusively in the last ten years, then clearly it would not have been a new edition; it would have been a new book – a different ship.

A major reason is related to the original aim of the book: to introduce the business of philosophizing about education. To that end, provided the examples are not so foreign as to be incomprehensible to the reader, it really doesn't matter what issues, what authors, or what arguments one uses, since the primary purpose is to illustrate philosophy in action and to have material on which to practice (i.e. get thinking). That reason would be sufficient to justify continuing to examine, for example, Peters' work on the concept of education or Hirst's work on forms of knowledge. Indeed, in the latter case, Hirst himself, if he hasn't actually repudiated his original thesis, has certainly moved way beyond it. But that does not stop it still being an intriguing and persuasive thesis, and one which may serve as an excellent way of introducing the question of the nature of knowledge and the significance of the question for curriculum.

But sufficient though that reason alone would be, I must in honesty add one more. While philosophy of education continues to thrive, not very much has been done in recent years that really adds to the primary analytic work done thirty to forty years ago, at least at a basic level. If I look at a recent issue of the *Journal of Philosophy of Education*, for example, I see a number of excellent articles, but none of them speak to the issues in this book. This is not to set the stage for a confrontation between different types and styles of philosophy. It is simply to say that this book is predicated on the belief that it is desirable that all teachers and educators should recognize the importance of, and become reasonably adept at, analysing the key concepts in education; that, and secondarily suggesting a particular view of what such analysis leads us to recognize as genuinely educational, is what this book is about, and most of the work focused on that was indeed done some years ago. Does this make the book old fashioned? No. This – analysing the key educational concepts – is something that each generation has to do for itself anew.

Robin Barrow
Vancouver
2005

Foreword

This Foreword consists of the Prefaces to the second and third editions, which are retained largely for historical reasons. Apart from registering when various specific changes and additions were made, they provide a record of the continual debate among philosophers as to the precise nature of analysis, and remind us of the constant need for those who are committed to the view of rationality that underpins this book to defend it against those who, however incoherently, seem to question it, whether in the name of relativism, nihilism, Marxism, sociology of knowledge, or postmodernism.

Preface to second edition

The invitation from our publishers to update and revise our *Introduction to Philosophy of Education* gives rise to the question of the nature of philosophy, for it is not the kind of subject that dates in the way that physics or even history may do. There are revolutionary thinkers in philosophy who open up entirely new paths of inquiry, but they are exceedingly rare, and even they do not often falsify the past so much as move away from it. Philosophy is less about generating knowledge of new matters than about providing greater understanding of what we are already familiar with. Seldom are there new discoveries or new interpretations that make previous work in the field unacceptable. What, for example, Plato had to say about love or justice over two thousand years ago has not been invalidated, replaced, or rendered obsolete by the work, of, say Wittgenstein in the last century. Plato's writings really do have as much pertinence today to the questions with which they are concerned as any contemporary work, in a way that the writings of early Greek doctors or scientists, for all their intrinsic interest, do not. There can of course be specific criticism in philosophy that shows arguments thought to have been sound to be untenable, but that kind of shift of view scarcely applies at the level of an introductory text.

Out initial aim was to provide an introduction to the business of philosophizing in the context of educational problems; in line with that aim we concentrated on pursuing an examination of the main concepts in the domain of education (or, as I should now prefer to say, schooling, since I take education to be merely one of many possible concerns of school, although most of the topics treated here are to do with the more specific concept of education). The intention was to conduct a rigorous investigation of the ideas of education, knowledge, culture, etc., so that a fuller picture of them and a greater awareness of the implications of each concept would emerge, or sometimes, so that the inadequacy of an idea or slogan might be exposed. In so far as what we originally wrote was to the point and coherent, the passing of time – at any rate, so brief a period of time – does not much affect it. If there was the logical possibility of distinguishing between influence generally and indoctrination specifically five years ago, there will be still. If our conception of education involved knowledge and understanding then, it does now in all probability. If the creativity of a Beethoven was distinct from the self-expression of a young child last year, there will be good reason to maintain that distinction this year. So, in design and broad outline this edition retains the format and flavour of the first, not because we are complacent, but because material changes in the world do not often affect conceptual truths and points of logic.

None the less some changes have been made. First, there are a number of small but not insignificant stylistic alterations; and a number of grammatical infelicities have been corrected. Allusions and references have in many places been brought up to date: nothing dates quite as obviously as the name of a defunct pop group or a forgotten political event. Examples, too, have sometimes been brought up to date, although here again it must be remembered that the function of examples in philosophy is very often such that neither their being up to date nor their practical likelihood matters very much. For instance, when a philosopher considers whether a historian who knows nothing other than history should be considered as educated, he is not interested in the likelihood of there actually being such a person, but in whether, *if* there was, he would count as educated. He is interested in what might intelligibly be conceived, more than in what happens to be the case in the physical world. It is important to realize at the outset that examples are used for the purpose of testing logical possibilities rather than actual probabilities in order to avoid the mistake of assuming that philosophers are out of touch with the everyday world. When we ask whether a person could be in two places at the same time, we are not questioning the possibility of a physical body such as yours or mine being entirely in Oxford while also being entirely in Cambridge; rather we are raising the question of the senses in which a person might conceivably be said to be in two places at the same time. (Suppose your body minus your heart is in Oxford, but your heart is keeping another body alive in Cambridge.) In other words we are really raising the question of what constitutes being a person, and not asking about material factors in the everyday world at all. When we ask whether an individual could be considered creative if he were to spill paint accidentally onto canvas in such a way as to produce a beautiful pattern, we are not concerned with whether anyone has done or might do such a thing, but with throwing light on what is involved in the notion of being creative. (Again, *if* someone did that, would we classify it as a creative act?) Likewise, nobody that I know of would behave in some of the ways used as examples in the chapter on rationality in this book, but to consider examples, however bizarre, allows us to fill in the details of, or to question, our conceptions. (Incidentally, one reference that I have not bothered to update is that made to the launching of the first sputniks. It is true that some readers may not have heard of sputniks, but in terms of technological breakthrough, which is the point of the reference, some of the early steps in the space race represent more significant achievements than later, more dramatic steps. For that reason the example does not need bringing up to date, and for that reason younger readers ought to be presented with it.)

Once or twice changes in our own thinking brought about by thought and discussion and with the passing of time have necessitated alterations to the substance of an argument. Or issues to which we were not previously alert, such as the widespread immoral treatment of animals, have impinged on our consciences and required a mention. However, such changes in substantive content are not extensive, if only because, while the original text was the work of two of us, this revision has been solely my responsibility.

The main weakness of the original edition, in my view, was that we did not draw a very clear distinction between words and concepts or between verbal and conceptual analysis. More simply, we did not, perhaps, make it entirely clear what we took philosophical analysis to involve. In particular, we made a number of references to 'linguistic usage' and to 'objectivity' and 'correctness', without making it clear to what extent linguistic usage *determines* conceptual meaning (as opposed to reflects it, coincides with it, influences it, etc.), and without explaining in what senses of the words an analysis can be said to be 'objective' and/or 'correct'. On this broad but vitally important matter of methodology Woods and I have, we think, slightly different views although we have never satisfactorily resolved wherein the difference lies. This may partially explain the slight vagueness, not to say odd sign of tension, about our procedure in the previous edition.

I have argued extensively elsewhere that although there are a number of very important questions to be asked about verbal matters (the features and functions of words and our use of them), it is important to distinguish them from conceptual questions.[1] Questions about linguistic usage may lead to illuminating answers of direct relevance to conceptual issues, and should therefore be asked by philosophers. But none the less they are distinct from questions about concepts as such, and should therefore not be the philosopher's only interest. As words and concepts are not identical, so linguistic analysis cannot be coextensive with conceptual analysis. We may ask how people tend to use the word 'educated' and that will certainly throw light upon what is generally involved in being educated, at any rate as conceived by our culture. We may find that all people use the term in exactly the same away, or we may find that, despite variations, there is a common core to all uses of the word. Consequently we might, if we chose, talk of a correct or objective sense of the word 'educated' (i.e. the sense of the word sanctioned by usage in our culture). But such linguistic exercises, though they may in some cases incidentally reveal all that there is to be said about the concept behind the word (the idea behind the label), do not necessarily do so, and in fact are less likely to do so in proportion to the complexity and sophistication of the idea in question. Two problems, at least, may very likely remain – problems that need tackling and which very obviously belong to the domain of philosophy: people may use a word in widely different ways, sometimes to the point at which there does not appear to be even a common core, and people's use of a term may fail to reveal a clear and coherent conception on its own terms. Thus 'educated' might conceivably mean something quite different for two people (in which case we are dealing with distinct concepts labelled with the same word), and anybody's notion of being educated, including one's own, might just be insufficiently clarified and worked out. I should be strongly inclined to conclude that talk of a correct or objective concept is therefore meaningless, unless one merely means a widely shared concept. One may reasonably ask whether my use of the word 'educated' is correct according to standard practice in my culture, but the question to ask about my concept of being educated is how well formulated or articulated it is.

The task of the philosopher, having taken what hints and clues he can from linguistic patterns, is to arrive at a set of clear, coherent, and specific concepts. We need to clarify our concepts in order to asses them; until we painstakingly spell out what we understand by being educated we can say nothing about it, and obviously our unpacking must lead to a clear exposition, so we know that we are saying something and what it is. Coherence is necessary, both within and between concepts, so that our ideas make sense and can stand up: we do not want a conception of being educated that when clearly articulated turns out to be self-contradictory or to carry with it implications that we cannot for one reason or another accept. Specificity is necessary in order to facilitate talk with teeth in it. That is to say, in order to be able to make telling comments on the world, in order to gain a fuller understanding, one needs to develop an armoury of specific as opposed to general concepts. The ability to discriminate between the various species of a genus, in any field, rather than to see the world only in terms of genera, represents power when it comes to knowledge.[2]

In line with the distinction referred to between words and concepts, the device of using quotation marks round single words or phrases, rather overworked in the first edition and not adopted consistently, has here been systematized. When the word is being referred to, quotation marks are used; when the concept is being referred to, they are not used. Thus we discuss the logical features of knowledge, but the emotive force of the word 'knowledge'. Occasionally quotation marks are also used as 'sneer quotes' to suggest an ironic or otherwise not quite literal use of a word or phrase.

Another change I considered was that of replacing the generic use of the word 'he' (to mean 'a person') by 'she' or by some newly coined neutral term. But I rejected this in the end on the grounds that correct English provides us with the word 'he' meaning 'a person of either sex', and it would be more appropriate for the few who do not appreciate this to learn it, than for the rest of us to devise new terminology. To replace 'he' by 'she', as some authors now do, seems the worst of all worlds and a good example of the incoherence of what is sometimes termed 'reverse discrimination'. If 'he' were an immoral or otherwise unacceptable usage, then so must the use of 'she' be immoral, as well as incorrect.[3]

One or two additional comments, sometimes substantive, have been made, but economic factors have necessitated that most of them be added as notes at the end of the chapter in question.

But what, the novice may ask, about the effect of recent currents of thought and shifts of ideology and perspective? Marxism, for instance, has made great inroads in the philosophy of education in Australia since this book was first written. In Britain in the same period interest in phenomenology and existentialism has increased. In the study of education a number of sociological critiques have tried to suggest that the type of philosophy here practised is just one more class-based act of special pleading. Should not these and other similar tides of thought be reflected in some way in a new edition? The simple answer is, no. The various movements, ideologies, and methodological critiques that come and go are attempts to interpret the world in one particular way. They are therefore to be contrasted with, rather than opposed to, a book such as this which does not seek to explain the whole field of education, let alone the world or human experience, but to contribute to a greater understanding of some ideas and arguments related to education.[4]

Of course some work in other fields does suggest criticism of our methodology. Some, for instance, have argued, though quite unconvincingly, that knowledge is a *purely* social construct, and that our attempt to be detached and objective is necessarily but one more socially determined pose. Others, more reasonably, have made points to the effect that our procedure is in various ways less value neutral than we might wish. These latter kinds of criticism, involving argument directly related to certain practices or assumptions, are fair comment and, in so far as they are convincingly argued, to be taken note of. But a general sociological thesis, presented without reference to the arguments of particular philosophers, to the effect that the would-be autonomous and independent-minded philosopher is actually inevitably the product of his social environment, no more requires a philosophical rejoinder or the abandonment of philosophical practice, than a Freudian account of why an individual seeks love in the ways he does obliges the lover to start loving in a new way. It is, incidentally, most unfortunate that, given this quite common tendency to fail to see the difference between sociological attempts to explain, psychological types of explanation, philosophical inquiry, and historical accounts of events, and the consequent tendency to believe any one of them to be more significant than it is, we have for the most part failed to institutionalize the study of at least these four subjects as crucial to the study of education. Had we done so with more success there might be fewer people around who believe that to explain why somebody believes something in sociological terms is to dispense with the question of whether the belief is reasonable. (At the University of Leicester, while preaching the importance of the disciplines, we have in fact moved from requiring students to study all four ten years ago, through a period of requiring that they study only one, to a state in which they study two. This is to be welcomed, I suppose, on the grounds that half a loaf is better than none. But the adage is misleading. When the point of the exercise is to develop in people a capacity to recognize logically different aspects of a matter, giving people awareness of only half the possibilities is more like giving them half a sixpence than half a loaf.)

It was, then, never the purpose of philosophy (our conception of it, that is) or a book such as this to offer to interpret the world. Its aim was, and remains, 'to attempt to show philosophy in action' with 'the stress on how to do philosophy'. For this reason it is of secondary importance what particular concepts and arguments are focused upon. We might have elected to add chapters on topical themes, but to have done so would only have been to reduplicate work done elsewhere. As to the original issues we chose to discuss, it is difficult to see how a philosopher of education could not but throw out at least passing reference to education, understanding, and knowledge, and we still believe that rationality, culture, creativity, indoctrination, and the notions of readiness, discovery, needs, and wants (collected together in Chapter 10), deserve to be carefully considered by any prospective teacher.

Robin Barrow
University of Leicester
1982

Notes

1 See in particular my *The Philosophy of Schooling* and 'Five Commandments for the Eighties' in *Educational Analysis*, ed. Barrow, R. vol. 4, no. 1, 1982.
2 See Barrow, R., *Injustice, Inequality and Ethics* (Brighton, Wheatsheaf, 1982) ch. 1.
3 On this topic, see further Barrow, R., op. cit. [For the third edition I have left this paragraph and left the generic 'he' in the body of the text. I regonize, however, that, rightly or wrongly, I am likely to lose this argument in practice, in the long run.]
4 [But note, since these words were first written, a recent review of the author's *Critical Dictionary of Educational Concepts*, which refers to an 'individualistic lack of interest in the social dimension'. *Times Higher Education Supplement*, 29 May 1987.]

Preface to third edition

In the Preface to the second edition of this book I wrote 'At the University of Leicester, while preaching the importance of the [foundation] disciplines, we have in fact moved from requiring students to study all four [philosophy, psychology, history, and sociology]..., through a period of requiring that they study only one, to a state in which they study two.' Time passes, and now Leicester, in common with many other departments of education, requires nothing in the way of disciplined academic study. Indeed, both Ron Woods and myself, in common with other theoretically inclined educationalists, have now left the University of Leicester, nor is it likely that we will be replaced.

That, as some readers may appreciate, is about par for the course. It is particularly gratifying, therefore, to be invited to produce a third edition of this *Introduction to Philosophy of Education*, at a time when philosophy departments in universities are being closed down and education departments are all too often turning their backs on anything except 'hands on' courses dictated by government (to what good purpose we have yet to be told). The fact is not only that having some adequate grasp of philosophy is essential for making sense of daily educational activity, and sorting out the coherent from the absurd, but also that, *mirabile dictu*, there is a market for it!

Mention of the previous Preface brings me on to the point that Woods, who is now happily cultivating his garden both literally and metaphorically, and who for that reason left the preparation of this edition to me, has none the less voiced an opinion on that Preface. He thinks that it should be omitted from this edition. 'I cannot think', he writes, 'that a rarefied dispute about philosophic techniques is of interest to anyone except people like you and me – and we are rare!' He is referring to the comments made there about the distinction between words and concepts, and he may well have a point, at least so far as the manner of drawing attention to that issue goes. None the less, I have retained the Preface, including the passage in question, though with a few modifications and omissions. This is because, in my judgement, the question of what philosophical analysis is – what one is trying to analyse, why and how – is supremely important. It is obviously important theoretically since an understanding of what one is about must have some effect on the doing of it. But it is also important in practical terms, since lack of competent philosophizing in educational contexts is due partly to ignorance of what is involved.

In particular, many, if not most, people still seem to equate analysing a concept with defining a word in the sense of attempting to provide some verbally synonymous phrase for the word in question. The Preface to the second edition draws attention to the view that (i) philosophical analysis is ultimately concerned with the clear and coherent articulation of ideas rather than with definitions of words (although the latter may have a part to play in contributing to the former), and (ii) consequently, so-called ordinary language philosophy and linguistic analysis can be at best only part of the business of philosophy. To illustrate this as succinctly as possible: while our style of philosophy here is indeed closely associated with the clear use of everyday language, the book is not concerned simply with attempting to tabulate how people generally use such words as 'education', 'creativity', and 'culture'. Rather it is concerned with trying to explicate and unfold ideas or concepts such as those of education, creativity, and culture.[1] The object is to explore and iron out obscurities, contradictions, confusions, absurdities, and so forth that may be involved in particular people's hazy grasp of the ideas in question, rather than to say how various words either should be or are used.

What Ron Woods will feel about this tenacity on my part, I do not know. But I do wish to take this opportunity to record my affection and admiration for him. He is, *au fond*, a very private man, but he was a fine colleague and I miss him a great deal professionally.

In this edition I have made minor revisions throughout and updated the Bibliography (which incidentally was previously inaccurately and absurdly called 'a comprehensive bibliography of worthwhile writing in the field' – it was not comprehensive, nor is it now; furthermore, some indubitably worthwhile writing was not mentioned, and some of what was mentioned was not obviously worthwhile). But the major change is to be found in the addition of two completely new chapters (Chapters 3 [5] and 11 [13] on 'Curriculum Theory' and 'Research into Teaching', respectively).

These chapters are not in quite the same mould as the rest of the book. The original chapters are all concerned with the analysis or elucidation of a concept (or concepts), with the aim, as was stated in the introduction, 'to attempt to show philosophy in action' with 'the stress on how to do philosophy'. While the new chapters do add a little to the general discussion of conceptual analysis (including some quite important points referred to but not illustrated in the Preface to the second edition), they are more concerned with claims about the confusion and logical incoherence of much of the current practice in the domains of curriculum and empirical educational research.

Curriculum is a branch of educational study that has come into its own more or less as institutional interest in philosophy has declined. This seems to me very sad. (And I suspect the change in their official fortunes is connected. Work in curriculum very often looks like a combination of bad philosophy and bad science, but it's very much easier to pass oneself off as a curriculum expert than a competent philosopher.) If curriculum is a relatively flourishing area, empirical research is rapidly becoming a *sine qua non* of respectability. Lecturers and professors are increasingly evaluated by reference to the amount of grant money they bring into a department (even if it is quite literally wasted) rather than by reference to an estimate of the wisdom they purvey. Yet, as I shall argue, a great deal of empirical research in education is misconceived, inappropriate, and quite simply irrelevant to advancing our understanding of the educational enterprise and thereby contributing to good practice.

I hope that the new chapters do not upset the pattern and the flow of the book as a whole too much. But it seems to me that philosophers should be applying themselves more than they sometimes have in the past to the practices and assumptions of those around them, that it is important in an introductory text to draw attention to the huge practical value of philosophy (as pinpointing, and hence allowing one to avoid, gross folly of one sort or another), and that their addition should therefore improve the utility of the book in respect of courses in education departments.

I toyed with the idea of cutting out some of the original chapters, as I did when preparing the second edition, but again felt disinclined to do so. Some of the words that form the chapter headings may be less in vogue than they once were, but the concepts and the issues surrounding them are quite certainly still around. For example, people do not actually say 'I believe in child-centred education' in the dewy-eyed way they did in the innocent 1960s and early 1970s. None the less, and whatever words they use, plenty of people do still emphasize the importance of children's needs, interests, and readiness and other features that once were referred to as the tenets of child-centred education; and furthermore they act in the light of their beliefs about such things. Consequently, it is as important as ever to get individuals to think more closely and carefully about these concepts and others that are discussed in Chapter 8 [10], but it is no longer entitled 'Child-Centred Education'. Similarly, 'creativity' may not be on educators' lips to the extent that it was when the book first appeared, but creativity tests are still an integral part of such things as empirical research into teaching quality, and a very large number of teachers, particularly at the primary or elementary school level, still proceed to put an inordinate amount of time and effort into what are hazily thought to be creative activities.

Of course, the fact that educationalists in general are still concerned with certain concepts does not necessarily mean that philosophers are. A case in points is provided by indoctrination. With the exception of my good friend Tasos Kazepides, philosophers have more or less stopped writing on the concept, because so much was written (a lot of it very good stuff) in the 1960s. But the issue of indoctrination is obviously still very much with us – one thinks of the upsurge of fundamentalism and creationist legislation in America, the recent trial of a teacher in Canada who maintains that the holocaust did not exist, and some of the 'educational' aspirations of the Department of Education and Science in Britain[2] – and in a textbook such as this it is therefore right and proper to study the concept.

There are certainly some omissions that might ideally be rectified. For example, there is no chapter on intelligence, which, quite apart from the fact that IQ tests are still with us and that the vogue word 'giftedness' at times seems a mere synonym for it, is surely one of the basic or key concepts of the educational enterprise. I decided against adding something on this particular topic, because I think that ideally it requires a fuller, book-length, treatment. (Within the limits of a chapter, a useful analysis is provided by John Kleinig in his *Philosophical Issues in Education*.) But more generally, having flipped through my own recent *Critical Dictionary of Educational Concepts*[3] for possible ideas, I decided against any attempts to cover the ground more thoroughly than we did initially. Philosophy is not about jumping on each passing wagon. The educational philosopher's task is to select the seemingly central or key concepts, those that help to constitute and organize his field, and stick with them.

In short, I am back with the contention that whatever one's particular views may be, anybody who professes to be able to talk reasonably about education and to proceed in practical term in ways that can be shown to be reasonable, will need to be able to show that he has a pretty good grasp of such concepts as education, understanding, indoctrination, rationality, culture, needs, interest, and wants, which in one way or another are central to the enterprise in question. Such concepts remain the core of this book.

Robin Barrow
Vancouver
1988

Notes

1 Throughout the book we continue to use inverted commas when referring to a word (e.g. 'gay' is a confusing word), but not when referring to the concept (e.g. many gays are sad).
2 I have in mind the charge that some would make, to the effect that recent initiatives combine to transmit the values of free enterprise and industry as if they were uncontentious. One might add the concern of some that such subjects as peace studies and sex education may become exercises in indoctrination.
3 Barrow, R. and Milburn, G., *A Critical Dictionary of Educational Concepts* (Brighton, Wheatsheaf, 1986).

Introduction

This book is intended as an introduction to philosophy of education for students in colleges and university departments of education who have had little or no previous instruction in philosophical methods and techniques. We shall, therefore, be at pains to explain as clearly and as accurately as is necessary any technical or semi-technical terms introduced in the course of the exposition. There will not, as a matter of fact, be many such terms and readers need have no fear that we shall blind them with jargon. Anyone with a modicum of common sense who is prepared to exercise thought should find no great difficulty in understanding what we have to say, always provided that he or she comes to the book with an open mind and not predisposed to regard philosophy as an essentially esoteric and difficult study capable of mastery by only a few gifted individuals.

The aim of this book is not to provide readers with information on a set of topics for regurgitation in an examination, but rather to attempt to show philosophy in action. Of course, we believe in what we have positively to say; but the stress is on how to do philosophy. Hence we have not attempted to review the literature in the field, and the topics chosen for analysis are, in a sense, simply vehicles for the exercise of philosophizing. One of our main objects will have been achieved if we can help readers to become more skilful at philosophical debate, able to think about and discuss in a philosophic manner issues which they have not met before and on which they have not read what other philosophers have to say. We should like to contribute to making philosophers in ways specified by John Wisdom (adding the rider that the second way to which Wisdom refers is not, to our mind, quite so inadequate as he implies):

> In a sense, philosophy cannot be taught – any more than one can teach riding or dancing or musical appreciation. However, philosophers can be made. They can be made in two ways, namely by practice and by precept. The first method is the one usually adopted by lecturers in

philosophy or performing philosophers. They themselves perform philosophic antics in front of their students, interlarded with anecdotes about the antics of contemporary performers. This is called giving a course in modern philosophy. Or, they tell stories about performers of the past: then they are giving a course in the history of philosophy. Sometimes their students are able to imitate these performances; they are the 'good students'. The second method of making philosophers, namely, the precept method, has not been much used. This is because even good philosophers have been confused about what it is they are trying to do, and have been, like many good riders, unable to say what it is about their methods which makes them good.[1]

But if philosophizing is a skill, then as with skills generally probably the best way to get people to command the philosophic skills is to insist on their being practised, and this will involve writing and talking philosophy, having one's arguments and conclusions subjected to the criticism of one's peers and tutors, having to defend one's arguments, and so on.[2] Obviously, simply to read this book is not to engage in these sorts of activity, and hence *pari passu* with the reading must go talk and discussion. No opportunity should be lost to follow up the arguments deployed in the ensuing chapters in conversation with others, for not only will this result in increased expertise but it will lead also to an increasing realization that anyone who is prepared to take time and trouble can come to advance ideas, theories, and arguments *of his own* as opposed simply to repeating parrot-fashion, the ideas, theories, and arguments of others. This brings us back to the suggestion that philosophy is not to be thought of as a fixed body of information waiting to be digested but as an activity through the exercise of which men and women can think things through, in concert with others, for themselves. In this connection the following description of the existentialist notion of 'inauthentic existence' is, perhaps, pertinent, although the reader would do well to discount the portentous theological overtones:

A man who is leading an inauthentic existence is in a condition of *Verfallensein*. He is in a fallen state.... Such a man ignores the reality of his own relation to the world. There is an ambiguity in his dealing with reality. He partly knows what things are, but partly does not, because he is so entirely caught up in the way other people see them, the labels attached to them by the world at large. He cannot straightforwardly form any opinion, and his statements are partly his own, partly those of people in general....

It may be that a man can go through the whole of his life in the inauthentic state, and he may never emerge from it. But reflection may bring his attention to the true state of affairs and may open his eyes to his position in the world, which is above all a position of responsibility. Realizing, that is, the uniqueness of his position as a human being, he may see the force of his own reflective capacity, namely that he and he alone is responsible for the world's having significance.[3]

Although we shall deal with any technical philosophical points as and when they come up in the text, it is appropriate at this point to make one or two observations about philosophy in general and about philosophy of education in particular. A fair amount of talk is heard these days about the sterility of philosophical analysis, about how it is that once upon a time philosophers used to debate fundamental questions concerning God, Freedom, and Immortality until one day hard-headed, tough men called logical positivists came along and said that all such debates were nonsense. Really, talk of this kind is somewhat superficial and inaccurate. There are very good grounds for thinking that a philosopher worthy of the name *must* indulge in a certain amount of analysis or to put it another way, *must* have regard to the meaning of words and concepts. Further, a great deal of evidence can be adduced to support the contention that this concern with meaning is not a recent phenomenon – that it did not first appear on the scene in the 1930s but has always been a part of the tradition of philosophizing, at least as far as the Western world is concerned. Thus, consider this passage from Plato's *Republic*:

'What you say, Cephalus, is excellent.' I said. 'But as to this justice, can we quite without qualification define it as truthfulness and repayment of anything that we have received; or are these very actions sometimes just and sometimes unjust? For example, if we have been given weapons by a friend when he was of sound mind, and he went mad and reclaimed them, it would surely be universally admitted that it would not be right to give them back. Any one who did so, and who was prepared to tell the whole truth to a man in that state, would not be just.'
'You are right.' he said.
Then this is not the definition of justice – speaking the truth and restoring what we have received.[4]

This passage makes it quite clear that one of the things Plato was up to in the *Republic* was to get at the meaning of justice, and this concern on his part links him directly with a great many contemporary philosophers, for as Gilbert Ryle observes, 'The story of twentieth-century philosophy is very largely the story of this notion of sense or meaning.'[5] What is true of Plato, incidentally, is true also of many other distinguished philosophers of the past.

Readers must not, then, be surprised to find that we engage in a certain amount of analysis in this book, and that we spend some time trying to ferret out meaning of one kind or another. Note that we say 'of one kind or another'. For most people dictionaries spring to mind when meaning is mentioned and the kind of meaning that dictionaries are commonly thought to trade in is what might be called 'verbal equivalence'; for example, 'quadruped' means 'four-footed animal'; the meaning of an unfamiliar word is given in terms of other words with which we are familiar. Now, for philosophic purposes meaning as verbal equivalence is an inadequate conception and it is necessary – particularly, as we shall see, as far as philosophy *of education* is concerned – to recognize other kinds of meaning and to recognize the possibility of one kind being mistaken for another. The matter is of sufficient importance to merit detailed treatment here and now.

It was Wittgenstein who drew attention to the connection between the meaning of words and their use and hence to the connection between different kinds of meaning and different uses of language. Thus, consider the seemingly fact-stating statement, 'Education consists of moulding individuals into obedient members of the state'. A moment's reflection shows that this statement is not a statement of fact but gives utterance to an evaluation – 'Education *ought* to consist of...' – on the part of the person making it. We need, then, to distinguish fact-stating language (we shall refer to it as the descriptive use of language) from the evaluative use of language. Further, we shall also need to say something about the emotive use of language, a use which is not unconnected with the evaluative use. Briefly, then, the descriptive use of language, or descriptive meaning for short, is concerned with supplying information about things in the world. For example, 'This book is on the table by the lamp', 'Snow is white', 'Jones is the new Professor of Astronomy' and so on.

Simple classification resting ultimately upon awareness of similarities and dissimilarities between objects and properties plays a large part in this use of language. We can get a little clearer about the nature of descriptive meaning by comparing it with emotive meaning. If someone, when asked how long the film 'Crash' lasted, said 'It lasted just over 1 1/2 hours', then this would be justly characterized as a descriptive statement. But if, when asked what he thought of the film, he said 'It was a sickening, disgusting piece', then it might well be justifiably claimed that in saying this he was giving vent to his feelings – he felt sick and full of disgust. Hence because of the reference to his, the speaker's, feelings, this utterance is classified as an instance of the emotive use of language. Further, suppose he said of 'Crash', 'It wasn't a particularly good film', and at the time of saying this had no feelings about the film at all, then it could be claimed justifiably that he was evaluating the film, attempting to rate or grade it in comparison with other films. If you like he was indulging in cool, dispassionate evaluation, where the words 'cool' and 'dispassionate' suggest complete absence of feelings of love or hate and suggest an attempt on his part to be, as we say, objective.

Now let us complicate matters slightly. Our hypothetical 'he' says, evaluatively, of 'Crash', 'It wasn't a particularly good film', but this statement of his has a strong, emotive, effect on the girl to whom he is talking. She is *upset* by his remark. This simple example brings out the fact that speakers *and* listeners are involved in discourse and hence that the same statement can be justifiably classified as evaluative as far as the speaker is concerned but as emotive as far as the listener is concerned. Hence the remark in the last paragraph to the effect that the emotive and evaluative uses of language are connected. All sorts of interesting possibilities now arise. As we have seen, an evaluative statement (speaker) may have an emotive effect (listener). Further, an emotive statement (speaker) may have no emotive effect (listener) but may simply be interpreted by the listener as an evaluation on the part of the speaker. Thus, the statement (emotive) to the effect that 'Crash' is a sickening, disgusting piece is interpreted by the listener as meaning that the film is not rated at all highly and he simply discounts the emotive impact of the words. Again, without feeling strongly for or against something, someone may want, for some reason or other, to make other people feel strongly against that something. Hence strongly charged emotive words are deliberately chosen in order to bring about the desired effect in the audience. And so on.

One final point here on the interrelations between descriptive, evaluative, and emotive meaning. If, as was suggested above, the evaluative use of language (speaker) betokens some concern with objectivity in the sense of saying what things are really like, then what is the difference between the evaluative and descriptive uses of language in that description must surely be concerned with saying what things are really like? The answer to this would seem to lie in the fact that, in general, the question 'Why?' can sensibly and legitimately be posed about a given evaluative utterance whereas this question is not appropriate in the case of a descriptive utterance. For example, 'Why?' in response to the descriptive statement 'Snow is white', is puzzling. Snow just *is* white. But the same is not true of 'Why?' in response to the evaluative statement, ' "Crash" is a good film'. All that 'Why?' does here is to demand the reasons for rating the film as good, and this is not at all puzzling.

The distinction between descriptive and evaluative/emotive meaning is one that finds application in several branches of philosophy and perhaps most particularly in philosophy of education. This is not really very surprising when we remember that much educational talk is shot through with considerations to do with value. As Max Black puts it: 'All serious discussion of educational problems, no matter how specific, soon leads to a consideration of educational *aims*, and becomes a conversation about the good life, the nature of man, the varieties of experience.'[6] This being so, educational discourse will provide us with endless examples of the evaluative/emotive uses of language and the sooner we recognize the main language use categories for what they are, the better. This book, simply because it is partly concerned with the analysis and critical appraisal of *educational* arguments, will give ample opportunity for the reader to treat his ability to distinguish the categories.

Meaning, then, is quite properly going to be part of our concern in the following chapters. Additionally we shall engage in critical evaluation of other people's arguments, looking to see if they are valid or invalid, trying to see what the arguments presuppose or assume, and so on. These sorts of activity are traditionally part of the philosopher's role and are usually summed up in the one word 'criticism'. Now, the connotations of this word are such that it is often assumed that philosophers are simply out to do a destructive job, that their main preoccupation consists in exposing to ridicule well-meaning people who are trying to put forward positive proposals for educational action. Certainly this will sometimes be the case, but in our view philosophers, operating under the banner of 'critical evaluation' have also a duty to try to advance, just like the well-meaning people referred to, con-structive suggestions relating to education. In line with this view our criti-cism of other writers will be made, not simply for the sake of criticism, but with the hope of reaching positive conclusions of our own. And from the pedagogic angle we hope also that the text, containing an amalgam of criti-cal comment and positive proposal, will serve the double purpose of engen-dering the critical spirit and providing the wherewithal upon which to exercise it.

In the following chapters we have adopted the use of the first person sin-gular rather than the first person plural. This is partly for stylistic reasons, and partly in order to distinguish clearly between the authors' claims and opinions and the use of 'we' that signals a suggestion to the reader about the claims and opinions of people in general. For example, 'I should argue that education means *x*.' 'We (people in general) surely would not accept that education means *x*.'

Notes

1 Wisdom, J., *Problems of Mind and Matter* (Cambridge University Press, 1963) p. 2.
2 But is philosophizing a skill? 'Skill' is an increasingly widely used word. But what is a skill? Are intellectual abilities well termed as skills? See Barrow, R., 'Skill Talk' in *Journal of Philosophy of Education*, vol. 21, no. 2, 1987.
3 Warnock, Mary, *Existentialism* (Oxford University Press, 1970) p. 57.
4 Plato, *The Republic* (Everyman edition) p. 5.
5 Ryle, G., *The Revolution in Philosophy* (London, Macmillan, 1956) p. 8.
6 Black, M., 'A Note on "Philosophy of Education"' in Lucas, C. J. (ed.), *What is Philosophy of Education?* (London, Macmillan, 1969) p. 11.

Further reading

No attempt is made in the Introduction to say at length what philosophy of education is. Fuller accounts of the nature of philosophy of education will be found in Robin Barrow's *The Philosophy of Schooling* (Brighton, Wheatsheaf, 1981), and in R. G. Woods (ed.), *Education and Its Disciplines* (University of London Press, 1972). On meaning, Charles L. Stevenson's *Ethics and Language* (Yale University Press, paperback edition, 1960) has much to offer the advanced student. All students would benefit from reading Chapter 9 on persuasive definitions. John Wilson, *What Philosophy Can Do* (Basingstoke, Macmillan, 1986) provides a valuable contribution to the debate on the nature and purpose of philosophy. Robin Barrow and Geoffrey Milburn, A *Critical Dictionary of Educational Concepts* (Brighton, Wheatsheaf, 1986) may prove useful in relation to a number of concepts not dealt with in detail in this book.

1 Thinking about education

> All 12-year-olds at a comprehensive were told that homework is being scrapped…[The Headmaster] who has already scrapped subject teaching…told them that, to make their schooling more 'relevant to life in the 21st century', they are to be given responsibility for 'managing their own learning'…[The School] is testing a futuristic project… which rejects the notion that a teacher's role is to transmit a body of knowledge to pupils. The project aims instead to encourage pupils to 'love learning for its own sake.'
>
> (*Daily Telegraph* 2005)

For those new to philosophy, the subject is likely to seem somewhat abstract and removed from day to day concerns at first, and I therefore want to begin by drawing attention to the quotation above. Here is an example of an actual policy decision: Students will no longer do homework (and apparently are no longer taught 'subjects'). The decision is driven by a point of view or theory to the effect that schools should be relevant to contemporary life, that in order to achieve that students need to 'manage their own learning', and that the object of schooling is not to 'transmit a body of knowledge' but to encourage pupils to 'love learning for its own sake'. I hope that most people will agree that, in broad terms, this is an interesting contention – something manifestly worth arguing about, and, particularly if you happen to have children at school, something that you might feel pretty strongly about, one way or the other. The kind of argument this decision might give rise to is decidedly *not* 'airy-fairy', 'merely academic', 'purely theoretical' or 'irrelevant' to practical matters.

Ultimately, it is dealing with claims and counterclaims such as this with which philosophy of education is concerned. But it does not go straight to the question of whether it is correct or incorrect, for example, to claim that 'managing one's own learning' is necessary for a 'relevant education'. It starts a step earlier. It tries to make sense of this 'argument'. It asks, in particular, such questions as what is meant by 'an education that is relevant to life', by 'managing one's own learning' and by 'love of learning for its own sake'? It asks why there is a presumption that loving learning for its own sake is incompatible with learning subjects. It asks what is the argument for saying that the teacher's job is not to transmit a body of knowledge. (It might also ask what scrapping homework is supposed to have to do with any of this.) Only by making sense of the argument, in particular understanding what some of the key words and phrases are supposed to mean, can we proceed to assess its merit or lack of it. And that is what philosophy is concerned with: making sense of arguments and ideas.

Philosophy is directly concerned with real live issues, but to learn to do the philosophical job we have to take it slowly. So I hope the reader will bear in mind that by the end of this book we should be in a better position to assess the coherence of this example and other similar arguments about education. But first we have to position ourselves.

The sphere of education

The sphere of education today is extensive and education is generally highly valued. In most countries, in addition to a developed system of state schooling, there is a rapidly expanding system of higher education, including institutions focused on such diverse things as art, computing, cooking, fashion design, and business, and a constant call for further qualification and accreditation in a variety of practices and pursuits, such as the hospitality industry, paralegal and paramedical services, mechanics, psychological services, accountancy, and horticulture. Alongside the state system a number of private education establishments at all levels, from primary to teacher training, has arisen. Self-education manuals and books are one of the more lucrative sides of publishing, and educational programs of one kind or another abound on television and the net. Governments, by and large, maintain or increase their spending on education regularly, and proclaim it to be one of their first priorities. Similarly, world organizations and authorities ceaselessly emphasize education as crucial to poor or troubled areas throughout the world. A great deal of money, too, is pumped into educational research of one kind or another, in addition to the enormous basic investment in educational establishments of all kinds. Education, in short, is widely pervasive, takes a good slice of our resources, and is fairly indiscriminately valued. It is very big business, although we seldom think of it in that way.

But do we have a common understanding of what this thing called 'education' is? Is your assumption about what educating yourself involves the same as your neighbour's? Is studying the history of Greece 'education' in the same sense that learning how to cook is 'education'? If we have different understandings of what education involves, are these various views all equally clear, and, if they are, are they all equally important or valuable? There is nothing necessarily wrong with our having some very general and vague idea of education, in the light of which we each have different particular educational ideals or focus on varying specific aspects of the educational enterprise. After all, we do something like that in the case of politics: it too is a general word covering a multitude of particular activities, some of which we, as individuals, variously approve or disapprove. The fact that fascism, Marxism, liberalism, and conservatism are all species of political theory, or the fact that there is a difference between politics as practiced by government and the politics of the local sports club, does not cause any particular problem. But then we don't allot a substantial part of our tax revenue to something vaguely called 'politics'; we don't assume that politics is in itself a good thing, as we tend to do with education; we don't seek to induct everybody into some form of politics.

Whatever the differences and similarities between politics and education, it is surely clear that in the case of the latter we do need to know what the word means. If we do not know what counts as being educated, how can we make judgements as to whether we are being more or less successful in our various attempts to educate people? If we are not clear what constitutes education, how can we assess whether a new course in health, a new programme on road safety, or a new college for aspiring comedians should be regarded as educational? Debate about whether physical education deserves more curriculum time than mathematics or chemistry, or whether we can reasonably forego teaching grammar in English classes, cannot coherently take place in the absence of a clear idea of what is involved in a successful education. And how on earth can we design research into such things as the most effective methods of teaching or classroom organization, let alone evaluate the significance of our findings, except in the light of some notion of educational success?

Whether we ultimately agree on a definition of education is not the primary concern. We can get along, understanding one another and even making reasonable accommodation to one another, provided that each of us can make clear to others what we presume educating people involves. (There is, though, a strong case for saying that the more successfully we clarify our individual ideas, the more likelihood that we will recognize similarity in our views). But we must at least clarify our own idea or conception of education if we are going to do any further thinking about it. It is the primary, the crucial, question in educational thought; and if practice is going to be based on sound reasoning, then it follows that it is the fundamental question for any educationalist, whether he sees himself rather as a practicing teacher or as a theorist. If you cannot give an account of what you mean by a 'well-educated person', then we can make no sense of any claim you go on to make about education, such as that it matters, that it is well-provided in this school, that another isn't really contributing to it at all, or that good teachers should proceed in this way rather than that.

I have deliberately used a variety of phrases as synonymous with 'knowing what education means': 'knowing what it is to be educated'; 'knowing what constitutes education'; 'what education is'; 'what we presume education involves'. For our purposes at the moment it is safe to regard these different phrases as interchangeable, along with some slightly more technical formulations such as: 'recognizing the defining criteria of education'; 'analyzing the concept of education'; 'establishing the necessary and sufficient conditions of being educated'. All of these different ways of speaking have this in common: they refer to the need to define the word education, not in the way that the dictionary does it (which usually simply refers to some examples of the word's use and provides a broadly equivalent synonym or synonymous phrase), but in the sense of establishing what is essential to its meaning. How do we distinguish education from other related but distinct concepts such as training, indoctrination, or socialization? To use my own preferred way of phrasing it: what precisely counts as being well-educated?

The funny thing is that raising and answering this question is the least common, and the least well carried out, aspect of all our thinking about education. Everyday, one can encounter people who will readily tell you that studying poetry is a waste of time, that in today's schools we should focus on technical knowledge, that students should learn how to learn rather than learn particular subjects, that instruction doesn't work, that this school is better than that, that this teacher is useless, another brilliant, that home-schooling is the way forward, that University is a waste of time, and so on. Yet these same people, as likely as not, cannot begin to explain, let alone justify, the idea of educational success that they have in mind in making such judgements. They know, apparently, that this is more effective than that at achieving or contributing to a result, but they have no clear idea of what result they are talking about. Nor is this simply a problem for the proverbial man in the street: equally commonly, we find educational researchers claiming to have demonstrated or proved that a particular method of teaching is or isn't effective, without providing any explicit account of what we should be looking for in students who have been effectively taught, not simply in the sense of, say, being able to retain information, but in the sense of taught in such a way that they have become better educated.

My first premise, then, is that the first and one of the most important tasks for those who wish to understand and contribute to sound educational policy and practice is to analyse the concept of education; to give an account of the idea; to determine what precisely counts as being well-educated.

Training, socialization, and education

We refer to the 'educational system', but that organization of schools, colleges, and universities in fact does a number of other things besides educate. Conversely, education doesn't only take place in some part of the system: people's education may be advanced in all sorts of ways, through their friends, by travel, on the web, by reading, by experience, by parents, or by self-reflection, to name but a few. So, before we attempt to analyse the concept formally (see Chapter 3), it may be useful to distinguish between education and some related concepts which, though distinct, may also be the concern of the educational system.

A typical dictionary definition of education might refer to it as 'upbringing' or 'acquiring knowledge'. In this sense practically anything one experiences, hears, or reads may be said to be part of one's education whether sensible or silly, coherent or incoherent, true or false, and regardless of how one came by the knowledge. It is in this sense that we refer to the education system, implying no distinctions between various things that might be learnt or how they might be taught. The most telling aspect of this broad concept of the educational system is that it is value-free. By contrast the concept of education itself is evaluative; it is by definition a good thing; (it is what is technically sometimes called a normative term). Why it is necessarily desirable and what makes it so, will be examined when we analyse the concept fully, but for the moment we need only note the distinction between the value-free concept of the educational system and the normative concept of education itself.

Schools and other educational institutions have many purposes and do a number of things besides educate. Some of what they do may not be the result of anybody's deliberate or conscious aim so much as a by-product of having a system of education at all. For instance, schools do as a matter of fact serve to some extent as child-minding facilities, regardless of whether that was either the community's or the parents' intention or wish. Similarly, at least in most systems, they play a part in categorizing and stereotyping individuals: schools just do tend to throw up the class clown, the computer geek, the sporting and the intellectual type, and they play a part in making individuals see themselves in particular lights, without anyone necessarily wanting to mould particular people into particular forms. More broadly, schools clearly contribute to classifying people as clever, dumb, hard working, lazy, etc. The educational system also makes a significant contribution to the immediate and often the long-term happiness, confidence, and character development of people. Many would argue that schools should be taking some active steps in regard to the emotional development of students, though it is usually the case that schooling has a far greater effect in this respect in ways that are not consciously controlled by educators than through deliberate interventions; but in either case, the business of emotional development needs to be distinguished from the business of educating.

But there are also purposes that we consciously expect the school or similar institution to serve and deliberately try to enhance. Emotional development may be one of these, as we have just noted; socialization, training, and character development are three more. Character development differs from emotional development, in that the latter is concerned with achieving a satisfactory emotional equilibrium: it is a personal internal matter to do with reacting in an appropriate way and to an appropriate degree to varying situations and events. One is emotionally developed, for example, insofar as one recognizes cause for but can nonetheless handle upset; one is emotionally undeveloped, if one is laid low by any disappointment or sent into a rage by the slightest obstruction. Character development refers to the cultivation of a wider range of habits and dispositions, such as being kind, truthful, or determined.

I am not at present trying to analyse these concepts or give a full account of what is involved in these notions. If I were, I could and should be criticized both for doing no more than giving examples, and for failing to address questions of value. You cannot define a term simply by giving an example of it: to say that ' being courageous' is 'to seek out and attack an intruder in one's house' is not to tell us anything about why this is courageous, which is what we need to know if we are to understand courage: what is it about 'seeking out and attacking an intruder' that is courageous, is the question. By the same token, any attempt to answer that question will have to tackle the implicit value question: courage is, by definition, a commendable quality, but is it actually commendable to seek out and attack an intruder in one's home? (It may well be. My point here is simply to illustrate that to define a term or analyse a concept, you need to do more than give examples, you need to explain why they are examples and, if values are involved, you need to support the implied value judgements with reasoning). So, all I am doing at this juncture is drawing attention to some functions the school and similar institutions may perform, which can be distinguished from education and each other, without attempting to fully understand them.

Just as schools in most people's view should be partly concerned with character development even though that is not the same thing as education, so it would be hard to deny that they both do and should train and socialize. To train is to perfect by practice, the most straightforward example being physical training, whereby the body is kept fit and develops various basic skills through repeated exercise. Indeed the change of name in educational writing from physical training (PT) to physical education (PE) in the last fifty years illustrates an aspect of the point. 'Physical training' was and probably still is a more appropriate phrase for much of what is actually taught, but those with an interest in the subject were quick to see that if 'education' and 'training' were recognized as distinct, and the former being value loaded had more cachet, then what they did would have more prestige if known as 'physical education'; to bolster the claim to education, in many cases the teaching changed to include study of more theoretical matters such as physiology, fitness, or sport itself. Be that as it may, some of what goes on in schools, particularly at the more junior levels, should more properly be seen as physical training than physical education.

Schools train students in a variety of basic skills, particularly at the elementary level. In teaching the young to tie their shoelaces, do press-ups, form letters, recognize numbers, raise their hand to ask a question, and in other cases where we attempt to inculcate a discrete or self-contained skill without necessarily involving explanation or understanding, we may be said to be training them. Even as adults, a great deal of our behaviour remains 'trained', as when we look both ways before crossing the road, clean our teeth for a minimum of two minutes, use a library reference system, keep our household accounts, sew on a button, greet people politely, or burn the garden rubbish.

Training can be more or less complex and relate to more or less important skills, and the line between educating and training is not always straightforwardly clear in practice: the good historian, for example, is partly a product of skill training (how to locate references in the library, how to present references) and partly a product of education (coming to understand history), and sometimes it is hard to disentangle the two (e.g., should we talk of training a person to use historical sources, or is that a part of educating them?). There is an important general lesson here: we must not make the mistake of thinking that, because there are border line cases when we don't know whether to describe someone as bald or not, it follows that there is no distinction between baldness and hairiness. In the same way, while it may be difficult to classify some human abilities as being clearly the product of training or education, there is nonetheless a clear distinction to be made between perfecting particular self-contained practices by repeated exercise, and grasping or understanding patterns of reasoning. The former constitutes training, the latter provides us with an initial statement of what education involves.

Socialization might be said to be a species of training, but relating specifically to acceptable social behaviour. What is meant by socialization is the development of certain attitudes, habits, and behaviours that are regarded as an integral part of the culture or society in question, primarily by a process of example and expectation, without any particular attempt to provide understanding of or any reasoning to support such behaviour (other than along the lines of 'this is how we do things', or 'you wouldn't like people to do that to you'). No doubt a large part of who we are, judged in terms of how we behave, what we expect of ourselves and others, even what we think is right and wrong or true and false, is the product of socialization. Most people are socialized into the habit of being co-operative or polite long before they cultivate any views or arguments relating to the question of whether they should be or whether there is good reason to be. Once again, the basic distinction is between acquisition of attitudes and beliefs through the example and influence of the environment, and the acquisition of some degree of understanding relating to our assumptions, which characterizes education.

I am not suggesting that because some functions of school, such as childcare, training, and socialization, are distinct from education that they are unimportant. The value of some of them, such as categorization or stereotyping of individuals, might be debated, but training and socialization seem in themselves to be desirable, even necessary and unavoidable, aspects of upbringing. (Of course, one might take exception to features of a particular culture into which people are socialized. But to object to socializing people into the ways of the Nazi state, for example, or to training people to torture, is to object to Nazis and torture rather than to socialization and training). There are other possible functions of the school, such as conditioning, indoctrinating, and closing the mind, which are inherently objectionable and antithetical to education, as we shall see (Chapter 6). But training and socialization seem proper and desirable functions of schooling.

However, I want to suggest from the outset that the provision of education needs both to be distinguished from these other functions and to be recognized as the most important purpose of schooling. A system of public or state schooling is not in fact necessary to education, nor is it to training and socialization. All of these functions can be provided, and historically often have been, by the family, self-study, or some other informal means. But it is far easier for most parents to teach basic skills, to train their children, and to socialize them than it is for them to educate them, given that at minimum this means helping them to understand complex and abstract bodies of thought: I can take my child to the library and teach her how to look for and take out books (training) rather more easily than I can teach her the history, literature, and science contained in them. Similarly, she can teach herself science, literature, and history, by reading the books, but most people will not make much progress without the help of other trained and educated people. (Why do I say both 'trained' and 'educated'? Because, to anticipate, I would argue that to become a good teacher one needs to be trained in some respects, for example, to write legibly on a board, to project one's voice, but overall one needs to be educated oneself, particularly in the subjects one teaches. It is a surprising fact that in many places people are able, sometimes required, to teach subjects that they have never themselves fully or adequately studied. A small part of the implicit argument of this book is that that makes no sense at all and borders on the scandalous). So at rock bottom I am claiming that the justification for a public or state system of schooling is the utilitarian or practical one that this is the most likely way to ensure that all children, of whatever background, have an equal opportunity to enter an educational environment, and that the main emphasis should be on the educative rather than other functions of schooling. In other times and places it has been clearly demonstrated that socializing and training the young to follow in the father's trade can be effectively done through the family. However, there is little reason to suppose that most people (especially the poor and relatively disadvantaged) will have a realistic chance of becoming well-educated without a (free) public system of schooling.

The rational tradition

Any school system, and any theory or argument about schooling and education, takes place within a particular social and historical context. This, without any question, has a bearing on what may be said and done. The educational practice of medieval religious communities owed something to the fact that that is what they were, just as the very different educational practice and thought of the Enlightenment owed something to the changed nature of society and general beliefs in the eighteenth century. Schools in the Soviet Union during the twentieth century provided a quite different kind of upbringing from that provided in Europe at the time (so different that one might question whether they provided a true education at all, although they undoubtedly trained and socialized citizens effectively); that difference arose out of the extreme differences in culture or the nature of and beliefs about society and people. Within Europe there were of course also differences between individual countries or, sometimes, between different religious, non-religious, or other distinguishable communities, and these too led to differences in schooling. There was a period (during the 1960s) when it was fashionable to focus on the importance of cultural difference and to argue that everything – all opinions, judgements, knowledge, and hence all consequent practical decisions – were simply a product of their time and place, and, in a different form, this rejection of a standard notion of truth or knowledge has returned under the name of 'postmodernism'. This extreme position, which will be considered in more detail below (Chapter 9), is quite untenable, indeed is rather childish in its wilfulness and overstatement.[1] But it is important to acknowledge that to some extent we are all products of our place in history and have to make an effort to see beyond it. It is also necessary to recognize from the outset that we are heirs to a particular tradition of thought, centuries old, that emphasizes and values rationality and believes that through detached and abstract reasoning we can hope to distinguish between sense and nonsense, between the plausible and plainly false, between the reasonable and unreasonable, and between what there is good reason to presume is true and what there is not.

For these two reasons – the fact that we are part of a particular historical tradition that needs to be acknowledged, and the fact that that happens to be a tradition that values rationality – I want to conclude this chapter with a brief skeletal account of the rational tradition. For, notwithstanding globalization, the revolution in communications, the multicultural nature of our world, and the distinctive cultures within many countries, the system of schooling and the view of intellectual activity in most English speaking parts of the world belong to and have been predominantly shaped by what is generally referred to as the Western tradition. It was not always and everywhere this way and it does not have to be this way. There have been, and are, societies that do not practice rational argument or scientific inquiry, relying instead on magic, religious inspiration, ideology, the commands of others, or tradition. Where does our commitment to rationality come from?

The Western tradition effectively begins in Athens in the fifth century BC. What may reasonably be said to be the beginning of civilization, implying living in a settled and ordered community as distinct from, say, a nomadic existence, is usually identified with the appearance of the cities of Uruk and Ur in Mesopotamia (a Greek word meaning between rivers, namely the Euphrates and Tigris), which is modern Iraq, in about 3500 BC. From here come the earliest examples of writing, consisting essentially of symbolic pictorial representation of commodities, and not of use for much more than inventories or lists. Between about 2500 and 2000 BC the Egyptian pyramids were built. While all of this attests to thought and design, it was not until somewhere between 1800 and 1600 BC that we find our first evidence of some kind of science, in Babylon where systematic planetary observations are made. In Greece, at about this time, the Minoan culture, associated with the famous palace at Knossos on Crete, is superseded by the Mycaenean Age, centred on the city of Mycenae, where King Agamemnon, according to tradition, was king. It was Agamemnon who led the Greeks to Troy to recover his brother Menelaus' wife Helen, and it is of this period that the Homeric poems, the *Iliad* and the *Odyssey* tell, although they were probably composed and certainly written down later.

For comparative purposes, we may note that in China this was the period of the Shang Dynasty, during which there is evidence of extensive cities and the development of bronze work and writing, but the latter is still limited to strictly practical uses as, for example, on oracle bones and inscriptions. There is no evidence anywhere of the use of writing to tell stories, let alone to engage in discursive reflection. It is some time between 1400 and 1500 BC that an alphabetic script first emerged in the Middle East, and this, having reached Greece, is used in writing down the Homeric poems at Athens in the seventh century BC.

This brings us to the truly remarkable story of Athens in the fifth century BC. Greece was not then a unified country as it is today. It consisted of a number of quite independent and small city-states, with different histories and sometimes different racial backgrounds, and often at war with one another. The city-state of Athens covered an area of about 1000 square miles, and had somewhere in the region of 50,000 adult males (outnumbered by 100,000 slaves and 20,000 resident foreigners, not to mention the women). Yet within a period of little more than one hundred years this tiny state gave to the world democracy, trial by jury, tragedy, comedy, history, theology, art as an aesthetic category in the form of architecture, pottery and pottery painting, and sculpture, grammatical study, rhetoric, medicine, and natural science. This last was really the culmination of inquiry that had its roots in Babylon and Egypt, and which then developed among the Greek speaking thinkers of Ionia (modern Turkey) at the end of the sixth and beginning of the fifth centuries. The major concern of these first scientists was not really what we associate with science today, although they were immersed in mathematics and, for example, predicted an eclipse in 585 BC; but they did not do much in the way of empirical investigation, and focused rather on the speculative question of how the world originally arose, and how change could come about, culminating in the first version of an atomic theory put forward by Leucippus and Democritus.

Here then is the beginning of systematic rational inquiry into questions to do with the nature of the world, though it should be noted that many did not write anything down, many of those who did still used poetry rather than prose, and all of them, however 'scientific' or 'modern' we may judge them to be, still reasoned in ways that made a lot of reference to gods, goddesses, chance, and necessity.

Then came Socrates, Plato, and Aristotle, who are the true known founders of the Western tradition. Socrates wrote nothing down himself, but is credited with being the first to emphasize the importance of moral and humanistic questions rather than scientific or natural ones. Plato, a disciple or pupil of his, did write, however, using a dialogue form that involved the character of Socrates, and it has been said and often repeated that there is a sense in which all of philosophy is a series of footnotes to Plato.[2] At any rate, Socrates, Plato, and Aristotle (who was not a native Athenian, but studied with Plato before founding his own school) between them gave birth to what we know as philosophy.

Plato's theory of Ideas or Forms insists (as did many of his scientific predecessors) that the world of the senses is not to be trusted: a stick looks different from different angles, or if placed half in water, or as time passes, so we can never apprehend the true stick – the stick as it really is – with our senses. In fact, the senses often deceive, as when a person with an amputated limb nonetheless feels the presence of the limb. Looking for certainty and truth, Plato put forward the view that while no particular stick could be said to be perfect, there is an Idea or Form of a stick (or of stickness) to which all everyday sticks conform to an imperfect extent; similarly while no human action is entirely, uncontentiously, unequivocally courageous, courageous acts are courageous in so far as they partake in the Form or Idea of Courage. The Ideas are real, unchanging, permanent, and as such must be the proper objects of knowledge, while about the shifting, deceiving, sensible world we can only have a belief or opinion: these opinions may sometimes be correct, but correct opinion is not the same thing as knowledge.

The theory of Ideas is not without its critics (and never has been, Aristotle was among the first to criticize parts of it), but it may be said that one's view of its plausibility depends mainly one how one interprets it. What is indisputably the case is that embedded in this theory is the claim that thought on any subject can only advance with absolutely clear conceptions: you cannot talk about, observe, or otherwise investigate anything from education to elephants without being clear about what counts as education or an elephant. And at one straightforward level it is correct to say that the idea of elephant is more 'real' (it is certainly more precise and timeless) than any actual elephant, though perhaps it would be better to say that it is more 'perfect' than more 'real', since for some the latter necessarily implies corporeal form (which Plato did not attribute to his Ideas).

There are those, even within the Western tradition, who deny even the basic assumption that one can meaningfully or usefully recognize or describe the characteristics of a concept, such that one can give an account of what an elephant or an education ideally is. And there are certainly other traditions of thought, that do not place the same or perhaps any value on the giving of reasons. But, essentially, the Western tradition has been forever and consistently shaped by the two most important assumptions of the Greeks: that there are rational aspects of the Universe, which we should seek to understand, and that a necessary and vital part of understanding anything is to have clear concepts.

Notes

1 For a recent study of this important topic, see Simon Blackburn, *Truth: a Guide* (Oxford: Oxford University Press, 2005).
2 The remark was originally made by A. N. Whitehead. For a recent study of Plato's educational philosophy, see Robin Barrow, *Plato: his Precursors, Educational Thought and Legacy* (London: Continuum, 2006).

Further reading

There are many books that consider the scope of education in a broad social and political context. Harold Entwistle's *Education, Work and Leisure* (London, Routledge, 1970) is still worth reading. More recent volumes of interest include Ruth Jonathan's *Illusory Freedoms* (Oxford, Blackwell, 1997), James Tooley's iconoclastic *Reclaiming Education* (London, Cassell, 2000), David Carr's *Making Sense of Education* (London, Routledge, 2003), and Christopher Winch and John Gingell's *Philosophy and Educational Policy* (London, RoutledgeFalmer, 2004).

2 What is it to be human?

Humans form a unique species. We are not just animals, although we are a species of animal, and we are not super-complex machines, or, more specifically, computers, although some analogies may be drawn between our brains and computers. Though some other animals have both brains and genetic codes that are very similar to ours, none has exactly the same brain or code. More to the point, notwithstanding many fascinating discoveries in the field of animal research, it remains clear that there are things that humans can and others animals cannot do. Only a human has the ability to use a language that allows us to do such things as hypothesize, imagine, predict, and lie. Washoe the chimpanzee, for example, has been 'taught' to 'recognize' ('react to'?) certain signs, and other animals could similarly be said to have acquired a language in the minimal sense of allowing some form of communication or at least response or reaction between them and us; as every dog owner knows, the sound 'walk' can produce a reaction. But there is absolutely no evidence to support the notion, and absolutely no reason to suppose, that any non-human animal can formulate thoughts of the type 'you promised to take me for a walk, and now you have broken your promise'. An animal can certainly experience pain, but it cannot say to itself 'if you would just stop hitting me' or 'if you would return my sister to me, I would feel fine'. Similarly, while computers can calculate to a degree and at a speed that is amazing, no computer can 'say' to itself 'oh, I'm so tired of this calculation; I'm going to take a break; see how you people feel about that'.[1]

This is not because we haven't yet designed computers that can formulate such thoughts or because non-human animals have not yet mastered a complex enough language. It is because, so far as we know, no other animal has the capacity to use our kind of language, and because computers are, however sophisticated, programmed calculating machines that do not use our kind of language (although we tend to confuse the issue when we use human terms in talking about them). To say this is not to challenge or disparage the work that has been done in recent years on the brain, artificial intelligence, computers, and animals. It is simply to say that what this research shows, time after time, is that human beings are unique. Whatever the similarities that truly exist or the analogies that less securely may be drawn between non-human and human brains, artificial and human intelligence, computers and people, and other animals and ourselves, there remains this ineluctable difference: the capacity to use a unique kind of language. From an educational perspective, we can add that if this is ever shown to be incorrect, if, for example, another species of animal is found that does have this capacity, or another familiar species develops it, or somehow a computer acquires it, what follows is that the animal or computer in question has become in this respect 'human' and therefore needs to go to school, because the distinctive linguistic ability of humans is at the core of the possibility of their being educated. You can design or program a machine and train a monkey, but, strictly speaking, you can educate only a human, or, to be precise, a being with a capacity for a hypothesizing language.

We are animals, then, and as such we have physical bodies that can be scientifically studied and explained. We have brains, which are also physical and can likewise be studied and explained in terms of cause and effect. Our brains in fact differ only slightly from those of certain other animals, so it is probably fair to say that it is not in our brains that our uniqueness really lies. It should also be acknowledged that we can identify certain parts of the brain with certain types of activity. But here we have to make an important distinction between a necessary and a sufficient condition. Science has established that part of the brain is associated with creative activity, for example. What this means is that without this part of the brain functioning properly one cannot display creativity; it is therefore a necessary condition of being creative. What it does not mean, what is not in fact the case, is that to have this part of the brain in good working order is sufficient to give rise to creative activity. Being creative means more than having a certain part of the brain functioning. A complete description of the brain can never capture the whole of the idea of creativity, rather as the quality and elegance of a champion tennis player is not captured in a description, however full, of her physical movements.

We are also genetically endowed individuals. Current evidence suggests that the particular people we are, our individuality, owes a lot to this personal genetic endowment. But we are not simply the product of that endowment, and we should not think in terms of being determined by it. Our individual genetic endowment is refined and modified by experience. The answer to the old question (very old; it was considered extensively by the Greeks) of whether nature or nurture makes us who we are, our innate self or the environment, is both; it is a matter of our given nature being developed in a specific way by its distinctive nurture. We are not determined by our genes; they are rather potentialities or tendencies that place limits on who we can become, but do not dictate specifics. To take a straightforward and simple example: I may have been genetically disposed towards some kind of cerebral way of life, and it may be that my friend, being differently constituted, could never have successfully and happily followed a cerebral career. To that extent we are both partly where we are today because of our genes. But it does not follow that I could not have done other than pursue a cerebral career. I might not have had the opportunity to develop in such a way as to follow my genetic bent.

But now we come back to the crucial point: the most important thing that humans and humans alone are genetically endowed with is this capacity for a distinctive kind of language. It is this ability to formulate propositions that may be true, false, or imaginary, and by extension, to promise, imagine, and hypothesize, and the consequent ability to explain our world and to some extent predict and control it, that makes us who we are. There are other ways that one might try to define humans (e.g., by reference to a soul if one is religious, or in purely physiological terms if scientifically inclined), so I do not propose this as the definition of a human being. But it remains the case that this is the most striking unique feature of humans, and it is difficult to think of anything more powerful and important.

The nature of our language, as contrasted with the communication systems of other animals, has enabled us to build up an understanding and explanation of our world. But the formidable web of understanding and insight that we have built up over the centuries includes truths that once articulated come to have control and direction over us. We have come to see, for example, that prime numbers have certain properties: having seen that, there is nothing we can do about it; we can't change anything; they have the properties they have. We have grasped that any argument of the form 'All men are mortal; Socrates is a man, therefore Socrates is mortal' (i.e. any syllogism of the form All As are B; C is an A, therefore C is a B), must be valid, just as any argument of the form 'All cows are four-legged; this is four-legged, therefore it is a cow' (All As are B; this is a B, therefore it is an A) is invalid. We, you might say, 'discovered' this or even 'invented' it, but that does not alter the fact that now we recognize that it must be so, and therefore here again we are subject to knowledge that we initially developed.

Humans, then, uniquely employ and can respond to reason. Being animals we also behave sometimes in terms of simple stimulus-response; but our distinctive characteristic is the use of reason. That is our essence: our mind, as distinct from brain. (Usage of the words 'mind' and 'brain' unfortunately doesn't follow any consistent pattern, particularly where different disciplines such as psychology and philosophy are concerned. The distinction that matters, however, is between the physiological organ that is necessary to but is not to be identified with the various aspects of reasoning, which I refer to as the 'brain', and the 'mind' which I reserve for the non-corporeal notion of our actual reasoning capacity in its widest sense. Fairly obviously, if you don't have a brain you can't have a mind; but having a brain does not guarantee having much of a mind.)

It is in virtue of the fact that we have minds that we may be said to have 'autonomy' which, though often thought of as 'freedom' actually means 'self-governance' or 'self-direction', as opposed to being directed, governed, or driven by external factors, whether inanimate or other people. Other animals have a limited number of responses to various stimuli; they are therefore in a literal sense governed by circumstances. So, no doubt, are we very often, but we are also able to act in response to our own reasoning, and in so doing we control rather than respond to circumstance; in so doing we are free in the specific sense of 'not a victim of circumstance'. (We are not here talking of free will and determinism as traditionally conceived. That is historically and primarily a problem for certain religious views. If God is all knowing, he knows what is going to happen; if he knows what is going to happen, in what sense can I be said to choose? Interesting as such a conundrum may be, it need not detain us here.) The argument here is simply that, notwithstanding the fact that we are partly shaped by our genetic inheritance, insofar as we follow the dictates of our minds we are autonomous in the sense of self-directed rather than other-directed.

There is another point to be made about our current understanding of genetics. Given the extent to which we are genetically endowed and given the close similarity between our individual genetic codes, some might be inclined to conclude that we must all be in reality very similar and that there is little room for individuality. Nothing could be further from the truth. Despite the fact that it has been calculated that the difference between individual DNAs is on average 0.1 per cent, the evidence suggests that the consequence of the interplay between each DNA and its unique environment ensures a real and ineradicable difference between each one of us: our individuality is both explained and seemingly guaranteed by our understanding of genetics.

Individuality is not the same thing as autonomy, but it too has potential significance in respect of educational debate. Some educational research, inasmuch as it seeks to establish universal laws or at least widely applicable generalizations relating to teaching and learning, needs to presume the kind of identity that the natural scientist takes for granted as existing among all instances of this chemical, mineral, or whatever. But each human being is unique. If I can establish that in certain circumstances mixing two chemicals causes an explosion, I can reasonably infer that in the same circumstances it will always cause an explosion. To say the least, a similar inference will be less secure, if I assume that because this teaching technique had this effect on one class it will do so on another class of different individuals. (The problems facing empirical research in education will be further considered in Chapter 13.)

The main conclusion to be drawn from a consideration of our understanding of genetics is surely that education is the most crucial thing in the world for us: it might be broadly and loosely defined as that part of experience that succeeds or fails in developing our unique reasoning capacity, hence our minds, hence our essential humanity, and hence our autonomy. Only humans can be educated. Only through some form of education can we fully realize our individual selves. It is now time to give detailed consideration to the concept of education itself.

Note

1 For more on Washoe and research into apes generally, see Paola Cavalieri and Peter Singer (eds), *The Great Ape Project: Equality beyond Humanity*, (Fourth estate, 1993). On computers and minds, see, for example John Searle, *Minds, Brains and Science*, (Harvard University Press, 1984).

Further reading

Matt Ridley *Nature via Nurture* (London, HarperCollins, 2003) is a key text on the current state of genetic research. Taking a very different view to that presented in this book is John Gray *Straw Dogs* (London, Granta, 2002). To different degrees, still wedded to a material view of mind are Rodney Cotterill *No Ghost in the Machine* (London, Heinemann, 1989), Steven Pinker *The Blank Slate* (New York, Viking, 2002), and Antonio Damasio *Looking for Spinoza* (Toronto, Harcourt, 2003). See also Rainer Born (ed.) *Artificial Intelligence: The Case Against* (London, CroomHelm, 1987), J. Z. Young *Philosophy and the Brain* (Oxford University Press, 1987), Robin Barrow *Language, Intelligence and Thought* (Sussex, Edward Elgar, 1993) and John Searle *Mind* (Oxford University Press, 2004).

3 The concept of education

What do the terms 'education', 'educate', and 'educated' mean? The hope must be that in answering this question we shall not simply find satisfaction in a job well done (undertaking the inquiry just for the sake of it) but also provide hints and clues for those engaged in education concerning the sorts of things they ought, as educators, to be doing and the ways in which they ought to do them. The situation *seems* to be parallel to someone wanting to be a shoplifter while not knowing what 'shoplifting' means. He is told, and then knows what to do in order to become a bona fide shoplifter. If only the parallel were exact.

A quotation from R. S. Peters will serve as a starting point for an inquiry into the meaning of 'education' and associated terms ('educate', 'educated'). But it should be stressed that Peters has been concerned with the notion of education for many years during which time he has modified his views to some extent. I shall concentrate on an early statement of his position, since his ideas are cited only as a way into the discussion of education. It is not my purpose to review his work and no attempt will be made to chart his subsequent changes of view or emphasis.

In *Ethics and Education* Peters asserts that the word 'education' has 'normative implications'. It has 'the criterion built into [it] that something worth while should be achieved'. In elucidation of these remarks he continues:

> It implies that something worth while is being or has been intentionally transmitted in a morally acceptable manner. It would be a logical contradiction to say that a man had been educated but that he had in no way changed for the better, or that in educating his son a man was attempting nothing that was worth while. This is a purely conceptual point. Such a connection between 'education' and what is valuable does not imply any particular commitment to content. It is a further question what the particular standards are in virtue of which activities

are thought to be of value and what grounds there might be for claiming that these are correct ones. All that is implied is a commitment to what is thought valuable.[1]

Peters is surely right in what he says. Vast sums of money are not spent on education simply because no other uses can be found for it, or just for the hell of it, or in the hope that positive harm will result. In general, money is spent on education because people think that education is a good thing, the linguistic corollary here being that the term 'education' has favourable emotive meaning or, in Peters' terminology, has 'the criterion built into [it] that something worth while should be achieved'.

On the other hand, if Peters is right how can it be that it makes perfectly good sense to say something like 'Education is a waste of time and money', or 'You get a rotten education at that school'. Surely, if the concept of education has 'built-in value' then to say 'You get a rotten education at that school' is to say, 'You get a valueless (rotten) valuable thing at that school', and this is a logical contradiction and therefore doesn't make sense – just as to talk about married bachelors doesn't make sense. This objection to Peters' analysis will not stand up. Of course, as we well know, there will be disagreement among people as to what things ought to be done in the name of education, as to what things are valuable or not valuable. Assuming that the teachers in a school are responsible, serious-minded people, they will believe that the curriculum of their school treats of valuable things, that benefit accrues to the pupils who study that curriculum. But this belief of the teachers is consonant with the fact that other people may well think such a belief misguided and that only harm results from study of the school's curriculum, and this contrary belief finds expression in a statement like, 'You get a rotten education at that school'.

Consider another example illustrating this general point. John Holt in his book *How Children Fail* writes as follows:

> Behind much of what we do in school lie some ideas, that could be expressed as follows: (1) Of the vast body of human knowledge, there are certain bits and pieces that can be called essential, that everyone should know; (2) the extent to which a person can be considered educated, qualified to live intelligently in today's world and be a useful member of society, depends on the amount of this essential knowledge that he carries about with him; (3) it is the duty of schools, therefore, to get-as much of this essential knowledge as possible into the minds of children. Thus we find ourselves trying to poke certain facts, recipes and ideas down the gullets of every child in school, whether the morsel interests him or not, even if it frightens him or sickens him, and even

if there are other things that he is much more interested in learning. These ideas are absurd and harmful nonsense. We will not begin to have true education or real learning in our schools until we sweep this nonsense out of the way. Schools should be a place where children learn what they most want to know, instead of what we think they ought to know.[2]

Here Holt attacks what we might call the 'essential knowledge' view of education and argues for what we might call the 'children-learning-what-they-most-want-to-know' view. This latter is Holt's *positive* conception and to mark the difference between this conception and the 'essential knowledge' conception he refers to *true* education or *real* learning. The words 'true' and 'real' are often employed in this way. They serve to ram home the speaker's conception of the phenomenon under discussion – as it might be love or democracy or education – and to belittle the opposition's conception, for the opposition is not concerned with the real thing. Now we can amplify Peters' central point in the following way. Anyone who cares to think about education will come to have a positive view however vaguely formulated and this positive view, embodying what the person concerned takes to be valuable, will be what education is, or ought to be, really about. Opposition views, reflecting what other people take to be valuable, will either be refused the title of 'education' ('That's not education'; 'You don't call *that* education!') or, if the title is granted, it will be a worthless title because it is not 'real education'. If the latter course is taken, 'education' in statements like 'Education is a waste of time' or 'All institutions of education ought to be razed to the ground' will be no more than a way of referring descriptively to what is the prevailing view, embodying the prevailing view of what is valuable, of education.

So far we have concentrated on Peters' claim that education implies that worthwhile things are to be transmitted. What about the processes of education, the ways in which these worthwhile things are to be put over? Well, the parallel between content and process when it comes to analysing education is a pretty exact one. Developing this point in detail, consider a simple analogy between education (as process) and gardening. When I am pruning, or digging, or weeding, then in each and every case what I am doing is legitimately described as 'gardening'. It doesn't make sense to say, 'He was pruning the rosebush, not gardening', for the simple reason that gardening is, to use philosophical jargon, a polymorphous concept; that is, 'gardening' is a generic term under which fall terms for particular gardening activities – weeding, pruning, and so on. Now, Peters holds, with justification, that education (as process) is a polymorphous concept and that it is a mistake to think of 'educating' as the name of one, and only one, particular activity.[3] Thus, ~~one is educating when one gets children to find out things for themselves,~~ when one drills them (recitation of tables, for example), when one instructs them (chalk and talk, showing them how to do things), when one gets them to make things, and so on. Each of these activities can be distinguished one from another but they are all instances of the educative process. It is not, then, logically legitimate to ask a teacher, 'Were you educating those children or merely instructing them?' (and note the emotive import of 'merely'!), for this carries with it the implication that educating is one particular kind of activity and instructing a different particular kind of activity.

The analogy with gardening, like most analogies, won't quite hold. It is difficult to imagine anyone wanting to maintain that pruning isn't gardening or that weeding isn't gardening, but it is not difficult to imagine someone maintaining that the activity of, say, instructing is not educating. We need only think of someone who is wedded to the idea of children finding out for themselves to the extent that he wants to propound this as a universal technique of educating. It is at this point that a *value* element – and hence a dimension of evaluative/emotive meaning – enters in. He who favours discovery techniques to the exclusion of all other techniques will want to retain the positively emotively charged term 'education' for the process he favours and will want, indirectly, to denigrate other processes by withholding the term from them. Without necessarily going to the lengths of the 'discovery' advocate, most of us would want to hold that a technique consisting of the use of torture is not an educational technique. The man who walked into the classroom idly tossing a pair of thumb screws must have been kidding. Torture repels us. To refer to it as an 'educational technique' would be to imply that we favour its use and this we would most certainly not want to be taken to imply. So we withhold the epithet 'educational'. In sum, the use of the term 'education', as applied to a process, has, as with its application to content, necessary connotations of value. With respect to process we may, with Peters, characterize these value connotations by saying that for a process to be educational it must be morally acceptable.

In so far as it does justice to the value component which is inextricably bound up with the concept of education, the opening statement of the passage from Peters quoted above serves as a useful – because pithy and accurate – definition of 'education'. (Education 'implies that something worth while is being or has been intentionally transmitted in a morally acceptable manner'.) But while on general philosophical grounds this seems to be an adequate definition, as far as would-be educators are concerned it is painfully inadequate. For would-be educators are looking for hints and clues concerning the sorts of thing they ought to be doing and the ways in which they do them, and we cannot pretend that Peters' definition provides any such hints and clues. It is accurate but uninformative; it provides no substantive guidelines; it leaves unanswered the two interesting and vitally important questions, 'What are the worthwhile things which are to be transmitted?' and 'How do we tell whether a manner of transmission is morally acceptable or not?'[4]

Perhaps we shall get answers to these questions if we turn our attention away from the concept of education, the analysis of which seems to be of limited value given what we want to know, and concentrate on an allied concept, that of the educated man. For surely the aim of the education game is to produce educated people. All we need do, then, is to establish what an educated person *is* and we shall have the hints and clues we want, at least is far as the first question is concerned. But since a correct analysis of this notion of an educated man involves an important philosophical distinction between meaning and criteria for use it is necessary first of all to make clear the basis of this distinction.

Suppose I attend a concert at the end of which I announce that I thought that the pianist was first-class. It happens to be the case that I thought he was first-class because he was technically equal to the demands of the concerto, his tone in the slow movement was perfection itself, he got just the right tempo for the scherzo and so on. Now, in one sense of the word 'means' it is clearly not the case that 'first-class' *means* 'technically equal to the demands of the concerto, etc.', for somebody else might pronounce the performance first-class and yet produce a different set of reasons for his pronouncement. Or, again, suppose I say that the performance is first-class and you say 'What makes you say it is first-class?', which is a perfectly straightforward, sensible, legitimate question. But it wouldn't be a perfectly straightforward, sensible question if 'first-class' *meant* 'technically equal to the demands of the concerto, etc.', for the meaning of 'first-class' would then be co-extensive with my reasons for using the term and your question would be redundant. Technical competence, getting the right tempi and so on, are my *criteria*, the satisfaction of which leads me to apply the term 'first-class' to the performance, but these criteria are not to be identified with the *meaning* of that term.

What, then, are we to say about meaning? Well, if we recall the remarks made in the Introduction about the mistake of assuming that all meaning is of the verbal equivalence kind, then we can characterize the meaning of 'first-class' by saying that to use this term of, say, a performance is to grade that performance – to indicate that the speaker rates the performance highly. Saying 'first-class' is like standing up at the end of the performance and applauding loudly. Anybody who pronounces a performance first-class but then says that he thought it awful – excluding the ironic use of 'first-class' of course – shows himself to be ignorant of the meaning of the term. He's like the man who claps vigorously as a means of showing his disapproval. Saying things like this is what it is to elucidate the meaning of 'first-class', and observe that this elucidation makes no reference to the criteria relating to the use of the term.[5]

Now 'educated' as employed in the expression 'educated person', is in some ways a term like 'first-class'. It is an evaluative term, generally used commendatorily; it is used to grade people, to indicate that the speaker, generally speaking, rates a person highly. It is a less general term of commendation than 'first-class' (we can use 'first-class' of a hundred and one different things, but this is not so with 'educated', although even here perusal of the sports columns of newspapers yields 'the educated left jab of Mohammed Ali' or 'the educated feet of David Beckham') nevertheless term of commendation it is, and we shall find it being differently employed by different people; that is, we shall find different *criteria* for its use being employed by different people. Thus, the little old lady informed her son that he had a visitor that afternoon; she didn't know who he was but he was well educated – he was well-dressed and spoke nicely. Are we prepared to say that she is misusing the term 'educated', that she doesn't know its meaning, in virtue of the fact that her criteria for the use of 'educated' – smartly turned-out and well-spoken – differ from ours? Again, are we prepared to say that a group of women at a bus-stop have no right to refer to 'uneducated' youths from the local school in virtue of the fact that the youths push to the front of the queue? ('Is that what they teach you at school?') Yet again, are we prepared to say of a man who regards knowledge of classical languages and literature as a *sine qua non* of being educated that he is ignorant of the meaning of the term? Examples like these could be multiplied almost indefinitely and the fact that this is so indicates that the criteria underlying the use of the epithet 'educated' are many and various and that different people tend to employ different criteria, but this is not to say that they are necessarily misusing the term 'educated' or are ignorant of its meaning.

Does, then, analysis of the concept of the educated man yield no more than analysis of the concept of education? Is it the case that just as people have differing positive conceptions of education so too they employ differing criteria governing their use of the commendatory epithet 'educated'? Is there any possibility of unearthing the *right* criteria? In terms of the familiar language of educational aims – related, obviously, to the language of positive conceptions of education and the language of criteria for being educated – isn't it simply the case that different people have different aims and there's an end on't? Perhaps the answer to this last question is 'Yes', but we have no right to conclude that it is without argument. For one thing it has already been suggested that 'educated' is, as a term of commendation, less widely applicable than 'first-class'. Further, the possibility exists that in addition to its evaluative meaning (commendatory) 'educated' possesses an element of descriptive meaning such that seemingly different criteria for its use on the part of different people do in fact have common elements, these common elements serving to identify the elusive descriptive meaning. Peters certainly seems at one time to have thought that this is so.

In *Ethics and Education* he writes that 'more has to be said about the formal requirements built into the concept of "being educated" '[6] and he then lists these requirements:

A. 'We do not call a person "educated" who has simply mastered a skill' (e.g. pottery). 'For a man to be educated it is insufficient that he should possess a mere know-how or knack. He must have also some body of knowledge and some kind of conceptual scheme to raise this above the level of a collection of disjointed facts. This implies some understanding of principles for the organization of facts.' Let's call this the body of knowledge and understanding of associated principles requirement or criterion.

B. The knowledge referred to under A must 'characterise [a man's] way of looking at things rather than be hived off. It is possible for a man to know a lot of history in the sense that he can give correct answers to questions in class-rooms and examinations; yet this might never affect the way in which he looks at the buildings and institutions around him. We might describe such a man as "knowledgeable" but we would not describe him as "educated"; for "education" implies that a man's outlook is transformed by what he knows'. I shall call this the transformation criterion.

C. The educated man must care about the standards immanent in his field of interest. Thus, 'A man cannot really understand what it is to think scientifically unless he not only knows that evidence must be found for assumptions, but knows also what counts as evidence and cares that it should be found. In forms of thought where proof is possible cogency, simplicity, and elegance must be felt to matter. And what would historical or philosophical thought amount to if there was no concern about relevance, consistency, or coherence? All forms of thought and awareness have their own internal standards of appraisal. To be on the inside of them is both to understand and to care. Without such commitment they lose their point.' I shall refer to this as the caring or commitment criterion.

D. The educated man must have 'cognitive perspective'. So, 'a man might be a very highly trained scientist [satisfying criteria A, B, C]; yet we might refuse to call him an educated man'. And what is lacking is cognitive perspective – 'The man could have a very limited conception of what he is doing. He could work away at science without seeing its connection with much else, its place in a coherent pattern of life. For him it is an activity which is cognitively adrift.' I shall call this the cognitive perspective criterion.

The first thing to note is that Peters' presentation of these 'formal requirements' is, surely, methodologically suspect. His formal requirements, or criteria, are to some extent based upon linguistic usage, the way in which 'we' speak. Thus, under A we find 'We do not call a person "educated" who has simply mastered a skill', under B we find 'We might describe such a man as "knowledgeable" but we would not describe him as "educated" ', and under D we find 'a man might be a very highly trained scientist; yet we might refuse to call him an educated man'. To whom does the 'we' in these three contexts refer? Presumably Peters does not use the 'we' to refer to himself and his colleagues but intends to refer much more generally to the English-speaking populace at large. But if this is so then doubts arise, for it is by no means clear that people at large, in all sections of the community, do in fact use, or in the cases under discussion do in fact *not* use, 'educated' in the ways specified by Peters. In sum, if his criteria are based to some extent on an appeal to ordinary linguistic usage then one may doubt the firmness of that base.

The point may seem to be a technical one but it is important, for if the appeal to ordinary usage is not allowed then we are being offered a preferred conception of education; we are being offered Peters' own positive conception of education (via the notion of the educated man) rather than a consensus view of education as reflected in linguistic usage.

In somewhat similar vein we might question particular criteria. Thus, with respect to C (the caring or commitment criterion) suppose there is a man who used to be committed to the study of, say, literature and history, but who now devotes himself to his garden and no longer cares about or is committed to the study of literature and history. Is it so obvious that we would say of such a man that he is uneducated? Is it that he ceased to be educated at the moment he ceased to care? Again, with respect to the cognitive perspective criterion, which seems to have to do with the notion of wide-ranging interests, it is not obvious to me that I have no right to describe as educated a man who talks intelligently and at length to me about Spanish literature but who turns out subsequently to be woefully ignorant about mathematics, science, history, French literature, and so on.

There are problems, then, about the validity and status of Peters' analysis of the concept of the educated man, but having drawn attention to them, let us now attempt to redress the balance by asking what there is in the analysis that transcends Peters' personal conception of education and points the way to a more acceptable, though perhaps more limited, account of the descriptive meaning of 'educated'.

First, it is surely the case that in the course of becoming educated a man is in some sense transformed or changed. This is a conceptual truth. To deny that this is so would be to hold that if at time t_1 a man is uneducated then he could be considered educated at time t_2 even though he is at time t_2 exactly the same *in all respects* as he was at time t_1.

More contentiously, the transformation to be achieved through education must surely involve more than a simple quantitive change in the stock of truths known by an individual. For example, the fact that I know many truths of such a type as 'H. G. Wells wrote *Ann Veronica*' counts as nothing in the scales which weigh the extent to which I am educated, or, put differently, the transformation to be achieved must involve change in the ways I behave *vis-à-vis* my fellow men, change in my ability to *understand* the world or particular facets of it, change in my ability to do things in the world. Herein lies the plausibility of Peters' version of the transformation criterion when he contrasts the knowledgeable man with the educated man, a contrast brought out more forcibly, and more exaggeratedly, by Lawrence Kubie:

> I have never been able to regard seriously partisan arguments that the study of any particular aspects of man's folly-ridden history will determine whether the scholar ends up with mature wisdom or with the pseudo-erudition of the idiot-savant. The conflict between education as we have known it and maturity as we can envisage it depends upon something more profound than whether we master this history of an art-form called painting or of an art-form called science. There is no educator who does not know scholars who lack the least quality of human maturity and wisdom, yet who are true masters of their own fields, whether this field is the humanities, art, music, philosophy, religion, law, science, the history of ideas or the languages by which men communicate ideas.[7]

This contrast between being knowledgeable and being educated is a most important one. It lies behind the criticisms levelled at much traditional schooling where very often the aim seems to be no more than to impart relatively recherché information for memorization and subsequent regurgitation in written examinations. This contrast *is* implicit in the linguistic usage of laymen. Take, for example, the case of the old lady referred to above whose visitor was smartly turned-out and well-spoken or the case of the women at the bus-stop and local school students. In both these cases the concept of educated that is operative involves more than mere knowledge; it involves things like consideration, manners, and abilities to do certain things and act in certain ways. In this connection, consider the use of a phrase involving the word 'educate' which occurs time and time again – 'We must educate the public.' With respect to AIDS, ecology, drugs, pollution, local government elections, banking procedures, behaviour at football matches, and a hundred and one other things we are constantly being told that the public must be educated, and the clear implication of this familiar way of speaking is that certain information is to be imparted, this information is to be understood and, in virtue of the understanding, what people do, or do not do, is to change.[8]

The contrast between knowledgeable and educated also crops up when progressive educationalists unite under the banner slogan of 'Education for Life'. Once more the direct implication is that education is really about people developing in certain preferred ways, living lives involving much more than the assimilation of knowledge for the sake of knowledge. Unfortunately, some progressives weaken their case by urging the wholesale dismissal of subjects or disciplines, or any kind of instruction, and take refuge in vague talk about discovery and inquiry. The point to be stressed here is that the notion of transformation, underlying the notion of the educated man, itself involves reference to knowledge and understanding. Surely it is just plain wrong to separate transformation (desirable) from knowledge and understanding (undesirable in the eyes of some progressives – at least as far as the knowledge component is concerned). Peters put essentially this same point in terms of a contrast between education and life very well:

> Those who make it [i.e. the contrast between education and life] usually have in mind a contrast between the activities that go on in classrooms and studies and those that go on in industry, politics, agriculture, and rearing a family. The curriculum of schools and universities is then criticised because, as the knowledge passed on is not instrumental in any obvious sense to 'living', it is assumed that it is 'academic' or relevant only to the classroom, cloister, study, and library. What is forgotten is that activities like history, literary appreciation, and philosophy, unlike Bingo and billiards, involve forms of thought and awareness that can and should spill over into things that go on outside and transform them. For they are concerned with the explanation, evaluation and imaginative exploration of forms of life. As a result of them what is called 'life' develops different dimensions. In schools and universities there is concentration on the development of this determinant of our form of life. The problem of the educator is to pass on this knowledge and understanding in such a way that they develop a life of their own in the minds of others and transform how they see the world, and hence how they feel about it.[9]

Peters' analysis of the notion of the educated man, while not acceptable in its entirety, does seem to contain the elements of a correct, objective analysis, summed up by saying that the educated man is one who has been transformed in ways delineated above, the transformation being integrally related to the concepts of knowledge and understanding. Of course, to say those things, although it enables us to conclude that 'educated' is a term of more determinate application than 'first-class', that there *is* an element of descriptive meaning involved in it, nevertheless leaves us operating at too great a level of generality. Nor does it seem likely that further analysis of the concept of educated will enable us to draw specific conclusions as to how we are to proceed as educators – it will not provide the more detailed hints and clues for which we are looking. But at least we are pointed in the right direction. We now know that in furtherance of our ends we have to explore the notions of knowledge and understanding. We know that we have to ask questions such as 'Are there different kinds of knowledge to be promoted', and 'Are there different kinds of understanding?'

In sum, endless speculation on education, educated, and educate is of limited value and the time comes when one must address oneself to conceptually related notions such as knowledge and understanding. However, the fact that the relation is a conceptual one means that one has not really abandoned the analysis of education; the focus of attention simply shifts.

Notes

1 Peters, R. S., *Ethics and Education* (London, Allen & Unwin, 1966) p. 25.
2 Holt, J., *How Children Fail* (Harmondsworth, Penguin, 1969) p. 171.
3 See, for example, Peters, R. S., op. cit., pp. 24–5.
4 I remind readers that Peters is well aware of these shortcomings in his definition. To see that this is so it is only necessary to read the whole of the passage from which the definition is taken.
5 For a fuller discussion of the distinction between meaning and criteria for use see Hare, R. M., *The Language of Morals* (Oxford University Press, 1964) ch. 6, pp. 94–110.
6 Peters, R. S., op. cit., p. 30. To avoid endless notes I observe here that the quotations from Peters which occur in the next few paragraphs come from *Ethics and Education*, pp. 30, 31.

   With respect to Peters' use of the phrase 'formal requirements' this seems to me to be yet another way of referring to the descriptive meaning of 'educated' or to what I have called the common elements underlying seemingly different criteria. For the record it is perhaps worth noting that yet another way of describing the inquiry on which we are engaged in the text is to say that we are searching for necessary and sufficient criteria for being educated, and the unearthing of these criteria will provide us with the 'hints and clues' referred to earlier, or so it is hoped.

7 Kubie, L. A., *Neurotic Distortion of the Creative Process* (Lawrence, University of Kansas Press, 1958) p. 128.

8 On the other hand, do not many people regard a champion on 'Mastermind' or 'Jeopardy' as being well-educated? Perhaps the appeal to ordinary usage here is not as secure as I imply in the body of the text.

9 Peters, R. S., 'What is an Educational Process?' in Peters, R. S. (ed.), *The Concept of Education* (London, Routledge & Kegan Paul, 1967) pp. 7, 8.

Further reading

Discussions of the concept of education are legion. R. S. Peters, as suggested in the text, is always worth reading on this concept and students should consult chapters 1 and 2 of *Ethics and Education* (London, Allen & Unwin, 1966), chapter 1 of *The Concept of Education* (London, Routledge & Kegan Paul, 1967), edited by Peters, and the first paper in the first part of R. F. Dearden, P. H. Hirst, and R. S. Peters (eds), *Education and the Development of Reason* (London, Routledge & Kegan Paul, 1972). W. K. Frankena's paper on 'The Concept of Education Today' in J. F. Doyle (ed.), *Educational Judgments* (London, Routledge & Kegan Paul, 1973) is measured and balanced. For hard-hitting objections to Peters' thesis it is worth consulting Professors Woods' and Dray's contributions to the volume *Philosophy and Education: Proceedings of the International Seminar March 23–5, 1966* (Toronto, Ontario Institute, 1967), which may also be found in R. S. Peters (ed.), *The Philosophy of Education* (Oxford University Press, 1973).

4 Knowledge and the curriculum

Towards the end of the last chapter I sought to establish a connection between the concept of education and the concepts of knowledge and understanding. The task before us now is to attempt to outline what kinds of knowledge we ought, as educators, to be concerned to pass on to students or, more generally, the kinds of thing we ought to seek to promote when teaching/learning takes place. This more general specification of the task will serve to remind us that we ought not to be concerned simply to transmit factual information but also, at the very least, to foster skills and abilities of various kinds. Or, in terms of knowledge, we shall be concerned not only with knowing *that* such-and-such is the case but also with knowing *how* to do various sorts of thing.

Just think for a moment of all the factual information that there is and of all the skills and abilities that there are. In addition to all the isolated factual items ('John Doe has a wart on his nose', 'Elsie Perkins didn't get the job at Marks & Spencer') there are all those factual edifices that get referred to as 'bodies of knowledge' – botanical classification schemes, histories of a hundred and one different things, geographical assemblages of fact, and the like. Further, as far as skills and abilities are concerned, we could, if we so chose, teach people to drive fast cars round Silverstone, make pancakes, mend fuses, fish for salmon in Scotland, solve differential equations, compose string quartets, and so on endlessly. It seems clear that, given this superabundance of knowledge of different kinds, one of the main problems facing us as far as curriculum matters are concerned is the problem of selection. What we want is a principle, or principles, by virtue of which we are able to select from the mass of knowledge those things that are in some way peculiarly relevant to education, those things that ought to be studied, taught, and learnt, in schools, colleges, and universities.

As a first move in attempting to unearth such a principle, or principles, consider the following phrases: 'uneducated hairdresser', 'uneducated bus-driver', 'uneducated dustman', 'uneducated greengrocer'. And consider also the following (fictitious) advertisement placed in the *Times Higher Educational Supplement* by a university. 'Applications are invited for the post of Lecturer in History. A medievalist is looked for. Only educated historians need apply.'

With respect to the first four examples there surely does not seem to be anything logically odd about them. It does not, for instance, seem contradictory to refer to an uneducated greengrocer. But if this is so, it follows that greengrocery is no part of what is to be educated, and that greengrocery is not the sort of thing that we should expect to figure as an item on the curricula of educational institutions such as schools, colleges, and universities. It is true, of course, that greengrocery, bus-driving, and so on *could* figure on the curricula of schools, but the implication of the above argument is that they would not be *educational* items and to that extent the school would not count as an *educational* institution.

But the situation seems different in respect of the university advertisement. Surely, historians are, by virtue of the fact that they *are* historians, educated. How can it be that a breed of men and women exist called 'uneducated historians'? And it is worth noting that the 'can' in the last sentence is what philosophers would call a logical 'can'; that is, it doesn't just happen to be the case that, as a matter of fact, there aren't any uneducated historians around, but it could *never* be the case that such people exist. For, putting the matter very strongly, to become a historian is, *ipso facto*, one way of becoming educated.

Let us hazard a generalization on the basis of the argument so far. The knowledge that should be the concern of educational institutions is knowledge related to things of the mind, to intellectual pursuits, to the development of the mind. The sorts of thing that will then be ruled in will be the study of physics, history, chemistry, literature, philosophy, biology, mathematics, and the sorts of thing that will be ruled out will be hairdressing, bus-driving, shopkeeping, and whatever. Even if the latter sorts of thing involve mental capacities – the dustman must *think* to remove the contents of the dustbin and not the contents of the car that happens to be standing next to it – these mental capacities are of such a low order compared with the mental capacities to be exercised by a physicist or a philosopher as to be classified in an entirely different category.

There are those who have argued that the considerations outlined in the last paragraph do, in fact, provide the principle of selection so sorely needed to enable us to determine curriculum content. Probably the foremost proponent of views along these lines is P. H. Hirst, and no inquiry of the kind on which we are now engaged would be complete without a critical appraisal of Hirst's central contentions.[1]

Knowledge, according to Hirst, is separable into a number of distinct forms. These forms of knowledge are not mere collections of information but rather 'complex ways of understanding experience which man has achieved' (p. 122). Again,

> by form of knowledge is meant a distinct way in which our experience becomes structured round the use of accepted public symbols. The symbols thus having public meaning, their use is in some way testable against experience and there is the progressive development of a series of tested symbolic expressions. In this way experience has been probed further and further by extending and elaborating the use of the symbols and by means of these it has become possible for the personal experience of individuals to become more fully structured, more fully understood. The various forms of knowledge can be seen in low level developments within the common area of our knowledge of the everyday world. From this there branch out the developed forms which, taking certain elements in our common knowledge as a basis, have grown in distinctive ways. (p. 128)

The developed forms of knowledge possess distinguishing features:

1   They each involve certain central concepts that are peculiar in character to the form. For example, those of gravity, acceleration, hydrogen, and photo-synthesis characteristic of the sciences; number, integral, and matrix in mathematics; God, sin, and predestination in religion; right, good, and wrong in moral knowledge. (pp. 128–9)

2   In a given form of knowledge these and other concepts that denote, if perhaps in a very complex way, certain aspects of experience, form a network of possible relationships in which experience can be understood. As a result the form has a distinctive logical structure. For example, the terms and statements of mechanics can be meaningfully related in certain strictly limited ways only, and the same is true of historical explanation. (p. 129)

3   The form, by virtue of its particular terms and logic, has expressions or statements...that in some way or other, however indirect it may be, are testable against experience....Each form...has distinctive expressions that are testable against experience in accordance with particular criteria that are peculiar to the form. (p. 129)

4   The forms have developed particular techniques and skills for exploring experience and testing their distinctive expressions, for instance the techniques of sciences and those of the various literary arts. The result has been the amassing of all the symbolically expressed knowledge that we now have in the arts and the sciences. (p. 129)

On the basis of these criteria Hirst originally catalogued the forms of knowledge, or disciplines, as follows: mathematics, physical sciences, human sciences, history, religion, literature and the fine arts, philosophy, and moral knowledge. Additional to the forms there are what Hirst calls 'fields of knowledge' which arise when knowledge that is rooted in more than one form is built up round specific phenomena. Unlike the forms of knowledge the fields are not concerned with developing a particular structuring of experience. 'They are held together simply by their subject matter, drawing on all forms of knowledge that can contribute to them. Geography, as the study of man in relation to his environment, is an example of a theoretical study of this kind, engineering an example of a practical nature. I see no reason why such organisations of knowledge... should not be endlessly constructed according to particular theoretical or practical interests' (p. 131).

The implications of this view for the secondary school curriculum are pretty clear.[2] Syllabuses and curricula 'must be constructed so as to introduce pupils as far as possible into the interrelated aspects of each of the basic forms of knowledge, each of the several disciplines. And they must be constructed to cover at least in some measure the range of knowledge as a whole' (p. 132). True, a sop is thrown to those people uneasy about what seems to be too rigorous an approach to general secondary education in the form of a mention of the possibility of using a project or topic approach. Thus, Hirst instances the study of natural, social, and political aspects of power, a practical project of design and building involving mathematics, science and the visual arts, a regional study involving geographical, industrial, historical, and social considerations – but the point is made that these kinds of approach have strictly limited value. Somewhere along the line project methods must give way to study of the disciplines, or forms of knowledge, themselves; understanding of the distinct approaches of the different disciplines – of physics, literature, mathematics, etc. – can only be properly had if they are taught as distinct and different.

Before passing to a critical evaluation of Hirst's argument let us clear up one or two points that are not strictly relevant to the overall argument in this chapter to date but which are none the less important. The first point concerns a charge often levelled at Hirst and others who share his views, namely, the charge that they are reactionaries.

The ground for this charge seems to be the claim that Hirst is concerned only with a certain type of pupil – the academically able. But this claim is simply false. Hirst's liberal education or general education is, as its name implies, for everyone. He is quite explicit about this,[3] and J. P. White, who shares some of Hirst's opinions on the issue under discussion, is even more explicit. In a paper entitled 'The Curriculum Mongers'[4] White asserts that 'radical' rather than 'reactionary' is the appropriate epithet to employ if one seeks to classify proposals such as his (and, for that matter, such as Hirst's):

> Radicalism...claims that there is no necessary connection between a professional career and access to the higher culture. This connection exists *de facto*, but is not rationally based. If most children will later have to do jobs which are not intellectually demanding, there is no reason why they should be taught only those things which will make them efficient workers – and perhaps efficient consumers and law-abiding citizens as well. For men are not only workers or consumers or good citizens: they are also *men*, able, if taught, to contemplate the world of a poem or a metaphysical system as well as to enjoy more easily accessible pursuits. If, as Tawney said, we think the higher culture fit for solicitors, why should we not think it fit for coalminers – those 'other inhabitants of places of gloom'?

Whatever reservations one may have about the idealistic strand in this kind of thinking – for example, one may have slight doubts about the possibility of all children coming to be able to contemplate the world of a metaphysical system, or that successful initiation into the higher culture is consonant with those so initiated being content to process peas or dig for coal – nevertheless the arguments here briefly presented do, surely, effectively rebut the charge that Hirst is 'reactionary' in the sense of being concerned about the minority only.

The second point to be taken up also relates to the reactionary charge but the ground now consists in the assertion that Hirst is perpetuating the 'Grammar School Tradition'. Not, as we have seen, in that he wants different curricula for different classes of children, but in that he is advocating a curriculum that takes no account of all the exciting new developments going on around us and which consists of the familiar diet of mathematics, physics, English language and literature, history, geography, and so on. In brutal terms, Hirst's proposals amount to no more than a plea for the retention of the tired old subjects that have always figured in grammar schools, and still do, in the grammar schools left to us. All that has changed is the name – for 'subjects' read 'forms of knowledge' or 'disciplines'.

There are at least three distinct elements in this second charge. First, there is the suggestion that simply because curricula have over a long period included disciplines like mathematics and history it is time for a change. This suggestion deserves short shrift. It is patently false and is on a par, in its logical force, with the deprecatory use of the expression 'That's an old argument', as if the validity of an argument necessarily decreases with time.

People who take up the suggestion are usually enamoured of change, but they make the elementary mistake of assuming that change is conceptually related to making things better; they fail to realize that things can change for the worse as well as for the better. Second, there is a tendency to identify Hirst's proposals relating to the teaching of separate, distinct disciplines with proposals to teach them, both as regards content and method, in the 'bad old ways'. That is, English consists of parts of speech, clause analysis; poetry is replaced by prosody; mathematics is computation; geography is capes and bays; history is dates, kings, and battles; and so on. Method is drill and, perhaps, in the last resort, recourse to authority in the form of the stick. Doesn't the very word 'discipline' connote all this? It *may*, but, if so, that's unfortunate. For there is no evidence in Hirst's writings to suggest that barbaric relationships as between teacher and taught are necessarily part of his scheme, nor to suggest that, as far as content is concerned, he is recommending the 'bad old ways'. Indeed, one reason for preferring the term 'discipline', or the term 'form of knowledge', is to oppose the notion of a subject. A school subject, in Hirst's view, is conceived of as a kind of translation of the corresponding discipline and the quality of the translation is often, as has been suggested above, suspect. Hirst would like to see a much closer connection between discipline and subject, and would like to see work done in various disciplinary areas with a view to sorting out the central concepts that must be got over to pupils if the discipline is to be properly presented. In all this one thing is clear. Hirst is saying that 'mathematics', 'history', 'chemistry', etc. are not just the names of things done in grammar schools over the past thirty to forty years. And in saying this he is quite right. The third element in the second charge need not detain us just now and it will, in fact, be taken up later on in this chapter. However, having mentioned it, I shall identify it. It consists, crudely in the assertion that even if they are viewed as 'forms of knowledge or 'disciplines' there are, nevertheless, matters of more importance with which curriculum-builders ought to be occupied than mathematics, literature, religion, philosophy, and the like.

Although to dismiss Hirst as a reactionary involves misunderstanding him, that is not to say that his position is unassailable. We need to examine the theoretical underpinnings of his curriculum proposals. With respect to his four criteria for distinguishing forms of knowledge – distinctive concepts, logical structure, testability against experience, and development of techniques and skills for exploring experience – at first blush it does seem that there is something in what he says. Consider, for example, a science such as physics. In physics concepts (mass, acceleration, density, force, etc.) are used to make statements comprising theories and these theories possess a logical structure in the sense that the statements which go to make up a particular theory can be so arranged that certain statements follow from others. And it is also true that, relatively speaking, well developed physical sciences have at their disposal refined experimental techniques so that the predictions made on the basis of working hypotheses can be checked with the object of falsifying the hypotheses – this constituting Hirst's notion of testability against experience. And similar sorts of observation would be true of mathematics – namely, pronounced degree of logical structure exemplified in some such pattern as 'If *a* is greater than *b*, and if *b* is greater than *c, then a* is greater than *c*.' But the radical difference between mathematics and the developed physical sciences lies in the fact that the statements of pure mathematics are not verified or falsified by reference to the external world. At no stage in pure mathematics reasoning does the mathematician break off to conduct experiments. Mathematics is essentially deductive. The pure mathematician is concerned with abstract symbolic systems in which regard is had to clarity and precision of definitions and assumptions, and by the process of deductive reasoning (exemplified in the 'If *a* is greater than *b*…' example used above) he explores the connections between axioms and postulates and conclusions.

So using Hirst's criteria we can distinguish physical sciences from mathematics. But it is the third criterion that is all-important. As Hirst says, 'The central feature to which they [the four criteria] point is that the major forms of knowledge, or disciplines, can each be distinguished by their dependence on some particular kind of test against experience for their distinctive expressions' (p. 130). But, and the but is a big one, the third criterion was not, in distinguishing physical science from mathematics, used quite as Hirst seems to intend. Mathematics simply does not make use of *any* kind of 'test against experience' in any sense that I can give to that expression.

The whole notion of testability becomes even more questionable when one turns to some of the other items that figure in Hirst's list of the forms of knowledge – religion, for example, or morals, or literature and the fine arts. In the case of religion what sort of 'experience' does one use to test statements of the order, 'God exists', 'Man has an immortal soul', 'There is a life after death'? These statements, although formally similar to the statements, 'Books exist', 'Man has a brain', 'There is decomposition of the body after death', seem to be quite unlike them in respect of testability. And this, not because the religious statements involve a different *kind* of testability, but because it is difficult to see if *any* kind of testability can be invoked in the case of such statements. Again, in the sphere of literary criticism, in what way is the notion of testability against experience to be employed when someone argues for the supremacy of *Daniel Deronda* over *Northanger Abbey* or for the essentially cardboard characterization which occurs in C. P. Snow's novels?[5]

The suggestion is, then, that it is far from clear that Hirst has succeeded in establishing that knowledge can be subdivided into these particular distinct forms.

But these criticisms of the theoretical underpinnings of Hirst's curriculum proposals do not imply that knowledge cannot provide the basis for a general curriculum. At most, if well founded, they reduce the Hirstian forms to the categories of mathematics (including logic), science, and arts, and there is no reason why curricula should not be constructed by drawing on these broad categories. However, in addition to the relatively technical criticism of the theoretical underpinnings there is a further, perhaps more serious, criticism to be made relating to the question of justification. For supposing that Hirst *did* manage to establish the existence of distinct forms of knowledge. What would then justify his asserting that they ought to be pursued, ought to be studied in educational institutions?

Hirst's answer to this question runs along the following lines:

1   The pursuit of the forms of knowledge is equivalent to the development of the rational mind.
2   Therefore, to ask the question, 'Why pursue the forms?', is to ask, 'Why seek to develop rational minds?'
3   But to ask such a question is to *assume the very principle* (rationality) that is being queried. 'The situation is that we have here reached the ultimate point where the question of justification ceases to be significantly applicable.' In other words it is not logically possible to ask the question, 'Why pursue the forms?'!

But the first step of this argument is suspect. For consider a number of mind-developing games – chess, for example, or bridge – or consider the possibility of inventing a number of mind-developing games; what principle of selection now operates in such a way as to validate the forms of knowledge as items in a curriculum for general education and operates so as to exclude actual and possible mind-developing games? Or, again, suppose it were the case that a particular branch of mathematics, as it might be some aspect of the theory of numbers, was known not to have any application, and suppose it was known that this branch of mathematics could *never* find application, what principle of selection now operates so as to enable us to decide the part to be played by this particular branch in a mathematics course as compared with other branches of mathematics known to have application – calculus, set theory and so on? The answer to these questions is that within Hirst's framework no such principle of selection operates and if we want a principle of selection we shall, as it were, have to import one from outside. I suggest that in very broad terms the principle to be imported is, in question form, To what end, or ends, do we seek to develop the rational mind among other things? To what end, or ends, do we advocate the pursuit of this or that activity?' This, in effect, is to say that we must import a utilitarian principle, in a very broad sense of 'utilitarian', and that we cannot rest content with justificatory arguments which, in the final analysis, rest upon an appeal to notions like pursuing activities just for the sake of pursuing them or pursuing them because they are valuable in themselves.[6]

Hirst wants to establish a conception of education 'whose definition and justification are based upon the nature and significance of knowledge itself, and not on the predilections of pupils, the demands of society, or the whims of politicians' (p. 115). One may sympathize with his desire to found curriculum proposals firmly on knowledge, but for the sorts of reasons adumbrated above this desire simply may not be realizable. Furthermore in framing curricula one surely cannot simply ignore society, more especially when one considers the extent to which practical problems – scarcity of available resources, for example – intrude on the scene. Nor is it obvious that one can simply override considerations to do with self-determination and autonomy by setting out to devise a curriculum without reference of any kind to the 'predilections of pupils'.

Reverting, then, to the question with which this chapter began – namely, what principle, or principles, enable(s) us to select those items that ought to figure on a curriculum concerned with general education – the answer I now give is, 'A utilitarian principle'. But, of course, this is a very general answer and needs filling out. As a preliminary, note that the principle is not to be interpreted crudely in terms of 'use'. For example, I do not wish to imply that if the pursuit of an activity does not lead to a positive material gain – a bridge built, a car made, a well-paid job got – then, by the utilitarian principle, that activity ought not to be pursued. The activity of philosophizing does not, in general, lead to hard material gain, and, indeed, is often a hazardous business, as Socrates found, but the utilitarian principle does not thereby prohibit philosophizing. All that the principle demands is that justification for the pursuit of an activity has regard to factors extrinsic to that activity, that justification couched solely in terms of intrinsic value – the activity is an end in itself, is worth pursuing for its own sake, is valuable in itself – is unacceptable, and unacceptable because it does not do the selection job that needs to be done. *Any* activity can be said by someone to be valuable in itself or worth pursuing for its own sake, and that someone cannot be gainsaid.[7]

We have to recognize that as far as the composition of a general secondary school curriculum is concerned, or any curriculum for that matter, the attempt to demonstrate or prove in the mathematical deductive sense of 'demonstrate' and 'prove' is doomed to failure. The only logic involved in arguments about this issue of composition is the familiar logic of, say, moral discourse where one adduces reasons for and against a line of action and in the light of these reasons decides how to act. There is, of course, nothing deductive about this – the relation between 'She didn't cook my dinner last night' and 'Therefore I ought to leave her' is *not* of the same type as the relation between 'Fred is taller than Bill and Bill is taller than Joe' and 'Therefore Fred is taller than Joe'. The world might be an easier place to live in if moral issues and curriculum issues could be settled in this cut-and-dried deductive manner, but unfortunately this does not seem to be the case, and with respect to these issues we are left with the difficult job of specifying reasons for and against lines of action, trying to weigh these reasons one against another, and so on. A messy, but unavoidable business.

Some philosophers have accepted the utilitarian principle espoused here and have seen that the sort of logic relating to curriculum selection is of the type specified in the last paragraph, and they have acted accordingly. Thus, when Nowell-Smith attempted to locate the reasons why universities ought to teach literature, history, and philosophy, he didn't take refuge in the stultifying concept of the valuable in itself, nor did he state baldly that literature, history, and philosophy were forms of knowledge or disciplines and that therefore further comment relating to the justification for teaching them was unnecessary. Rather, he attempted to specify the particular skills and abilities promoted by their study and to put forward reasons for thinking these particular skills and abilities worthy of promotion.[8] An important part of the job of the philosopher of education consists in following and critically evaluating arguments of the order of Nowell-Smith's.

I would not wish to imply that only philosophers ought to engage in the curriculum content debate ('Why do this rather than that'). True, philosophers will tend to be particularly interested, but, aside from this, it is open house. The fact that it *is* open house seems to have been increasingly recognized in recent years. In addition to practitioners of various arts, sciences, and crafts making incidental justificatory comments about their art, science, or craft it does seem that more and more people are beginning to face the justification problem head on, recognizing it as an important problem and trying to do something about it. Consider, for example, that thought-provoking Pelican, *Crisis in the Humanities*, in which a group of distinguished contributors debate the whys and wherefores of doing classics, history, philosophy, literature, *et al*. And from it, as an illustration of the kinds of thing with which it is concerned, consider these remarks of J. H. Plumb. Plumb bemoans the fact that in 'my own University of Cambridge' history teaching does not lead directly to students deepening their 'experience about the nature of man in society and the historical processes of change'. He continues, somewhat wistfully:

> He [the Cambridge undergraduate] will not…be led directly to such considerations. He will, for example, be expected to know far more about Tudor Chamber finance than the impact of the geographical discoveries, or the scientific revolution. Instead of being central to his education, the idea of progress will be incidental to it. What we can be certain about is that the social purpose of history will neither mould his studies nor help him to form his attitude to the past. He will be taught inexorably to distrust wide discussions and broad generalizations, to eschew any attempt to draw conclusions or lessons from history. He will be encouraged to read history and treat history as an intellectual pastime, with little rhyme and less reason. Those who go off to teach in schools go to instruct and not to educate. And worse still history fails to fulfil its social function, in government, in administration, in all the manifold affairs of men.[9]

And, in similar key, consider the following passage from a more recent collection of papers on curriculum matters. It comes from a paper on modern languages:

> Is there adequate justification for extending the teaching of a hitherto not particularly successful subject to a larger number of pupils? Can it be assumed that new methods based on a new rationale will avert the failures of the past? No one will question the country's need for more and better linguists, but is this objective reinforcing the circular career route whereby successful languages pupils automatically proceed to university in order to become language teachers, the whole self perpetuating process being masked by the system of external examinations? The time is certainly ripe for an investigation, and we can begin by posing a few more questions. For instance does language study provide an education experience that would otherwise be lacking? Can this value be identified? Do we need to teach the whole ability range, or can we isolate 'language aptitude'? Is the bilingual child intellectually at an advantage? Does learning a language at school increase intelligence? Can all children learn languages equally well? Do they have individual learning rates and can they be taught *en masse* or are they best taught in differentiated groups? What influences act upon their attitude to language learning?[10]

This passage, of course, ranges beyond the question of curriculum content and brings out well the fact that although one may begin an inquiry into curriculum hoping to restrict the inquiry to content it soon becomes apparent that other factors cannot be held at bay – for example, the teaching methods factor. Thus, it is clearly not sufficient simply to specify subject matters for a general curriculum, produce reasons for the specification and leave it at that. For suppose I argue that mathematics or history ought to appear in a secondary school curriculum. On the assumption that I am not arguing simply for the memorization of sundry mathematical formulae or sundry names, places, and dates, it follows that I am, presumably, arguing at the very least for something in addition to the mere transmission of factual information, certain mathematical and historical skills and abilities shall we say. In which case it would be difficult for me to avoid saying something about teaching methods if only because certain methods might be peculiarly effective in promoting the requisite skills and abilities and certain other methods peculiarly ineffective.

The passage also brings out the fact that curriculum discussion of the kind advocated in this chapter cannot, as has already been suggested, be left to philosophers alone. Sociologists, psychologists, and historians will all want, and rightly so, a say. Indeed, curriculum is a good example of educational theory to which philosophy, sociology, psychology, and history all contribute in their various ways. With this in mind I shall end this chapter by raising a number of debating points related to the issues already discussed and by tying up one or two loose threads. I make no apology if the reader objects that some of these points are not philosophical.

A. The chapter began with an explication and appraisal of Hirst's views on the place of forms of knowledge in the curriculum for general secondary education. In retrospect, and given the nature of the justificatory enterprise as I have spelled it out, *is* there a place for the forms in such a curriculum? Well, it may not be possible to define a form of knowledge, or discipline, in precise terms, but it does not follow that it is no longer possible to tell the difference between physics and history, or between chemistry, philosophy, and literary studies. If you undertake a course in theoretical physics you will not end up knowing a lot about the novels of Graham Greene. Nor does the inability to proffer precise definitions entail that we must begin to construct curricula *de novo*. The legacy from the past consisting of curricula comprising, broadly speaking, literature, history, science, mathematics, geography, languages, etc., is not simply to be dismissed overnight. The reasons for the existence of such curricula may be difficult to unearth and state in exact terms, but I find it hard to believe that there are no *good* reasons as to why curricula of this type remain with us today. No, we start, or continue, the overall process of evaluation from where we stand now, and possible candidates for curricular inclusion have to make out a case for inclusion, just as English studies had to make out a case for inclusion in university courses and just as sociology, more recently, had to do. If environmental studies appear on the scene, then we ask, 'What have these to offer that geography does not already offer?' 'What, if environmental studies were to replace geography, would be lost?' If inter-disciplinary or integrated studies of the humanities variety are put forward as replacements for the separate study of history, geography, and English, then we need to examine closely the specific proposals put forward and, once more, inquire of teachers of history, geography, and English what they think would be lost if their specialisms were to be merged into humanities. It goes without saying that this whole process of vetting applications for new curricular subjects not only puts the justificatory onus on the innovators but also on the sitting tenants and results in the periodic reappraisal of the claims on curriculum time of the teachers of traditional subject matters. No bad thing surely, always provided that the sitting tenants don't play an obscurantist game.[11]

B. What the procedure outlined under A brings out is that curricula are sensitive to time and place. In other words, it is not a question of searching for some ideal type, some kind of Platonic form, of curriculum which, once unearthed, will remain valid for all eternity. Ultimately curriculum decisions, like educational decisions generally, rest upon individuals' systems of value and these, varying with time and place, will bring about variations in the curriculum practices based on them. Thus it might *prima facie* seem that scientists will have an easy time of it playing the justification game according to the utilitarian rules. Don't we all of us know that our very standard of living in a technologically orientated world is dependent upon an adequate supply of scientists, mathematicians, and technicians? And in so far as the career route leading to becoming a scientist passes through the schools via their examinations to universities and polytechnics, schools *must* teach mathematics, physics, chemistry, biology, and so on. The justification for doing these things is writ large in rigid utilitarian terms relating to hard, practical gain. But all this holds good only on the assumption that we are committed to valuing things like relentless scrutiny of natural phenomena with an eye to their subsequent control and consequent benefits, and that we are committed, in some degree, to averting our gaze from the sometimes unpleasant by-products of technical and scientific progress. George Steiner puts the matter thus:

> For the first time (and one's conjectures here will be tentative and blurred), this all-governing axiom of continued advance is being questioned. I am thinking of issues that go far beyond the current worries in the scientific community about the environment, about

weaponry, about the mindless applications of chemistry to the human organism. The real question is whether certain major lines of inquiry ought to be pursued at all, whether society and the human intellect at their present level of evolution, can survive the next truths. It may be – and the mere possibility presents dilemmas beyond any which have arisen in history – that the coming door opens on to realities ontologically opposed to our sanity and limited moral resources.[12]

C. Is it, then, on the assumption that all of us, generally speaking, are prepared to go along with the technological society that science and mathematics find a place in the curricula of schools simply for the sorts of strict utilitarian reason sketched briefly under B? I think so. I hasten to add that this does not mean that *every individual* who studies mathematics and science does so for these sorts of reason. Some scientists might simply claim that they practise science because they like doing so, or because they are naturally curious, or because they find it intellectually challenging. But I do think that, given individual variation in the 'reason why', a large element of justification for the institutionalization of mathematical and scientific studies is of the strict utilitarian kind. I tend to agree with Michael Oakeshott when he says that:

> Flattered by circumstance and linked with ancient heresy, an attempt was made to promote 'science' as itself a 'culture' in which human beings identified themselves in relation to 'things' and to their 'empire over things', but it now deceives nobody; boys do not elect for the 'science sixth' expecting to achieve self-knowledge, but for vocational reasons.[13]

I think, further, that a number of scientists and mathematicians are themselves concerned that there is a high degree of truth in what Oakeshott says and that they are now seeking to find those elements in science and mathematics and, in some cases, beyond science and mathematics that transcend vocation or preparation for a useful job. I refer not only to the stress on aspects of biology which everyone ought to know (health, drugs, sex, etc.) but also to the importation into science courses of themes relating to the social responsibility of scientists, to pollution, to the moral implicatons of the scientist's work. I refer also to attempts on the part of mathematicians to define those parts of mathematics which, again, everyone ought to know and which go beyond low-level calculations of the social arithmetic variety.

Whether or not attempts like these succeed we shall simply have to wait and see. Just now it does seem that, if we leave the utilitarian justification to one side, mathematicians and scientists are at a disadvantage compared with their colleagues operating in the other great area of curriculum, namely, humanities. For the study of things like history and literature does not appear to be, nor need it be, geared to utilitarian ends. The broad claim here is that the humanities deal in matters with which every man and woman ought to be concerned. The claim will need ultimately, in my view, to rest upon broad utilitarian principles but no longer of the gross, pragmatic variety. As is the case with Graham Hough's observations on why have a literary education – incidentally, what he says about literature goes pretty well for history as well:

> What do we want of a literary education anyway? Scholarship and judgement of the highest kind for a few. And the few are no problem. But for those of unspecialized general intelligence who are the proper subjects of humanist education? We expect a literary education to expand their range of human awareness and sympathy; to enlarge their imagination beyond the limits of their own class and country; to show them that our problems and obsessions are part of a larger pattern of human experience, and assume a new meaning within the larger pattern. I should feel suspicious of the human competence of a leader or administrator who had not had at least a little of that sort of education. But it need not have made him a literary critic or historian, or an editor, or an emender of Shakespearean texts.[14]

D. The argument, then, leads us back towards the Hirst type of school curriculum, but for reasons different from those put forward by Hirst. The reasons are now of a utilitarian kind.

The question arises as to how, if utilitarian considerations are applicable to justifying some parts of a Hirst type of curriculum, such considerations operate to preserve, say, mathematics and science, but not to allow in a whole host of other activities – hairdressing, shorthand and typing, railway portering, bricklaying, plumbing, and so on ad infinitum. Relatively mundane reasons take over here. Schools happen to be places where mathematics and science get taught and they get taught to *everyone* relatively systematically from about the age of eleven on because it cannot be seen in advance which children are going to get to be good at them and which children are not. The fact, too, that these disciplines have a lot to them and that they demand, therefore, a high degree of structure in their teaching and learning, leads to their institutionalization in the interests of effectiveness as regards the output of people with the required skills and abilities. Physicists chemists, biologists, and mathematicians serve their apprenticeship in schools.

Compared with these activities a large number of vocational pursuits are essentially trivial (railway portering, dustmanship, shopkeeping, and many others – with apologies to porters, dustmen and shopkeepers) – there is nothing to them, or what there is to them could be dealt with summarily. A number of other vocational pursuits are best dealt with – in the interests of effectiveness – by agencies other than the school. If my son wanted to get to be a plumber or a bricklayer or an electrician I would advise him to take up an apprenticeship. Very often, to generalize this point, if a particular activity is put forward as a candidate for inclusion on the secondary school curriculum we need simply ask, 'Is it already done reasonably well by some other agency?'

E. But doesn't all this mean that we give no consideration at all to pupils' demands for a say in the school curriculum? Doesn't this mean that we cavalierly disregard the whole notion of choice? What of the boy who wants desperately to opt out of anything to do with mathematics, science, history, literature, etc., who is desperately opposed to the whole academic enterprise? This is surely in essence an organizational problem. Grave doubts may be had about the reality of 'choice' made by a twelve year old as between history and mathematics, or as between literature and slot machines, or as between the Bloodsport films and Hamlet. Choice between A and B when there is no knowledge and understanding of A is no choice at all. Such doubts would become much less grave, however, when it came to choice made by a fourteen or fifteen year old who had some relatively clear indication as to what he was choosing between. Organizationally, therefore, one might advocate a system of comprehensive education of the middle school, upper school pattern. The middle school would provide a common curriculum up to, say, the age of fourteen, at which point broad choice as between an upper school providing primarily academic courses and an upper school providing an alternative curriculum would be allowed to operate. The alternative curriculum would, as far as possible, take into account the diverse interests and predilections of pupils. On the other hand, the comprehensive pattern itself and the common curriculum to the age of fourteen would go some considerable way to the preservation of equality of opportunity and the prevention of so-called 'less able' pupils being fobbed off with a worthless and trivial programme of studies. There is no reason why there should not be built into such a system arrangements for the transfer of pupils (who so desire) from the alternative to the academic curriculum.

F. A deal of talk about curriculum matters, about the justification for doing this rather than that and so on, boils down in the final analysis to *claims* on the part of interested parties, claims which have no evidential backing; Musgrove embroiders this point. He cites the Jacob Report and asserts that:

> Jacob was forced to the conclusion that the curriculum in the social sciences and the humanities has little of the potency which is usually claimed; that little change occurs in the values of university students; and the changes that do occur cannot be related to the content of the curriculum.[15]

He also cites a modest piece of research undertaken by McNicol on history teaching as a result of which McNicol concluded, 'that history is not a fit subject for schoolchildren; that, like many other subjects, it is failing to make good the contribution to education which specialist teachers commonly claim for it'.[16]

Leaving aside the methodological difficulties which must face researchers into the effects on students of studying history, literature, philosophy, and what have you, it is true that it would be helpful to have some kind of positive proof that, for example, the study of literature does result in greater sensitivity, greater self-awareness, deeper understanding of oneself and other people. To this extent empirical research of the kind favoured by Musgrove is to be encouraged provided that we appreciate the necessary limits on the effectiveness of such research and the need for it to have a sound philosophical basis, and just so long as we realize that research of this nature will not settle any value questions for us nor will it necessarily lead to the wholesale jettisoning of particular subject matters.[17] It may, for example, do no more than pinpoint the inefficiency of particular teaching *methods*. This said, in the absence of appropriate research, what have we left as a basis for making curriculum content decisions other than the kinds of reasoning and thinking exemplified in this chapter? The only alternative seems to be not to think at all with the result that we lapse into doing this rather than that for no other reason than that our grandfathers did this rather than that. I am reminded of Harold Benjamin's delightful satire. Once upon a time there were fish, woolly horses, and sabre-tooth tigers, and so the curriculum sensibly incorporated fish-grabbing-with-the-bare-hands, woolly horse-clubbing, and sabre-tooth-tiger-scaring-with-fire. Later on, however, the waters were muddied and fish catching became difficult, the woolly horses were replaced by speedy antelopes and the tigers by bears. There were those in the community who adapted to these changes, but the wise men would not hear of curriculum change. 'With all the intricate details of fish-grabbing, horse-clubbing, and tiger-scaring – the standard cultural subjects – the school curriculum is too crowded now. We can't add these fads and frills of net-making, antelope-snaring and – of all things – bear-killing. Why, at the very thought, the body of the great New-Fist, founder of our paleolithic educational system, would turn over in its burial cairn.'[18]

G. Finally, we should not forget the implications of the argument of Chapter 2. Rationality is a uniquely human capacity, as far as we know; our ability to understand and control our world is of a different order from that of other animals and machines and is an essential part of what it is to be human. There is undoubtedly utilitarian value in understanding, but it is also the case that in developing it we become more fully human – we realize ourselves more completely.

There are dangers in an argument of this kind, which is sometimes referred to as a form of the naturalistic fallacy or the mistake of arguing that because something is the case it ought to be the case, or it is right that it should be the case. Clearly to argue, for example, that because a species is aggressive it is morally right that it should behave aggressively is suspect (although presumably it is not improper to argue that it is 'fitting' or 'appropriate' in some non-moral sense). But while we therefore should avoid an argument of the form 'human are characterized by their capacity to understand, therefore, they ought to develop that capacity', it surely is the case that to develop our specifically human as distinct from our animal nature, it is by definition necessary to cultivate our understanding.

While the details concerning forms may be intricate and disputed, it is certain that distinctions can be made between a certain number of different forms or types of understanding. Hirst chose to call these forms of knowledge, but he also refers to them as 'complex ways of understanding', and I suggest that the latter is to be preferred. They differ primarily in that 'knowledge' has connotations such that emphasis falls on that which is known – the body of knowledge – while the connotations of 'understanding' emphasize the reasoning behind the body of knowledge. It is true that if I 'know' in the full sense of that word that the angles of a triangle add up to 180° then I can give an account of this claim; but it is just a fact of usage that often a person may be said to 'know' such a fact meaning simply that they can repeat it. By contrast to 'understand' that the angles of a triangle add up to 180° necessarily implies that one recognizes and appreciates the nature of and the reasoning behind the claim, rather than that one can merely regurgitate the formula.

While the details of what forms of understanding there may be have not been settled, it is certain that not all types of phenomena can be understood in the same way, and that some of the distinct forms, notably science, mathematics, and philosophy, are fairly indisputable. There are, then, distinct types or forms of understanding, and this fact is of crucial importance in helping us to select from the vast array of human knowledge and information.

Combining this focus on fundamental forms of understanding with some concern for what is of most use to us in the widest sense and for what makes us distinctively human (as, for instance, understanding history does but being able to make tools doesn't), it seems justifiable to argue that we both can and should seek to establish a knowledge-based curriculum.

My object in this chapter has been to inquire into the sorts of knowledge that ought to figure in educational programmes. I have examined at some length the influential philosophical views of P. H. Hirst and I have, through consideration of a number of debating points, indicated the ways in which, and the extent to which, philosophical perspectives merge with and relate to broader perspectives. But it is now necessary to turn our attention to the wider world of curriculum theory.

Notes

1 As with Peters and education, so Hirst has written at length on curriculum matters at various times. Not surprisingly his views have been modified with the passing of time. I am not, however, intent on following through in detail the progression of Hirst's thought and I shall take as representative of his position his influential and often-quoted paper 'Liberal Education and the Nature of Knowledge' which is to be found in Archambault, R. D. (ed.), *Philosophical Analysis and Education* (London, Routledge & Kegan Paul, 1965) pp. 113–38. I shall not refer in these notes to specific pages of Hirst's paper; I shall instead give the necessary page references in the body of the text. The paper, along with Hirst's subsequent papers on the theme, has been reprinted yet again in Hirst, P. H., *Knowledge and the Curriculum* (London, Routledge & Kegan Paul, 1975).

2 Broadly speaking, Hirst's concern is with 'general' education; that is, with the education that *everyone* ought to get up to, say, the age of sixteen, and before they embark – if they do embark – on further, 'specialist' education.

3 See, for example, Hirst, P. H., 'The Logic of the Curriculum' in *Journal of Curriculum Studies*, vol. 1. no. 22, 1969, pp. 142–58. Note particularly pp. 153–5.

4 *New Society*, 6 March 1969, pp. 359–61.

5 In the case of the putative form of literature and the fine arts, it is by no means clear that Hirst is referring to propositions of this sort. He seems rather to regard the art work itself, the novel, symphony, or statue, as a proposition. See his 'Literature and the Fine Arts as a Unique Form of Knowledge' in *Knowledge and the Curriculum*.

6 In view of the fact that much of Robin Barrow's writing is concerned with the ethical theory of utilitarianism, which has a rather more precise meaning, we should like to stress the broad sense of the term as used here.

7 The notion of 'valuable in itself' is explored more fully in Gregory, I. M. M. and Woods, R. G., 'Valuable in Itself' in *Educational Philosophy and Theory*, vol. 3, no. 2, 1971, pp. 51–64.

8 Nowell-Smith, P. H., *Education in a University* (Leicester University Press, 1958).

9 Plumb, J. H. (ed.), *Crisis in the Humanities* (Harmondsworth, Penguin, 1964) pp. 43–4.

10 Jerman, J., 'Modern Languages' in Whitfield, R. (ed.), *Disciplines of the Curriculum* (New York, McGraw Hill, 1971) p. 94.

11 In practice, it may be felt, we have recently seen rather too many enthusiastic proposals for new areas of study, such as peace education, environmental education, and sex education, without adequate thought being given to their justification.

12 Steiner, G., *In Bluebeard's Castle* (London, Faber, 1971), pp. 103–4.

13 Oakeshott, M., 'Education: The Engagement and its Frustration' in *Proceedings of the Philosophy of Education Society of Great Britain*. vol. V, no. 1, January 1971, p. 69.

14 Hough, G., 'Crisis in Literary Education' in Plumb. J. H. (ed.), op. cit., p. 107.

15 Musgrove, F., 'Curriculum Objectives' in *Journal of Curriculum Studies*, vol. 1, no. 1, 1968, p. 8.

16 Musgrove, F., op. cit., pp. 9, 10.

17 See Chapter 13. See Barrow, R., *The Philosophy of Schooling* (Brighton, Wheatsheaf, 1981) ch. 6 and *Giving Teaching Back to Teachers* (Brighton, Wheatsheaf, 1984).

18 Peddiwell, J. Abner (alias Benjamin, Harold), *The Sabre-Tooth Curriculum* (New York, McGraw Hill, 1939) pp. 24–5.

Further reading

P. H. Hirst is always worth reading on curriculum. I suggest that readers consult his paper 'Liberal Education and the Nature of Knowledge' in R. D. Archambault (ed.), *Philosophical Analysis and Education* (London, Routledge & Kegan Paul, 1965), his contribution to J. F. Kerr (ed.), *Changing the Curriculum* (University of London Press, 1968), and his contribution to a collection of readings, *The Curriculum: Context, Design and Development* (Edinburgh, Oliver & Boyd, 1971) edited by Richard Hooper. See also his collected papers, P. H. Hirst, *Knowledge and the Curriculum* (London, Routledge & Kegan Paul, 1974). R. C. Whitfield (ed.), *Disciplines of the Curriculum* (New York, McGraw-Hill, 1971) consists of a collection of papers concerned with different subject areas – mathematics, history, art, etc. – and the reasons for their appearance in curricula. *Towards a Compulsory Curriculum* (London, Routledge & Kegan Paul, 1973), by J. P. White is provocative and very interesting, while Robin Barrow's *Common Sense and the Curriculum* (London, Allen & Unwin, 1976) offers a sustained critique of White as well as positive curriculum proposals. On the concept of understanding, see chapter 4 of J. F. Soltis *An Introduction to the Analysis of Educational Concepts*. See also Robin Barrow *Understanding Skills: Thinking, Feeling and Caring* (London, Ontario Althouse, 1990).

5 Curriculum theory

The previous chapter dealt with a key curriculum question – 'What content should be taught?' and also, since an immediate answer to that is 'knowledge', the logically prior question 'What is the nature of knowledge?'. However, in the years since this book was first published a relatively new subject within the study of education has come very much into its own, namely 'curriculum' or 'curriculum and instruction'.

Those who see themselves specifically as lecturers in or professors of curriculum have evolved their own framework (or frameworks) of inquiry and research, and some rather different priorities among the educational questions that might be asked. Some consider curriculum itself to be a discipline, almost a form of knowledge in Hirst's sense, rather than a mere subject or field of knowledge; and many do not regard the questions 'What is the nature of knowledge?', 'What should our aims be?', or 'What should the content of the curriculum be?' as specifically and properly curriculum questions at all.

The widespread development of curriculum as a branch of study in Britain (it has held sway for rather longer in the United States) calls for a chapter rather different in kind from the previous ones. Here what is required is a description of the field that draws attention to different viewpoints and clarifies some obscurities; we need to note the practical implications of adopting one conception of curriculum rather than another or of proceeding in this way or that, rather than attempt to delineate the logical properties of a particular idea or concept of curriculum. For, while with concepts such as education or knowledge, one feels that there is an idea that many of us more or less share, but that needs clarification and elucidation, when it comes to curriculum the word clearly means different things to different people, and what people do in the name of curriculum is equally varied.

Curriculum: the word and the concept

The first question we need to raise concerns the meaning of 'curriculum' itself, for obviously what counts as or what constitutes curriculum has some bearing on what constitutes curriculum theory. Furthermore, the question conveniently allows us to draw attention to and stress the distinction between a verbal question and a conceptual question, for the question 'What does "curriculum" mean?' is surely not a real conceptual question.

The word 'curriculum' is used in different ways by different people, ranging from its use to refer to a course of study of some sort, through its use as a term to pick out a set of intended outcomes, to its use to refer to a set of actual outcomes in student learning. But in none of these senses is there a genuine complexity about the idea of curriculum as there is about the idea of love or the idea of education. In the latter cases, although different people may turn out to have completely different conceptions (different ideas of what love or education are), the initial presumption is that they are talking about the same idea, but that each finds it difficult to articulate precisely what this idea involves. In the case of curriculum, it is evident that different people just have quite different conceptions – that is to say, they use the word to refer to quite distinct ideas or concepts (any one of which may or may not turn out to be conceptually problematic in the way that love is). There may be various reasons why people should come to use the word curriculum in different senses. The most obvious one is that they come from different backgrounds (cultural, social, intellectual), but a person may also adopt a particular usage for certain practical or political purposes. It is obviously useful to define key words in an enterprise, as curriculum is a key educational term, in ways that reflect or reinforce one's point of view. But whatever the explanation of the different senses of 'curriculum', the example usefully reminds us that concepts may be of different sorts – or rather that we have concepts of different types of thing. Some concepts are conceptions of what is to a large extent given and unalterable in nature: mountains, for example, are what they are, and, if it is the concept of mountain that one is trying to understand, one is to some extent governed by physical reality. Other concepts are primarily governed by laws of logic: whatever a circle is, it cannot be square. A third group of concepts are clearly man-made: they are ideas conceived, developed, and defined by man as, it may be said, the concept of chivalry has been. It is into this third category that curriculum surely falls.

It is not written in heaven how the word 'curriculum' should be used nor what features or properties any particular type of curriculum (or sense of the word) should have. Neither logic nor the laws of nature can decree that curriculum should be understood to mean one thing alone or that an actual curriculum should involve one thing rather than another. It is therefore not my intention to try and tease out the meaning or even a possible meaning of 'curriculum', as I shall do, for instance, in the case of creativity, where behind different uses of the word there does appear to be a particular idea or concept of some interest and complexity (see Chapter 11). But, while it would not be appropriate to pursue the question 'What is curriculum?' as if it had some fixed and determinate answer, one may none the less produce reasons that incline one to defining the term in one way rather than another. In this case, broadly speaking, I suggest that there are reasons for keeping our definition of curriculum simple, specific in scope, and, as it happens, old-fashioned in meaning.

The reasons in question are of three kinds. The first is etymological, the second is based on ordinary usage, and the third has to do with the advantages of specificity. The first two reasons are certainly not decisive in themselves. For instance, in Chapter 10, I shall specifically repudiate an argument based on etymology, suggesting that, whatever the Latin origin of the English word 'education' may be, it has no direct bearing on what the word means today or what education should be. Then again, if ordinary usage were taken to be decisive in determining what, for example, constituted justice, we might be in considerable trouble. What people say using the word 'justice' – how they ordinarily use the word – naturally enough reflects or incorporates their various shortcomings, prejudices, and confusions; ordinary language does indeed tell us what people think about a concept, but it does not necessarily provide us with a clear and coherent view of that concept. Certainly, as philosophers, we would be well advised to study and take note of the etymology and ordinary usage of words, for these provide many useful hints and clues, and no doubt in certain cases they can help to fix the actual current meaning of a word. Furthermore, if there is no compelling reason to reject the implications of etymology or ordinary language – no reason, for example, such as that ordinary usage has clearly departed from the original meaning of the word or that ordinary language shows itself to be incoherent or contradictory – then, as a general principle, it may be said that it is advisable to be guided by them, not least in the interests of improved communication. After all, if a word derives from a word or usage that is quite clear and straightforward, and if current usage is ordinarily consistent with that meaning, it would be somewhat perverse to attempt to put forward some new, idiosyncratic, usage. (Not that that hasn't happened, with mixed success depending on your point of view, with such words as 'gay', 'parameter', 'silly', 'stasis', and 'infer'.) None the less, one surely cannot accept the view that something about the usage of a word (be it its history or current usage) should necessarily determine the meaning of a concept.

The meaning of a concept can only be explored when the verbal issues have been settled. Once we know what usage we are concerned with – be it the romantic novelist's view of love as exemplified in his work, the putative ordinary person's, the psychologist's, or anyone else's – then the conceptual work can begin: then we can begin to explicate and see that the usage in question is clear, coherent, consistent with the laws of nature or logic, and adequately or fully enough characterized. To examine these points in respect of a particular meaning or usage of a word is to engage in philosophical or conceptual analysis.

A definition of curriculum

In the case of 'curriculum', therefore, although etymology and popular usage do support the relatively simple and narrow definition that I shall propose we should adopt, I do not claim that those are overwhelming or compelling reasons for adopting it. The main reason for resisting the temptation to define curriculum very broadly so as to cover, for instance, all the experiences that a child encounters at school, as some wish to do, is that it is useful in itself to have a number of relatively narrow or specific concepts to work with in a field or area that one is trying to understand. The more specific a concept is in relation to others in the same area, the more fully it characterizes or delineates something. For example, the general concept animal tells us far less about any particular animal, than the more specific concepts of duck, snake, rabbit, and so forth. Knowing what an animal is tells us less about animals than knowing what a duck is tells us about ducks. Of course we need general terms too, precisely in order to note and fix our attention on similarities. Without the concept of animal we might fail to note that by certain criteria ducks and rabbits are similar or comparable and to be distinguished from fishes, trees, and, perhaps, humans. But a proper understanding of a field is hampered by reliance on general concepts. It may, for example, be argued that it is difficult to have serious and illuminating discussions about popular music, precisely because the concept of popular music itself is so broad as to cover a variety of forms which do not really resemble each other in any way other than that they are classified as popular. The explanatory power of a concept is seriously affected by its degree of generality. As historians used to be taught, anything that allegedly explains everything (such as God or market forces) in fact explains nothing.

The desire and tendency to widen the concept of curriculum arose at least partially from an honourable cause. Those who were interested in the curriculum in the old-fashioned and relatively simple sense of the syllabus or programme of study saw, correctly enough, that what is on the syllabus is never totally identifiable with what is taught, still less with what is learned, and in some cases is barely comparable. The curriculum, in this sense, may be, for example, the study of the American war of independence; but what that actually comes to mean in classrooms and individuals' experiences throughout the land will vary enormously as a result of such diverse factors as who is doing the teaching, how they choose to do it, the material resources available, where it is being taught, who the students are, their backgrounds, their prior knowledge, and their frame of mind. To categorize the broad range of factors that may affect the nature of the curriculum, we may say that the form of the curriculum as it is actualized will depend upon psychological truths about teachers and students, sociological truths, truths about teaching, and political truths. And it obviously is the case that such factors do have a decided bearing on what students actually receive in the name of curriculum. There is therefore a perfectly straightforward and reasonable sense in which using the term 'curriculum' to mean the programme of study and to refer to such things as 'reading, writing, and arithmetic' in the elementary school, or 'quadratic equations and trigonometry' for a secondary maths curriculum, is less in touch with reality, or what actually happens, than some definitions based on what particular students actually get out of the provision of various courses with such titles.

However, the great disadvantage is that in lumping everything together the term 'curriculum' becomes unmanageable and diverts attention away from what is after all a key question – even if only one of many – what is the content that ideally we want to impart to students? Granted that it is also important to pursue such questions as whether particular styles of teaching or certain individual psychological states of mind may in various ways affect the outcome of our programme, we have to start with some idea of a programme. We want to consider what content or subject matter students ought ideally to study, not only because it is an important question in its own right, but also because our answer to this question is logically necessary to conducting inquiry and research into other related matters. Whether certain techniques of teaching are desirable, for example, may depend at least partly on what one is teaching and why – two questions that are at the heart of inquiry into content. Evidence from psychologists that children tend to fall asleep in classes devoted to Marxism would be irrelevant if we saw no reason to include Marxism in the curriculum in the first place.

My view is that the key question in the domain of curriculum, however the word is defined, is 'What should the content be?', and that consequently the term should be used to refer to the programme or content that we intend to put before students (which may, as far as meaning goes, be specified in greater or less detail). The main argument for this, as I say, is that it forcefully reminds us that we have to focus on that question, and that ideally we should do so in isolation from all the other kinds of question that will undoubtedly subsequently arise. Let us examine what happens when we teach x in certain situations by all means, but let us do it when we are certain that we *want* to teach x and clear about what we mean by teaching it.

Curriculum as a *sui generis* practice

The view set out in the previous section is not universally shared, particularly by curriculum specialists in the United States, who are usually generalists in search of a discipline, not above decreeing one when they find difficulty in getting on the inside of those that already exist. They have a marked tendency to see curriculum, not as an area of inquiry primarily concerned with what should be taught, but rather one concerned with how it (whatever it may be) should be organized for teaching purposes.

At this point certain other possible sources of confusion need to be sorted out. Phrases such as 'curriculum studies', 'curriculum theory', 'curriculum development', and 'curriculum and instruction', and 'curriculum' itself are not always very clearly distinguished. 'Curriculum theory' I take to be abstract inquiry into general principles affecting curriculum. It is thus not very different from educational theory. Precisely how different it is will depend upon how narrowly one conceives of curriculum itself. 'Curriculum studies' does not seem in practice appreciably different. Perhaps the phrase carries less of a suggestion that the area of curriculum represents a cohesive whole, and perhaps there is a hint of a more practical perspective, but the difference is slight. 'Curriculum and instruction' is more confusing. Sometimes used as a synonym for 'curriculum theory' or 'curriculum studies', it may also refer to an allegedly *sui generis* skill, or again it may simply refer to content and pedagogy. In addition to the different nuances of these different phrases and the possible different senses or interpretations of the school 'curriculum', we must note three quite distinct uses of 'curriculum'. It can be used to refer to the school curriculum; it can be used to refer to curriculum theory, as when someone says 'I study curriculum'; and it can also be used to refer to an alleged special facility to bridge the presumed gap between theory and practice.

This last use is very common in the United States, and, in one view, is what Schwabb meant when he referred to curriculum as 'the art of the practical'.[1] Whether Schwabb did mean this is not at all clear to me, but what is clear is that there are some people who understand curriculum experts to be people who are good at putting the ideas of others (theorists?) across to practitioners and thereby into practice. On the face of it, this sounds well enough – after all, it is a common complaint that theory and practice don't seem to relate to one another – but on closer inspection it is less satisfactory. Without anticipating the discussion of theory and its relation to practice in Chapter 14 too much, let me just say here (i) that it is not clear that the idea of a general facility or skill of putting theory into practice makes sense, and (ii) that, if it does, it is still not clear why the skill should be found amongst a specialist group of middlemen rather than amongst theoreticians or practitioners (assuming the latter two to be distinct). There are, of course, a number of popularizers in various fields – men such as Mortimer Adler, Simon Blackburn or Bryan Magee in philosophy and Isaac Asimov or Richard Dawkins in science who are also respectable scholars in their field, and others, such as the writer Bill Bryson, who are not. But these are popularizers in the sense of people who simplify ideas and present them entertainingly. They are not blessed with some special knack of expressing the profound easily. They simplify, which is to say they leave out some of the complexities of the views they explain. Popularizers are therefore to be distinguished from people who communicate complex and abstract ideas well without modifying or simplifying them.[2] But what sense can be made of the idea that there are on the one hand educational theorists, who are wise, clever, and profound in their abstract way, and, on the other hand, practical chaps who can cope with children, such that a special art is needed to communicate the wisdom of the former to the latter or to put the theory into practice?

Imagine that I am a good educational theorist: I have clearly worked out my aims and have articulated them with the clarity of a good philosopher. I also know about children and teaching, and, as a result of my understanding, I come up with a proposal of the form 'We ought to do x in schools'. Granted that some teachers may not be skilled in the kind of theorizing that I engage in, or may simply lack the time that I can devote to it, surely that does not mean that my ideas are not communicable and comprehensible to them? If it does mean that, then what exactly would the middleman do? It is sometimes suggested that he is needed to temper theory with practice or practical wisdom. But this, depending on what precisely it means, is either something to be strongly resisted or else something that each practitioner should do for himself. Suppose for example, that theoreticians conclude that we should do x in the school, but practical people are aware that there is no money to do x. If 'tempering theory with practice' means being 'realistic' in the sense of ignoring what we ought to do because it is in practical terms difficult or politically awkward, then obviously such 'tempering' should be resisted. It is part of our job as educationalists to insist on what ought to be done from an educational perspective and to argue against political obstacles; whether we win or lose such battles is another problem. The point here is that we cannot formally approve of cutting the coat of our ideals according to the cloth of politicians. On the other hand, if 'tempering theory with practice' means that a theoretical prescription, which will by its nature be general in form, will need modifications and adaptations in particular situations – well, every teacher (and every theorist) knows that; but particular modifications clearly have to be worked out by the people on the spot, the people who know the particular situation, rather than by some outside middleman. Besides, what would it mean to say that one was blessed with the art of modifying things in general? How does one acquire it? Is it not clear that one gains skill at modifying particular kinds of thing by knowing one's particular territory? And is it not equally clear that individual teachers should have this ability to interpret educational theory in the context of their own classrooms?

What happens in fact is that certain individuals become semiprofessional curriculum developers – that is to say they become practised, through experience, in going through various hoops typically associated with drawing up a new curriculum. For example, they become familiar with the idea of setting out aims in terms of various observable objectives or with the idea of testing the necessary resources for a particular curriculum proposal. But such people are not necessarily blessed with understanding and wisdom (not having studied education seriously in a theoretical mode), and they are not necessarily any more practical than professors. (It is a complete nonsense to imagine that because a person comes from the classroom he is necessarily more practical than those who don't. In any case, for the record, professors too work in classrooms – their own.)

In short I find it very difficult to see a plausible role for the curriculum expert as an identifiable middleman with a unique role to play. And I see more danger than advantage in leaving curriculum planning, design, and change to a group of specialists, rather than insisting that curriculum should be in the hands of teachers, provided that they get to grips with theoretical understanding of their enterprise.

Means and ends

And so we come to what for me is a most worrying tendency: the shift towards curriculum as a headless monster, which arises from the widespread acceptance of the idea that one can coherently pursue other curriculum questions independently of discerning one's aim or ends, combined with the more particular view that curriculum is a form of applied science.

Curriculum as an area of study started out by reference to some key questions, most famously enunciated by Ralph Tyler.[3] Since then it has become more ossified (as tends to be the way with ideas) and the domain is generally seen as divisible into the areas of development, design, implementation, and evaluation. The last two of these are fairly straightforward, though it should be noted that evaluation is concerned with the efficacy of a programme rather than with its educational worth. Evaluators are not in the business of estimating the educational success or value of curriculum change or practice, but in that of assessing the tendency of a given programme to be incorporated as intended and to attain the ends that it has, whatever they may be. Development and design are not always clearly distinguished, but design is primarily concerned with the manner in which a curriculum (conceived of, as we have seen, as anything from a programme of study through to an attempt to pinpoint student experiences) should be set out or presented to would-be users. Development is concerned either with improving one's own design (on an individual, school, or district level) or with improving the style of adoption in schools: that is to say, with looking at ways in which one's school might better adapt to more appropriate curricula. In this latter sense, it evidently shades into implementation.

But the crucial thing to note, and, I suggest, to be seriously worried about, is the extent to which these various branches of curriculum are pursued and studied, (i) independently of each other, (ii) independently of serious philosophical consideration of aims, and (iii) in the mode of the natural sciences. I must of course stress that there are honourable exceptions to the tendency that I draw attention to. For example, Denis Lawton writes about curriculum with some concern for the integration of various aspects, and ties up all that he has to say with some clearly enunciated arguments about content and aims. David Hamilton, to take another example, argues specifically for a humanistic, informal, model of curriculum development and research. The late Lawrence Stenhouse specifically repudiated the idea of behavioural objectives, which can serve like a millstone around the neck of curriculum.[4] None the less, although one could cite other exceptions too, the dominant trend in curriculum is undoubtedly towards a scientific view of the enterprise, such that curriculum specialists are deemed to be working on means to ends that have been determined by others, and research into means is seen as a scientific business.

What this means in effect is, first, that implementers carry out research into how various programmes may most successfully (compliantly?) come to be adopted, without, for example, being much concerned about evaluating the efficacy of the adoption. Evaluators, by the same token, tell us about principles that are supposed to govern those curricula that successfully meet their objectives, but rather ignore the question of how to get a curriculum adopted in a way that ensures that justice is done to it. Both are likely to proceed without direct reference to the third, distinct, branch of design. Designers very often include prescriptions in their design proposal for evaluation, but these are with reference to ensuring that in using the curriculum one is obtaining its objectives, which does not necessarily pertain to the question of whether the curriculum has been successfully adopted.

One might at this point raise the objection that this just is an age of specialism. Why, it may be asked, should designers be expected to understand about implementation and vice versa? This brings me to my second, altogether more urgent, point: what one cannot reasonably do is proceed in any one of these branches of curriculum without a very firm and clear grasp of educational ends. It simply does not make sense to claim to have expertise in designing curricula without reference to some particular idea of educational success. More generally, one cannot say that *x* is a good principle in the abstract, because it can only be a good principle in the light of certain ends. To this we may add a quite distinct point which is that it is far from clear why so many people take it for granted that there are significant general principles of design, implementation, and such like. Surely the best way to design a science curriculum for ten year olds may be in many important respects quite different from the best way to design an English curriculum for sixteen year olds?

In general curriculum wallahs seem to take far too little account of the specifically educational nature of their sphere of interest, of the nature of the particular subject matter on any given occasion, and of the multifarious particularities of any given teaching situation. This is a point to which I shall return in Chapter 13.

For the moment this brings us to a more specific and more serious objection, namely the tendency of many curriculum persons to be wedded, thinkingly or otherwise, explicitly or implicitly, to an applied science view of the field. (There can be no doubt, I think, that this stems from the quite extraordinary dominance that pragmatism held in American philosophy and behaviourism in psychology. The intellectual culture of the United States is, deep down, characterized by a view of life as a series of surmountable technical problems and man as but one more, albeit highly developed, form of material being.) The ends are variously presumed to be given, unproblematic, the product of democratic consensus, self-evident, or, paradoxically, too complex for anyone but absent-minded philosophers to worry about. What they are not is firmly grasped, stated and connected to research, argument and prescription pertaining to means. Consequently, implicit in much of the curriculum work is a set of very dubious and ill-thought-out objectives or end states. Notions such as intelligence, imagination, understanding – specifically human attributes – are either ignored or travestied by operational definitions. Education itself and mind are more or less ignored. Instead we are presumed to be creatures with a brain, capable of being instructed rather than taught, assessable by reference only to such things as time on task. The world is seen as comprising only scientifically demonstrable means to unquestioned ends. Thus curriculum textbooks and lecturers tell one how to do a curriculum as culinary experts tell one how to prepare a meal. It is all recipes. But it may all be nonsense, as the cooking recipe might be, if one were to question the food value or the cost of the end result.

Values are central to the curriculum business and values are primarily a matter for philosophical inquiry. This is not, as is often wrongly supposed, because they are non-factual or necessarily part of the subject matter of philosophy. (Whether, to what extent, and in what way value judgements are or are not related to factual propositions is one of the issues that needs careful consideration. And there are plenty of other disciplines besides philosophy that may have an interest in values; for example sociology.) The reason that philosophers are needed at some point in any serious discussion of values is that many of the crucial questions in the area are conceptual. That is to say, the first main problem we face in arguing about aims is in getting clear what people mean by such claims as that the aim of education is to produce a critical thinker, a happy person, or whatever.

It is argued by some that settling our values is a forlorn hope, since value judgements are relative. But at best any such claim would have to substantiate itself by philosophical means. At worst (and I believe this to be the case) the claim is false and based on a confusion between 'arbitrary' and 'not empirically demonstrated'. This is not the place to pursue this particular issue (but see Chapter 9). Suffice it to say that certain values seem undeniable, and are not in fact disputed, many if not all of them being conceptually tied up with what it is to be human and what morality is all about. Furthermore certain more specific values are conceptually linked to the nature of education.[5]

Where does this leave us? Curriculum is very often instituted as a distinctive subject or discipline. Within it there are subdivisions. It is not clear how wise or well-founded this is, but if it is going to be done (and certainly one recognizes the usefulness of curriculum as a category on which to focus inquiry) it should start with the question of what we ought to learn. Everything else must then be pursued in the light of some specific answer to that question.

Notes

1 Schwabb, J., 'The Practical: A Language for the Curriculum', *School Review*, vol. 78, no. 1, 1969.
2 Incidentally, I subscribe to the view that if a thing is worth saying it can be said clearly, and am therefore mightily suspicious of people who talk deeply in the sense of incomprehensibly about even profound and esoteric matters. This is not to be confused with technical language: obviously the language of atomic physics is incomprehensible to one on the outside.
3 Tyler, R., *Basic Principles of Curriculum and Instruction* (University of Chicago Press, 1949).
4 Lawton, D., *Class, Culture and the Curriculum* (London, Routledge & Kegan Paul, 1975); Hamilton, D., *Curriculum Evaluation* (London, Open Books, 1976); Stenhouse, L., *An Introduction to Curriculum Research and Development* (Heinemann, 1975).
5 See further on these important issues Wilson, J., *What Philosophy Can Do* (London, Macmillan, 1986); Barrow, R., *The Philosophy of Schooling* (Brighton, Wheatsheaf, 1981) and *Giving Teaching Back to Teachers* (Brighton, Wheatsheaf, 1984).

Further reading

Robin Barrow, *Giving Teaching Back to Teachers* (Brighton, Wheatsheaf, 1984) offers a full analysis and critique of the field of curriculum theory, while Kieran Egan, *Education and Psychology* (New York, Teachers College Press, 1983) is pertinent to critical consideration of the contribution of psychology to curriculum. Paul Croll. *Systematic Classroom Observation* (London, Falmer, 1986) chapter 7, deals directly with some of the criticisms made here. Useful introductions to curriculum study are provided by Hugh Sockett, *Designing the Curriculum* (London, Open Books, 1976), D. Jenkins and M. Shipman, *Curriculum: An Introduction* (London, Open Books, 1976), and other volumes in Open Books' Curriculum Studies series. Examples of the kind of curriculum theorizing criticized here are provided by, for example, David Pratt, *Curriculum: Design and Development* (New York, Harcourt Brace Jovanovich, 1980) and D. Tanner and L. N. Tanner, *Curriculum Development: Theory and Pratice* (New York, Macmillan, 1980).

6   Indoctrination

When the first edition of this book was published in 1975 there was considerable interest in the concept of indoctrination among philosophers of education. This may have been partly because, being a notion that was on the face of it antithetical to education, it seemed a useful way to throw further light on the nature of education itself. But it was also because, in those years of Cold War and somewhat hotter engagements in places such as Korea and Vietnam, there was a genuine feeling that indoctrination and other related activities such as brain-washing were prevalent. At the time of preparing the third edition (1988), consideration was given to cutting out the chapter altogether, on the grounds that the word 'indoctrination' was no longer in common use and the practice perhaps not as significant as had once been thought. The first point was and remains broadly correct: newspapers no longer seem interested in lurid stories about brain-washing and people don't seem to talk much about 'indoctrination' as such. Whether the second point was correct at the time is debatable. It certainly isn't now.

Indoctrination is a very real thing. The evidence is suddenly widespread that the world is full of closed minds, ideologues and fanatics, which, though none of them are synonymous with 'indoctrinated', certainly take us relentlessly into the realm of indoctrination. Terrorists who believe unwaveringly that they are justified by their cause, people who are willing to bring death to their own supporters in their unyielding conviction that they alone have access to the truth, people who deny the Holocaust despite all the evidence, people who are incapable of critically examining their religious beliefs, those who cannot see beyond 'my country, right or wrong', those who are incapable of questioning either whether the United States is 'the great Satan' or 'God's Republic on earth', and those who do not seek to question as they carry out hideous atrocities on fellow humans in the name of some creed, faith or ideology – all testify to the reality of indoctrination in some sense and to some degree.

The essence of indoctrination, as I shall argue, is not to be found in the degree of conviction, nor in the desirability or otherwise of one's goals, but in the blind unshakeable commitment. There is something beyond argument, beyond reasoning, about indoctrination and that is why it is antithetical to education. Other things are different from and other things are incompatible with education, but indoctrination is education inverted. So it matters that we give consideration to the concept of indoctrination, partly because to do so will help us to understand education further, partly because indoctrination involves denial of the value of rationality, and partly because it is a very real phenomenon – and not only in terrorist cells. Some religious fanatics in the West appear to be at least as thoroughly indoctrinated as members of Al Qaeda.

But how does one distinguish between the honourably committed and the indoctrinated? What are the criteria that enable us to determine whether your position is based on sound reasoning or on indoctrination? What are the defining characteristics of indoctrination?

If it is agreed that education should involve only morally acceptable ways of teaching, then most people will immediately conclude that it should not involve indoctrination. 'Indoctrination' is a term pregnant with emotive meaning, and, for most people, it is a condemnatory term. But what is its descriptive meaning? If *prima facie* it seems that teachers ought not to indoctrinate, it becomes rather important for them to know what indoctrinating is. An analysis of what it is to indoctrinate may also help to explain why it is generally regarded as an objectionable practice.

Indoctrination clearly involves causing people to hold certain beliefs. If a teacher has responsibility for a particular child for a year and by the end of that year he has not imparted any beliefs to him of any sort, then whatever he has been doing or trying to do he has not indoctrinated him. Indoctrination is therefore to be distinguished from conditioning. To condition someone is to cause him to behave in certain ways and does not necessarily involve any reference to beliefs at all. We talk of conditioning rats, for example, to respond in specific ways to various stimuli, but we do not talk of indoctrinating rats, on the assumption that rats do not have beliefs.

But equally clearly the fact that a teacher has imparted certain beliefs to children is not a sufficient indication that he has indoctrinated them. If I cause you to believe that there is a world energy crisis, it does not automatically follow that I have indoctrinated you. It is a necessary condition of indoctrination that beliefs should be imparted, but it is not a sufficient condition, which is to say that not any way of imparting any kind of belief is *ipso facto* indoctrination.

What other conditions necessarily have to be present, then, for one to conclude that indoctrination is going on? What does the concept of indoctrination involve besides the imparting of beliefs? What distinguishes it from other teaching activities whereby children come to hold certain beliefs?

Let us start with a paradigm case of indoctrination. By a paradigm case is meant an uncontentious example, an example that virtually everybody would concede is an example of indoctrination, notwithstanding the fact that different people have different views as to what is essential to the concept. By separating the various strands involved in the example and considering each one in turn it may become easier to form a judgement as to which of them are necessary to indoctrination and which of them merely contingent.

Imagine a Catholic school in which all the teachers are committed Catholics and where all the children come from Catholic homes and have parents who want them to be brought up as Catholics. Imagine also that the teachers are determined to try to bring up the children as devout Catholics. They deliberately attempt to inculcate in their pupils an unshakable commitment to the truth of Catholicism and of the various claims or propositions associated with it. They thus bring up the pupils to believe in the unquestionable truth of such propositions as 'The Pope is infallible', 'One should not use artificial birth-control methods', and 'God (defined in terms of the Catholic conception of God) exists'. They bring them up to believe in these and similar propositions in such a way that the pupils come to regard those who do not accept them as true propositions as being simply mistaken or in error, and in such a way that no reasoning put forward that might cast doubt upon their assurance that Catholicism and the propositions related to it are incorrigible truths can cause them to reconsider their assumptions. They are, let us assume, drilled by their teachers in the answers that explain away any possible doubts about or objections to the claims of Catholicism. The techniques used by the teachers to evoke this commitment to Catholicism may be many and various: some of the propositions presented may be put forward with rational explanation, but others will be cultivated by means of the example set by the teachers, the use of praise and blame or the withholding of approval by the teachers, or simply the use of their authority to reinforce their insistence on the undeniable truth of the Catholic view of the world and man's place in it.

It is difficult to conceive of anyone seriously doubting that these teachers are indoctrinating. But the question remains: why 'indoctrinating'? What is it about what is going on here that indicates that it is an example of indoctrination? Do all the features of this example have to be present for one to describe it as a case of indoctrination, or might one still regard these teachers as indoctrinators even if some of the details in the example were changed? To find an answer to these questions it is necessary to examine the various features of the example in isolation.

Content

One notable feature of this example is that the beliefs which the children are being brought to accept are of a particular sort. Catholicism is a doctrinal system of belief, that is, it consists of an interrelated set of ideas, based upon certain propositions or postulates that cannot be demonstrated to be unquestionably true, which taken together have repercussions for the way in which the believer views the world and for the way in which he lives his life.

In referring to a proposition as one that cannot be demonstrated to be unquestionably true, one is not necessarily denying that it is true. An unprovable proposition cannot be demonstrated to be unquestionably false either. The distinction is between propositions in relation to which, whether they are in fact true or not, there is no disagreement as to the sort of evidence that would count to show whether they were true or false (provable propositions), and propositions in relation to which there is no such agreement (unprovable propositions). Thus propositions such as 'Metals expand when heated', 'Trollope wrote *Can You Forgive Her?*' or, 'There is a planet made of green cheese' are all provable propositions. All are in principle verifiable or falsifiable, even though some or all of us may not in fact know for certain whether they are true or false. We all agree on the sort of evidence that would count in favour of or against the truth of such propositions, even if we do not actually have the evidence to hand.

Examples of unprovable propositions might be 'God exists', 'The Pope is infallible', 'The meek shall inherit the earth', 'All men ought to be free', 'Economic considerations are the fundamental determinant of social change'. There is no general agreement over what would count as evidence for or against these propositions or on how to interpret the supposed evidence. For me, as a non-Catholic, there is fairly strong historical evidence that the Pope is not infallible; but to a committed Catholic this evidence can be explained away: it doesn't count. For some the fact that there is suffering and misery in the world is a strong argument against any notion of an omnipotent and loving God; but the believer does not deny the existence of suffering, he merely denies that it counts as evidence against the existence of such a God, and he explains the evidence away at least to his own satisfaction. More generally every piece of evidence produced by the religious sceptic against the notion that there is a God (we cannot see him, hear him, touch him, and so on) is dismissed by the believer as irrelevant, until it is not clear to the sceptic whether anything even in principle could be allowed by the believer to count as evidence against the existence of God. But if *nothing* could count as evidence in principle, what kind of a belief is it? Certainly not a belief that is demonstrably true or false. Similarly one who is committed to an exclusively economic interpretation of social change simply interprets the history of social change in the light of that commitment. It is entirely unclear what would count as evidence against this interpretation, just as it is entirely unclear what would count as evidence to establish or refute fundamental moral claims such as that all men ought to be free. These propositions which by their nature are neither verifiable nor falsifiable serve rather as guiding principles for interpreting the world. In each case it seems that for one who is committed to the truth of the proposition nothing counts as evidence against it, whereas for those who are not so committed quite a lot of evidence counts against it. The situation is thus quite distinct from that in which two people disagree about whether metals do or do not expand when heated, but would none the less agree in principle upon what would count as evidence for or against the proposition.

It will be seen from this that all political, religious, and moral systems of belief are doctrinal, at least in so far as it is agreed that fundamental political, religious, and moral axioms constitute propositions the truth or falsity of which there are no generally agreed criteria for establishing. It should be stressed that this is not to say that those who are committed to a specific doctrinal system, be it Marxism, liberal-democratism, Catholicism, atheism, or whatever, are wrong or ought not to be so committed; indeed it is difficult to imagine a person who is in no way committed to any doctrine. Nor is it to say that people who are committed to doctrines are altogether irrational. Given the basic assumptions of a specific doctrinal system, an adherent of that doctrine may behave, argue, and generally proceed in an entirely rational manner. All that is being said is (i) that propositions such as 'There is an omnipotent God' are distinctive in that it is not clear how even in principle one could incontestably demonstrate their truth or falsehood; (ii) that a doctrinal system (or ideology) is a set of beliefs enjoining a particular way of looking at the world and a particular way of life on the believer that is based upon such unprovable propositions; and (iii) that Catholicism is an example of such a system.

Now it is arguable whether those philosophers who have claimed that only doctrines can be indoctrinated are correct. Some would argue that the etymological connection between 'indoctrinate' and 'doctrine' proves little, and that there is nothing conceptually odd about the idea of indoctrinating false or even true propositions. However that may be, it is clear that, whether it is a matter of logical necessity or contingent fact, it is in respect of doctrine that indoctrination is usually to be feared. That is to say, we tend to get more worried about teachers and parents instilling belief in doctrines than instilling belief in truths such as $2 \times 2 = 4$. Getting people to believe in falsehoods seems adequately characterized as just that (or 'lying' or 'talking nonsense'). For convenience, then, we may take indoctrination to involve the imparting of doctrinal beliefs. The next question, therefore, is whether imparting belief in a doctrine is a sufficient condition of indoctrination. Is anybody who in any way contributes to the formation of belief in a doctrine by another person thereby indoctrinating him?

I shall argue that the answer to this question is 'No' and that there are three other necessary conditions of indoctrination.

Unshakable commitment

Another striking feature of the paradigm case of indoctrination with which we started was that the teachers were concerned to implant an unshakable commitment to the truth of Catholicism. They were not concerned simply to present Catholicism and all it entails as a set of beliefs involving a particular view of the world and man's place in it and then to leave the children to decide for themselves whether they felt drawn to adopt this set of beliefs. The doctrines were presented as truths. And this surely provides us with another necessary condition of indoctrination. The most obvious hallmark of the indoctrinated person is that he has a particular viewpoint and he will not seriously open his mind to the possibility that that viewpoint might be mistaken. The indoctrinated man has a closed mind when it comes to the question of the truth or falsehood of the doctrines to which he is committed. If this condition (that to be indoctrinated involves having a closed mind) is not accepted as a necessary condition, we should have to accept the conclusion that we are all equally indoctrinated, since all of us in practice live our lives in accordance with some system of beliefs involving a way of interpreting the world. If we accept an analysis of what it is to be indoctrinated that leads to the conclusion that we are all inevitably indoctrinated, there is not much point in troubling ourselves further about the concept. But if to be indoctrinated is to have a closed mind, then to indoctrinate must involve causing someone to have an unshakable commitment to the truth of the beliefs in question.

In other words the claim here is that if the pupils had left school believing in Catholicism, but they were none the less aware that its truth was not incontrovertibly established, and were quite willing to engage in discussion on the question of whether it was true and how one would set about establishing its truth or falsehood, we should not regard them as having been indoctrinated. It is still of course possible that their teachers may have been *trying* to indoctrinate them and simply have failed. But in so far as the pupils, while being devout Catholics, do not regard the doctrines as having the status of incorrigible truths, the teachers have failed to indoctrinate them. And if they have failed they manifestly have not indoctrinated.

A second necessary condition, then, of indoctrination is that the indoctrinator should cause someone to have unshakable belief in what are in fact unprovable propositions.

Method

If the first two conditions are accepted it follows logically that a third condition relating to the method whereby the beliefs are imparted must also be accepted as necessary to indoctrination. If only doctrines can be indoctrinated (content), and if to be indoctrinated they have to come to be regarded as unquestionably true (unshakable commitment), then indoctrination must be a process of inculcating belief by non-rational methods. For clearly, if the basis of a doctrinal system is a set of fundamental propositions that cannot be rationally demonstrated to be true, commitment of an unshakable sort to these propositions cannot be based on rational demonstration of their truth. Therefore, although none of the *particular* examples of non-rational techniques of persuasion listed in the paradigm example may be necessary to indoctrination, some form of non-rational persuasion designed to bring about unshakable belief is necessary.

Intention

The teachers in the paradigm example *intended* to implant unshakable belief. Is such an intention a necessary condition of indoctrination or merely a contingent feature of some examples of indoctrination? Surely it is not merely a contingent feature; it is not the case, in other words, that the indoctrinator *sometimes* happens to intend to promote conviction. Intention is logically necessary to the concept of indoctrination. The mere fact that unshakable belief has already been put forward as a criterion suggests that intention must come into the picture, for it seems very strange to talk about bringing about, or producing, such belief without at the same time necessarily making reference to the intentions of the person engaged in bringing about the belief.

What causes difficulty in ready acceptance of intention as a necessary feature of indoctrination is the fact that it is not always *obviously* present. It is not always the case, for example, that an indoctrinator will admit to having the intention to produce unshakable beliefs. Sometimes he will claim that his intention is anything but this; he will claim, let us say, that he wants his pupils to think for themselves, to make up their own minds on the issue in question, and that all his efforts subserve this end. We are faced here with a distinction between avowed intention (what the indoctrinator *says* he is trying to do) and the real intention (what the indoctrinator is in fact trying to do), and as far as the latter is concerned evidence concerning it is only to be drawn from observation of the particular teaching situation concerned. In the very nature of the case it is impossible to get clear about real as opposed to avowed intention by asking the teacher.

Consider an example, borrowed from J. P. White, of the distinction referred to. White considers the case of a teacher of Marxism or Catholicism whose avowed intention is to get his pupils to make up their own minds on these difficult matters, and he asks, on the supposition that the teacher is an indoctrinator,

> Is it conceivable, that his avowed intention is also his real intention? If so, then if any of his pupils questions a fundamental proposition of the doctrine, like 'There is a God' or 'The course of history is predetermined', he will not fob him off with specious argument or use non-rational techniques of persuasion to get him to believe the proposition, but will try to explore with the pupil whether there are any good grounds for it. But if he is as open-minded as this, would we, seeing him from outside the system, say that he is indoctrinating?...If the teacher inside the system *is* an indoctrinator, it is therefore inconceivable that his avowed intention is also his real intention.[1]

In other words, the argument points inescapably to the conclusion that intention is logically tied to the concept of indoctrination. The nature of this intention is real intention which may, or may not, coincide with avowed intention. If there is coincidence then no problems arise, but if there is a lack of coincidence then real intention, based upon general contextual evidence, takes precedence over avowed intention.[2]

Indoctrination and the teaching situation

In the light of the above analysis let us now consider the extent to which indoctrination is, or could be, a significant element in the teaching that goes on day by day in the schools of this country.

One thing, at least, is fairly clear. If a teacher's subject matter is of the hard fact variety or, more generally, if at no stage he finds himself trying to get across essentially disputatious propositions (doctrine), then on the content criterion there can be no possibility of his indoctrinating. Take mathematics, for example. Whether the content consists in the multiplication tables, how to solve quadratic equations, how to bisect a line, or Euclid's geometrical proofs, what is clear here is that nothing remotely resembling doctrine is involved. As far as the content and techniques of mathematics are concerned there is agreement among mathematicians as to the truth of statements like '3 × 2 = 6' or the correctness of techniques in solving various types of equation. How strange it would be to say of someone who, as a result of attending classes in mathematics, could solve all kinds of differential equations that he had been well and truly indoctrinated!

Similar considerations apply to science teaching. The very nature of scientific activity precludes the possibility of indoctrination in science. Broadly speaking, scientific method consists in setting up a hypothesis designed to explain some phenomenon or other and then testing (by experiment) to see if predictions made on the basis of the hypothesis are correct or incorrect. If the predictions are shown to be incorrect then the original hypothesis is rejected; it will either be modified or abandoned altogether and the process of testing will be repeated with a new hypothesis. Clearly there is no room here for clinging on to a hypothesis through experimental thick and thin. If one allows nothing to count against a hypothesis, just as the teachers in the paradigm example allowed nothing to count against certain religious statements, then it would simply be the case that one is no longer doing science. A very good instance of this is provided by the celebrated Russian 'scientist' Lysenko. Lysenko held that acquired characteristics of an organism are subsequently inherited by succeeding generations. C. M. M. Begg in his *Introduction to Genetics* remarks of this theory that there was no 'supporting evidence' for it and draws attention to the 'difficulty of conceiving of a mechanism for such inheritance'. Why, then, did Lysenko's views gain ground in Soviet Russia to the extent that he 'became President of the Lenin Academy of Agricultural Sciences, and many "orthodox" geneticists disappeared from the Soviet scene'? Begg answers as follows:

> Suffice it to say that Marxism ascribes to the environment an over-riding significance in determining the course of history. It is a short, if not necessary, step to extend this idea to cover the whole living kingdom, and see in external conditions not merely an agency which directs evolution by weeding out the unfit and preserving the fit, but an active force which moulds animals and plants directly in each generation, the modifications so acquired being passed on at any rate in part to the progeny. For this view there seems to be no factual basis.[3]

In other words, the very nature of scientific activity runs counter to the possibility of indoctrination being practised in science. To teach Lysenko's theory as an unquestionable truth is to cease being scientific and to begin indoctrinating.

Of course, it might be that teachers of mathematics and science lay themselves open to the charge of indoctrinating, but this can never be so by virtue of the fact that they teach these particular disciplines. For example, a mathematician might claim that God is the supreme mathematician and that all mathematics stem from Him, or a scientist might claim that only science is worth doing and that arts subjects are a waste of time. In so far as the mathematician and scientist peddle these questionable doctrines they will run the danger of being labelled 'indoctrinators', but the important point to note here is that these doctrines have nothing to do with the nature of mathematics and science as such.

When one turns to other subjects that figure on the school curriculum the situation is rather different. Aspects of the teaching of literature, history teaching, civics, moral education, or religious education, all seem to have to do with essentially contentious subject matter and, therefore, teachers of them have to be on their guard if they do not wish to be classed as indoctrinators. I say 'on their guard' because it does not follow automatically that the nature of the subject alone decides the issue. Analysis of indoctrination showed that intention to bring about unshakable belief and use of fundamentally non-rational means were also necessary conditions additional to the content condition. It follows, therefore, that the mere fact that a teacher is a teacher of history or of religion does not of itself settle the question as to whether or not he is an indoctrinator.

In this connection a particular problem faces the teacher of young children. It is often said that young children – let's say aged between five and eight – are not capable of appreciating the reason why of things. They are incapable, for example, of understanding the reasons for not being spiteful to members of their peer group, for not lying, or for not breaking promises. And it is claimed that because of these facts about young children their teachers cannot help being indoctrinators. But this is plainly not necessarily so. In the first place even with young children one can give reasons up to a point: if the child asks why he should not steal one can offer an explanation in terms of considering other people's feelings. But even granting that such explanation might be meaningless to the child or that, in any case, one readily reaches a point at which it becomes meaningless (as, for example, if the child asks why he ought to respect other people's feelings), this still does not turn such teachers into indoctrinators. It is true that on these conditions they are trying to bring children to accept certain moral propositions by non-rational means; that is to say that in so far as rational explanation will be meaningless to the child they will have to resort to persuasive techniques such as setting an example or praise and blame. On the assumption that it is agreed, as it would be by most philosophers, that fundamental moral propositions are not known to be true or false or that they are essentially contentious, it does indeed follow that some of the necessary conditions for indoctrination are present. But they are not *all* present. So long as the teacher's intention is not to plant unshakable belief in the moral propositions in question he is not indoctrinating. He is merely influencing children towards the acceptance of certain patterns of behaviour. It may be that such influence is itself objectionable (a suggestion that we shall examine in Chapter 10), but that is a separate question: to influence is not in itself to indoctrinate. Provided that children are ultimately brought to examine for themselves the various moral values that are adhered to within a society and which they have been initially brought to conform to, they have not been indoctrinated. The danger lies in conveniently forgetting that the measures adopted with young children are conceived of as temporary and in never actually coming to the age of rational debate. At least it will then be clear that if rationality *never* supersedes authority the teacher's avowed intention was not his real intention, and he may properly be labelled 'indoctrinator'.

The example of the teacher of the very young can be generalized. It does appear to suggest that all teachers of all subjects to all age groups (including mathematicians and scientists in so far as they will inevitably find themselves treating of more than just strict mathematics and science) need to have an overall awareness of just what it is they are trying to do, of their overall aims and particular objectives, if they sincerely wish to educate rather than indoctrinate. This will involve not only thinking about their methods of teaching, how they go about putting things over, but also thinking about the logical nature of the subject matter with which they deal. Those who choose not to think about these matters will naturally not come to a view about them, and to that extent will not come to a view as to what kind of teachers they are.

Conclusion: what's wrong with indoctrination?

I said at the beginning of this chapter that the term 'indoctrination' is, for most people, a condemnatory term. I shall, in conclusion, probe further into why this is so or, more strongly, why it is right and just to condemn the practice. Additionally the opportunity will be taken to focus attention on the contrast between the twin concepts of education and indoctrination.

We have assumed that indoctrination inevitably involves doctrines but we have seen also that the presence of doctrines as subject matter in a teaching situation does not necessarily mean that indoctrination is taking place. In other words the presence of doctrinal subject matter is consonant with a situation being an *educational* situation. Thus it makes perfectly good sense to talk about religious education, political education, and any other kind of education involving essentially contentious or disputatious doctrinal subject matter. When then does, say, political education become political indoctrination? On the analysis presented the answer must be when the teacher ceases to present the various views held by different people on the controversial political issue under discussion and becomes intent on getting his *own* views on the issue taken as gospel by his students, an intent which will, again as we have seen, necessarily involve the overriding of the rationality of those same students.

We may consider briefly the relationship between indoctrination and Peters' definition of 'education' (Chapter 3) – 'It implies that something worth while is being or has been intentionally transmitted in a morally acceptable manner' – and raise the question as to why education is to be preferred to indoctrination. With respect to the content component of Peters' definition, the something worth while, it would surely be difficult to sustain an argument designed to demonstrate that religious, or political, or educational, or moral discussion and debate does not fall under the heading of 'worth while'. And this being so it follows that indoctrination differs from education not because it involves trafficking in doctrine but because it violates the process criterion stated in the second part of the definition. Indoctrination, in that it necessarily involves lack of respect for an individual's rationality, is morally unacceptable and hence fails to rate as education. And not only does it fail to rate as education, but to say that it is morally unacceptable is to say that it ought not to be indulged in.

The moral principle here appealed to finds its most forceful advocate in the great German philosopher Immanuel Kant (1724–1804). Kant stated the principle as follows:

> Now I say that man, and in general every rational being, *exists* as an end to himself, *not merely as a means* for arbitrary use by this or that will; he must in all his actions, whether they are directed to himself or to other rational beings, always be viewed *at the same time as an end*.[4]

Indoctrinators violate this principle in that essentially they treat their audience as means. People are to be *got to believe* the preferred doctrines and there is to be no detached consideration of them. Thus the *Sunday Times* of 2 September 1973 quotes *Pravda*:

> Peaceful co-existence does not mean an end to confrontation between the two world social systems. The struggle will go on until the full and final victory of communism on a world scale. Problems of ideological struggle cannot be a subject for negotiations between states.

And *The Times* of 6 July 1973 carries a report from Peter Nichols on the Catholic doctrine of infallibility. Worried by the criticism of this doctrine by the Swiss theologian, Dr Hans Küng, the Vatican's Sacred Congregation for the Doctrine of the Faith published a document reaffirming papal infallibility:

> The document deals with the circumstances in which the doctrine of the infallibility bestowed upon the Church and its teaching authority is necessarily immune from error.
>
> This occurs when the bishops scattered throughout the world, but teaching in communion with the successor of Peter, present a doctrine to be held irrevocably. It occurs even more clearly both when the bishops by a collegial act (as in ecumenical councils), together with their visible head, define a doctrine to be held, and when the Roman Pontiff speaks *ex cathedra*, that is, when, exercising the office of pastor and teacher of all Christians, through his supreme apostolic authority he defines a doctrine concerning faith or morals to be held by the universal Church.

In both cases, the political case and the religious case, the message comes through loud and clear, 'Think as we think and don't dare question'. Nothing could be more contrary to Kant's moral dictum and hence nothing more clear than that indoctrination is morally reprehensible and fundamentally anti-educational, unless one is prepared to defend the thesis that it is morally acceptable to treat people simply as means.

The preceding argument does not involve denying that we generally want students to share our values: to believe, for example, that certain works of art are superior, that science is valuable, that some conduct is morally unacceptable, or that the humanities matter. But we have to proceed by reasoning, trusting that students will come to see such things for themselves, and not by coercion or distortion. So it is not the natural desire to uphold and share our values that is at issue: it is determining to impose those values and beliefs so that they stick, come what may, that is reprehensible. That is what leads to the closed mind, that is what leads to fanaticism, and ultimately to the delusion that one is justified even in torturing and killing in the name of one's creed or ideology.

A number of issues that have been raised in this chapter will reappear and be examined in more detail in subsequent chapters of this book. One such issue is that of rationality. To date it has been appealed to as a principle but it has not been subjected to detailed analysis. It is time now to undertake this analysis.

Notes

1 White, J. P., 'Indoctrination' in Peters, R. S. (ed.) *The Concept of Education* (London, Routledge & Kegan Paul, 1967) pp. 182–3.
2 It does seem worth stressing that the intention in question is the intention to produce unshakable belief and *not* the intention to indoctrinate. The latter could not conceivably be part of the definition of indoctrination itself, any more than 'a cow with four legs' could be part of the definition of 'a cow'.
3 Begg, C. M. M., *Introduction to Genetics* (London, Edinburgh University Press, 1959) pp. 229, 231. I might add that, though what is said in the text still seems to me correct, I am a little uneasy about uncritical acceptance of the orthodoxy that the theory of evolution put forward by Lamarck, to which Lysenko's views are closely related, is obviously false. The approach of contemporary Creationists would be, perhaps, a better example, but it would take too long to document it.
4 H. J. Paton's translation of Kant's *Groundwork of the Metaphysic of Morals* (London, Hutchinson, 1949) p. 95. Translator's italics.

Further reading

The literature on indoctrination is extensive. Suggested texts are: (1) papers by J. Wilson and R. M. Hare in T. H. B. Hollins (ed.), *Aims in Education* (Manchester University Press, 1964); (2) a paper by J. P. White in R. S. Peters (ed.), *The Concept of Education* (London, Routledge & Kegan Paul, 1967); (3) A. G. N. Flew, 'What is Indoctrination?' in *Studies in Philosophy and Education*, vol. 4, 1966. This is a very good paper; (4) I. A. Snook, *Indoctrination and Education* (London, Routledge & Kegan Paul, 1972). See also anything by Tasos Kazepides on the topic, William Hare's *Open-mindedness and Education* (Montreal, McGill-Queen's University Press, 1979) and Diane Ravitch's *The Language Police* (New York, Alfred P. Knopf, 2003).

7 Rationality

In one sense of the word all men are rational, and therefore it seems odd to argue that education should be concerned to make men rational. It was Aristotle who first defined man as a rational animal, and he meant by this that man was to be distinguished from other animals in that he had the ability to think, calculate or reason. Other animals can respond to their environment, they can sense the heat from flames, for example, and withdraw from the fire. Instinctively they can seek shelter in appropriate places from bad weather or from enemies. Not only do they come to respond in a regular manner to specific signals, but they can also be conditioned by man to respond to artificial signals. The wild animal senses his prey and automatically responds with the appropriate hunting behaviour. The dog, taken over as a household pet, automatically responds to certain food-preparing activities on the part of the owner. In extreme cases, as in Pavlov's experiments, the animal is conditioned to respond to signals such as the ringing of a bell. But what animals cannot do is act purposively. They cannot decide to do this rather than that on certain grounds, they cannot work out what is going on, or reflect upon the possibility that the ringing bells may be part of some experiment on their behaviour. Man differs from other animals in that he is able to act purposively, to plan, choose ends and adopt means, and in that he is able to control his environment rather than simply respond to it. He is able to memorize, to imagine, foresee, to predict, to hypothesize. To use the imprecise term which in common language includes all such activities, man has the capacity to think. (That, it will be recalled, was the argument of Chapter 2.)

Except in rare instances we all have this capacity, and hence the statement that all men are rational. But the fact that all men have the capacity to think does not mean that all men are equally good at thinking, just as while virtually all men have the ability to see, they do not all see equally well.

Clearly, when people talk of aiming to promote rationality to make people rational, they mean that they want people to think well. And a great many educationalists do talk in these terms T. H. B. Hollins, for instance, in his introduction to *Aims in Education: The Philosophic Approach*, noted that all the contributors to the volume put forward as their 'chief aim of education the developing of rationality in children'. John McPeck in his *Critical Thinking* likewise provides testimony to the widespread interest in developing rationality. But if rationality is understood as good thinking and irrationality as bad thinking the question obviously arises as to how we are to distinguish between good and bad thinking.

The fact that rationality is inextricably tied up with the notion of thinking may lead one to assume that the proper application of the term is in the sphere of pure thought. Rationality may be seen as a quality reserved for academics and theoreticians. To be *really* rational, it might be said, one would have to be some kind of professional thinker. But this is surely not acceptable. It may be helpful for some purposes to make a distinction between theoretical reasoning, such as a philosophical argument or a historical dissertation, and practical reasoning, by which is meant thinking bound up with action (e.g. the sort of thinking involved in a game of chess or thinking about what to do in specific situations). But the thinking that goes on in each case is not in some mysterious way of a different type. We are not dealing with separate compartments of the brain that come into action on different occasions and proceed in their own distinctive manner. Whether one's thinking is geared to some activity going on at the same time or not, one is still thinking. And one can still do it well or badly. It seems quite clear that rationality and irrationality can be displayed in both theoretical and practical reasoning. An argument designed to elucidate the concept of education (or the concept of rationality, for that matter) may be more or less irrational; thinking directed towards deciding what to do in certain circumstances can be more or less irrational; and the thinking involved in playing a game of chess can be more or less irrational.

If, then, I were to argue that Aristotle was probably more rational than most people, it would be irrelevant for me to point to the fact that he did more theorizing than most people as evidence. If Aristotle was relatively rational, that does not necessarily have anything to do with either the *type* or the *amount* of thinking that he indulged in. We call a man rational or irrational in respect of the quality of this thinking *when* he thinks and in *whatever sphere* he thinks.

If a man's rationality is to be judged by reference to the quality of his thinking in some sense, it may be suggested that being rational is to be identified with being right. A rational argument would thus be one that leads to the correct conclusion, or the right answer, and rational behaviour would be behaviour that was right. But if we were to accept this view of rationality as good thinking in the sense of 'thinking that comes up with the right answers', there would not be a great deal of point in talking about the promotion of rationality as an aim of education. Of course it would be very nice if everybody could work out the right answers to everything for himself, but what are the right answers? There are vast areas of human experience, such as the spheres of religion, politics, morality, and aesthetics, where there is little or no agreement as to what the answers are, or indeed as to whether it makes any sense to talk of wrong and right answers. (For example, is there a right answer to the question 'Was Beethoven a greater composer than Wagner?') If we do not know or agree on the answers to certain questions, then we are in no position to judge whether people are being rational about these questions, if 'being rational' is synonymous with 'being right'. And if we cannot judge whether people are being rational or not, it is difficult to see how we could attempt to make them rational. If 'being rational' meant 'being right', then, in practice, aiming to make people rational would mean aiming to make them think in the way we do, so that they arrived at the answers of which we approve. This is certainly not what those who advocate the promotion of rationality have in mind. But fortunately the suggestion that rationality simply means the ability to produce the right answers is most implausible. It simply does not square with the way in which we use the words 'rationality' and 'rational'.

Consider first the notion of a rational argument. It makes perfectly good sense to describe somebody's argument as rational, even if we do not happen to agree with the conclusion of the argument or if we are unsure as to whether the conclusion is acceptable to us or not. It is quite possible to watch a debate between two people and to feel that the person who is defending the point of view that one happens to hold oneself is arguing less rationally than his opponent. If we identified rationality with being right, it would not make sense to do this. We should be unable to judge the rationality or irrationality of an argument except in those cases where there was only one correct answer and we knew what it was. In complex cases, such as arguments for and against communism or comprehensive schools (where, even though one may have adopted a point of view or an opinion on the matter, one may none the less feel that the issue is too complex to admit of an indisputably right answer), one would not be able to distinguish between rational and irrational arguments. But these conclusions are incompatible with the way in which we use the word. We can distinguish between a rational argument for communism and an irrational argument for communism. And we can do this whether we believe in communism or not. We may quite reasonably distinguish between one argument as rational and another as irrational even if both arguments end with the same conclusion.

These considerations indicate that a rational argument is not an argument that ends with the right answer. To describe an argument as rational is to say something about the *process* of reasoning involved in it. It is not to say anything directly about the conclusion of the argument, except that the conclusion does follow from the previous steps of the argument. Arguments proceed from certain premises towards a conclusion. To say that an argument is rational is to say that the chain of reasoning from premises to conclusion is valid. But of course the premises from which an argument starts may be false, dubious, or simply unproven hypotheses, and so it is that, although the conclusion may follow from the premises, and although the argument may itself be rational the conclusion may nevertheless be false or unproven. Conversely we may believe that the conclusion of somebody's argument is a true or correct statement, but none the less feel that his argument is irrational, if we feel that the chain of reasoning presented by him does not in fact lead to the conclusion, or is at fault in some other way.

A rational argument is therefore one that proceeds logically, that is to say in which each step of the argument as given does indeed follow from the preceding step, and in which the reasons that are used to move from the premises to the conclusion are good reasons. An argument may fall short of being rational in a number of ways: it may refuse to take account of pertinent evidence that would upset it; it may lay stress on irrelevant evidence; it may appeal to emotion rather than reason; it may contain contradictions and inconsistencies; or it may contain illogical steps (e.g. all cats are four-legged: this is four-legged, therefore this is a cat). But whatever the precise way in which a particular argument is irrational, what it clearly means to describe it as such is to claim that it proceeds without respect for the notion of giving good reasons.

Hitler's argument that all the great works of art throughout history have been the product of the Aryan race and that therefore the Aryans are entitled to dominate other races is irrational, because there is simply no connection between the two propositions. The 'therefore' is quite inexplicable. The fact that the Aryans produced the great works of art is not simply a weak reason for the conclusion: it does not seem to be recognizable as a reason at all. It seems no more relevant to the conclusion than the fact that Aryans do not come from Central Africa. But it is important to note that it is the lack of coherence in the reasoning that makes this particular – oversimplified – argument irrational. It is not the fact that the premise itself is nonsense. One might claim that the premise is also irrational, by which one would mean that the premise cannot be shown to be true by any rational argument. But there is a distinction to be made between an argument that is irrational, and an argument which, though it may be rational itself, is based upon an irrational premise. Hitler's argument happens to be culpable in both ways.

Use of the terms 'rational' and 'irrational' in respect of other things besides argument confirms the suggestion that the essence of rationality is the giving or holding of good or relevant reasons. Irrational hatred, for example, is hatred that is based on no recognizable reasons; irrational jealousy is jealousy that has no proper grounds. This is not to say that irrational hatred or jealousy are inexplicable. In theory some kind of explanation can always be given as to why people feel hatred or jealousy. To describe these feelings in a particular person as irrational is to say that they are not based on anything that could be regarded as a good reason for hating someone or feeling jealous of them. No doubt a good psychoanalyst could give an account of *why* a man feels jealous, even in a situation where we should still want to describe the man's jealousy as irrational, because he has no good reasons for harbouring the suspicions that cause him to feel jealous. But to explain that a man is prone to jealousy because, for instance, he has an insecurity complex, is not to say that his specific jealousy of a particular individual is well-founded. Again, when people say that love is an irrational emotion they mean that feelings of love do not necessarily arise in us for good reasons. People cannot help falling in love with other people who are in various ways most unsuitable objects for their affections, and who could not be said to be or to have done anything that constitutes a good reason for loving them. Falling in love is not an activity that takes note of the notion of giving good reasons at all, and that is why it seems appropriate to regard it as an irrational business.

More generally, rational behaviour is behaviour that can be rationally defended or explained. If we refer to somebody's behaviour as rational we do not necessarily imply that he has actually thought about what he is doing. His behaviour may be rational either in the sense that he has a rational account to give of why he is behaving in this way or in the sense that we feel that it possible to give such an account, despite the fact that the agent acted without conscious reflection. But whichever is the case, for behaviour to be correctly described as rational, as with argument it must be explicable in terms of good reasons. Irrational behaviour is behaviour for which there is no good reason. Of course, as with the specific instances of irrational hatred or irrational jealousy, to say that behaviour is irrational is not to say that it is inexplicable. In one sense behaviour can perhaps theoretically always be explained. That is to say some kind of a reason can be produced that tells us why a man behaves in a particular way. But to tell us why a man does something need not be to show that the man had good reason for what he did. For example, a man who has excellent qualifications for a post as a mathematics lecturer might be turned down in favour of a weaker candidate on the grounds that he is Roman Catholic. The fact that he is Roman Catholic explains why he was turned down, but we should still say that the employer who turned him down for that reason was behaving irrationally inasmuch as we cannot see that being Roman Catholic constitutes a relevant reason for being denied this particular job.

Some people might prefer to describe the employer's behaviour in this instance as unreasonable, and the question now arises as to whether there is any distinction between the concept of unreasonableness and the concept of irrationality.

It is clear that if what is meant by irrational behaviour (or argument or feeling) is behaviour that is based on irrelevant reasons, then the concept of irrationality does not exhaust the ways in which behaviour may be regarded as ill-founded. For as well as behaving in certain ways, allegedly for reasons that are in fact irrelevant, people may (and very often do) act in certain ways for reasons that are not irrelevant but merely weak. For example, it is irrational to beat up your wife because you have lost your job. It may be explicable in terms of your violent psyche, but it is irrational in that the fact of your losing your job does not in itself constitute a relevant reason for beating up your wife. (Perhaps it would be safer to say that most of us would regard it as irrational. There is a problem, which I shall examine below, about who decides what reasons are relevant reasons.) But suppose that you beat up your wife because she has been unfaithful? Now we may disapprove of this, we may not think that her behaviour is a sufficiently good reason for your reaction, but we should not call your behaviour irrational. It makes sense; it involves reference to a reason that is recognizable as a reason; it is the right *kind* of reason. Some people may even feel that your behaviour is quite reasonable in the circumstances. But there are surely many who, while conceding that it was not irrational, would want to say that your behaviour was unreasonable. In other words they would concede that you had a reason that was recognizable as such (in a way that the man who beats up his wife because he has lost his job does not have), but would claim that it was none the less not a good enough reason for your behaviour. In the same way it is irrational to assume that everybody hates you in the absence of any evidence for this assumption. But it is only unreasonable to assume that your boss hates you on the evidence of his refusal to promote you. He *may* hate you, you *may* be right, but your opinion seems unreasonable because, in the absence of further information about the situation, the reason you produce for holding it looks weak.

The suggestion is, then, that a person is irrational in so far as he behaves or argues without concern for reasons or by reference to irrelevant reasons, whereas he is unreasonable in so far as his behaviour or argument is backed by reasons that are not obviously irrelevant but which are none the less weak and insufficient to justify his argument or behaviour. But now we come to the problems.

First of all it may be pointed out that although in principle there obviously is a distinction between what I have termed 'irrationality' and what I have termed 'unreasonableness', in practice it may be exceedingly difficult to distinguish between them. Suppose, for example, you beat up your wife because she has failed to do the washing-up. Is that irrational or unreasonable? Is your reason merely weak, but recognizable as a candidate for the title of good reason, or is it so pathetic that it does not count as a reason at all? Tied up with this is a second, more serious problem. Some people have argued that although the formal outline of 'irrational' and 'unreasonable' as given here (or some similar outline) makes sense, in practice not only can one not distinguish between them, but one cannot be sure that any behaviour or argument is either. The paranoiac, for instance, may behave in ways that we regard as irrational, but surely, given his way of looking at things, his behaviour may be entirely rational. Are we entitled to call a man irrational who shoots somebody on the grounds that the person is a member of a certain race? *We* may think that an absurd non-reason, but he has a view of life such that it constitutes a good reason. Do we not therefore either have to admit that a lot of so-called irrational behaviour is not irrational, or else openly confess that by rational behaviour we mean behaviour that we regard as rational, which is to say behaviour that we regard as backed by good reason – which means effectively behaviour that we approve of?

It begins to look as if the cynic who claims that we call people who agree with us 'rational' and people who disagree with us 'irrational' may be right up to a point. Naturally we tend to use the word 'rational' to describe people who see things in a similar way to that in which we see them. How can I regard what does not for me constitute a good reason for a certain action as a good reason, just because somebody else thinks that it is? I do not think that the mere fact that a man has lost his job, depressing though it may be, is relevant reason for him to beat up his wife. I therefore regard people who think that it is as irrational. Furthermore it is probably true that as a matter of fact the term 'rational' has emotive overtones and that one part of what one is doing in describing a person as rational is indicating approval of that person.

But the fact remains that the cynic is talking about a tendency of ours in using the word, and he is not talking about the meaning of the term. 'Rational' does not *mean* 'seeing things my way', even if it may be difficult sometimes to attribute rationality to people who do not see things my way. In the same way, we tend to describe only those people whose actions in certain situations we admire as brave, but 'brave' does not mean simply 'actions that I admire'. What is true, however, and what those who are sceptical of the promotion of rationality as a feasible aim (or who see it as a covert way of maintaining the status quo) sometimes confuse with the generalization that 'being rational' is 'seeing things in the accepted manner', is that it may occasionally be very difficult to judge whether an individual is being rational or not.

In order to judge whether a man is being rational we have to know what his premises are as well as observe his behaviour or listen to his arguments. For it is only in the light of premises that we can assess reasons as good or relevant reasons. One's natural assumption, for instance, would be that a man was being irrational if he pounced on a man and beat him up simply because the latter had bent down to tie up his shoelace. But it might transpire that the man had had considerable experience of some out of the way community where people kept knives tucked away in their shoes and that therefore, to him, the fact that a man reached down to his shoes provided a very good reason for responding quickly and violently. In the same way, to someone who has grasped no more about soccer than that there are two opposing teams trying to kick the ball into each other's net, it would seem quite irrational for a player to stop just as he was about to score, simply because somebody blows a whistle. It is only on the assumption that one recognizes and accepts the rules of soccer that the fact that the referee blows a whistle constitutes a relevant reason for ceasing to storm on towards the goal. It is therefore sometimes difficult to know whether a person's behaviour is rational or not, when one is in ignorance of the assumptions on which that behaviour is based.

But the cynic may want to go further than this. He may point out, quite rightly, that it is not only that we sometimes do not know the premises on which another man bases his behaviour, but very often we know another person's premises but do not share them. The premise of a religious man might be that one should not interfere with what God ordains. His child is sick. God ordains it thus and therefore, he concludes, medical aid should not be provided. What are we to say about such a person? There is nothing faulty or irrational in his argument or behaviour, if his premise is granted. Are we entitled to call him irrational simply because we do not share his premise? We may say that his premise is irrational, but here we would be on much trickier ground, for how are we to decide what count as good reasons or relevant reasons either for holding or for rejecting this premise? But if we do not call him irrational, then one might have to accept that certain madmen, as we should conventionally term them, were not irrational either. A man might shoot me on the grounds that a pigeon flew by the window and none the less avoid the charge of irrationality by explaining that his premise is that God expects and demands that people shall do precisely what they feel like doing whenever He causes a pigeon to fly by the window. Does this kind of consideration lead us to the conclusion that we cannot meaningfully distinguish between rationality and irrationality, and that we either have to allow that all men are equally rational or else concede that in picking out some people as more rational than others we are simply picking out those who see things our way and that there is no objectivity in this selection? Of course it does not.

In the first place there is still room for distinguishing between rational and irrational argument or behaviour, even if we ignore the question of what premises people hold. If a man contradicts himself, produces an incoherent argument, or appeals to considerations that are irrelevant on his own terms, he is being irrational and that is all there is to it. It is one thing to point out that somebody *could* construct a world view in terms of which it would be rational to shoot people when pigeons fly by, and quite another to say that therefore we cannot regard anybody as more or less rational than anybody else. We can certainly distinguish between the relatively rational and the relatively irrational man, at least in many cases, because some – probably most – irrationality is displayed in people's inconsistency or lack of coherence given their own world view. If I am very anxious to become a doctor, work hard for my medical exams and then fail to turn up to take them, then *prima facie* I am being irrational. Somebody else might construct some elaborate theory about the iniquity of the examination system in an attempt to show that there was good reason to refuse to take exams, but so long as this theory is not mine, and so long as there is not some other good reason, such as my being ill, to explain my absence, then in failing to turn up I am being irrational. If I criticize the prime minister on the grounds that he changes some of his policies and refuse to criticize the leader of the opposition when he does the same thing, I am being irrational.

Second, despite what was said above about the difficulty of knowing in some cases what would count as relevant reasons for establishing or rejecting certain premises, there are surely some premises or some world views that we simply will not accept as rational. It is of course quite true that in saying that it is irrational to base one's behaviour on a premise such as 'God expects us to shoot when pigeons fly by', or 'The Aryan race is entitled to preferential treatment', one is appealing to others to adopt one's view of the sorts of thing that do not seem to be supported by anything that could count as good reasons. It is not clear how one could prove that it is not true that God expects us to shoot people when pigeons fly by. But we may still argue that it seems to us an irrational belief, since we cannot see anything remotely resembling a good reason for believing it.

Finally, and most importantly, a rational man (as opposed to a rational argument or rational behaviour considered in isolation), being a conscious creature, must surely be one who has *respect* for the idea of giving good reasons. A man may adopt an idiosyncratic point of view, but, if he is a rational man, he must at least be the sort of person who attempts to produce reasons for that point of view and who takes notes of arguments against it. What seems to be forgotten by those who delight in raising bizarre examples about people who shoot on the strength of seeing a pigeon is that in practice, in nine cases out of ten, what indicates the irrationality of such madmen is not so much the holding of a peculiar premise as the fact that they cannot and will not consider alternatives or the problem of justifying their point of view.

Those who argue that education should aim to promote rationality are, therefore, arguing that we should aim to promote in children a respect for the notion of giving good reasons, for thinking (and hence behaving) in a coherent manner and, as a natural consequence, for evaluating the arguments, ideas, and opinions of others by reference to their coherence rather than by reference to their emotive appeal, the status of the person arguing or any other irrelevant consideration. It is perhaps true that to some extent this will in practice lead to the assumption or adoption of opinions, attitudes, and ways of behaving that are not idiosyncratic and that coincide with what we happen to regard as rational opinions and behaviour. But this is not a necessary consequence and it is not the aim of those who advocate the development of rationality as an educational objective. For the aim of promoting rationality is not the same thing as promoting commitment to those opinions and judgements that we regard as rational.

In fact to set up rationality as one of one's educational aims is automatically to oppose the practice of educating children in such a way that, as adults, they become unreflective individuals who act and think in response to the dictates of authority figures. Implicit in placing a value on it is the idea that people should act in a certain way or hold particular opinions because they see good reason to do so and not because they have been told to do so.

This is not to say that the aim is to deter people from taking any notice of what experts or authorities in any particular sphere may have to say. There is a distinction to be made between being *in* authority and being *an* authority. To be in authority is to be in some position by virtue of which one has authority in the sense of a degree of power, as, for instance, a headmaster has authority over his school, parents have legal authority over their children, and the government has authority over us all. (There is also a distinction to be drawn between formally being in authority, and hence technically having authority, and actually having authority. A headmaster might in fact lack authority, despite his position, because of his weak character, whereas one of his pupils, though technically not in any position of authority, might actually have considerable authority with other children. But this distinction is not germane to our purpose here.) To be an authority in a particular sphere, on the other hand, is to be one who has knowledge and expertise in that sphere, as, for example, doctors are authorities in medicine. Clearly an individual might be in authority without being an authority in any sphere, and vice versa.

It would presumably be foolish for most of us to ignore as a matter of policy what authorities, in the sense of experts, have to say in various spheres. In general we should be well advised to take note of what the doctor, being an authority in medicine, has to say about our health, for instance (although even here it has to be remembered that authorities in a particular sphere often disagree and the mere fact that somebody is an authority does not automatically make him right). But to give particular attention to what *an* authority says is one thing; to give particular attention to what those *in* authority say is quite another. The aim of those who advocate rationality is not to do away with any concern for what authorities in various spheres have to say, so much as to deter people from assuming that the fact that somebody or some group has authority, in the sense of having some degree of power, in itself makes that person or group right or even particularly worth listening to on whatever issue is pronounced. The fact that parents, teachers or governments have authority does not mean that they are more likely to be right in their views of any issue than anybody else. The object of stressing rationality as an educational aim is to attempt to do away with the tendency of children to assume that something must be true, or right or good because teacher says so, and of adults to make similar assumptions because the party leader, the newspaper editor or the vicar says so.

This aim invites two further questions: How does one do it? Why should one be concerned to do it? The former is largely an empirical question, depending for its answer on the collection of evidence as to what effect various practices actually have. But there are one or two points that follow logically from the analysis of the concept. Since a rational man is, by definition, one who approaches matters with a concern and an ability to assess them by means of relevant reasoning, he needs ideally to have, besides this disposition to be concerned, understanding of the type of reasons that *are* relevant in various logically distinct areas, at least a certain amount of information, an ability to conceive of alternative ways of looking at things besides that with which he is familiar, and a questioning attitude. These characteristics may be illustrated by reference to a proposal for comprehensive education. Imagine that such a proposal is put to a man who has no experience of comprehensive education and to whom the idea is essentially a novel one. First and foremost, if the man is rational, he will regard the suggestion as up for questioning. He will neither oppose it simply because it is new to him or unfamiliar nor approve it automatically because it is advocated by people whom he happens to respect. He will want to examine the issue and to examine it on its own merits. But in order to do that he will need to have or to acquire certain information – information, broadly speaking, about child psychology, sociological factors, and whatever empirical evidence there may be about the actual consequences of schooling on a comprehensive model. One mark of the rational man will be that his judgement on the issue will be more tentative in proportion to the degree in which he lacks such information. It is not, of course, part of the meaning of being rational that one should have such information; it is a mark of the rational man to recognize the need for it before an informed judgement can be made. But such information alone will not decide the issue, since the question of comprehensive education also involves value judgements: one needs not only to know that a particular system, let us say, is likely to produce greater social cohesion than another, but also to have considered the question of the relative value of social cohesion and various other objectives that might be better served by other educational systems. In order to deal rationally with this dimension of the problem the man in question will need to be able to distinguish between issues that are essentially to be determined empirically and evaluative questions which are not. If he were to make the mistake of thinking that the fact that most people happen to think that social cohesion is relatively important as an educational objective is a relevant reason for concluding that it is then his procedure would in that respect be irrational. Likewise if he were to object to a comprehensive system of education simply on the grounds that he would find it aesthetically displeasing to see a lot of new schools being built and that the system proposed would necessitate such new building, we should say that he did not understand the sorts of reason that were relevant to an educational issue and those that were not. Finally, even when he had formed his judgement, it would be a continuing indication of his rationality that he was open to the consideration of alternatives that might be proposed.

It follows, from the recognition of these features as characteristics or aspects of a man that are necessary for him to be able to make rational decisions and to behave rationally, that rationality is not likely to be promoted by any educational system that involves a concerted effort by teachers to instill in children unthinking acceptance of all that is set before them and all that is demanded of them. If willingness to question and concern for relevant reasons are to be promoted in children, then presumably they must to some extent be encouraged to question and to appreciate the reasons for various things, rather than be fobbed off with remarks such as 'Because I say so' or 'It just is true, that's why'. Now this point seems to have been well grasped by a number of radical educationalists such as Postman and Weingartner, who in their *Teaching as a Subversive Activity* demand that we throw away the notion that we (the teachers) know best and know what things are worth doing, and instead throw everything open to the children's questioning and in this way teach 'the most important and intellectual ability man has yet developed – the art and science of asking questions'.[1] What does not seem to have been grasped by Postman and Weingartner is that simply to pose questions and give answers is a pretty feeble sort of exercise if those answers do not have to measure up to any standards of rationality.[2] If we are after the asking of meaningful questions and the search for rational and significant answers, we shall presumably have to do more than sit around enthusing over the sound of each other's voices (which at times one feels would be the characteristic of the Postman and Weingartner ideal teaching situation). If we really wish to promote rationality then we shall also have to see to it that children acquire information, acquire knowledge as to what sort of information is appropriate to what sort of question and how one sets about dealing with different kinds of question, and, above all, acquire the formal notion that there is a distinction to be made between good or relevant and weak or irrelevant reasons. Thus, although we cannot say precisely what the best way to achieve these ends is without a degree of empirical research, we can say that the nature of the concept of rationality demands that the teacher shall make some positive effort to discriminate between children's responses and opinions as relatively coherent or incoherent, to provide information, and to initiate children into at least some of the various forms of knowledge.

Turning to the question of why we should want to promote rationality we have first to distinguish two possible confusions that may be involved in the claim that rationality is not an important objective. First, it is not uncommon to come across people who claim to be hostile to the aim of rationality, but who are in fact hostile to the promotion of certain views or opinions which society in general may happen to regard as rational. However, as we have seen, to object to the promotion of particular views which are allegedly rational is quite distinct from objecting to the promotion of rationality itself. Second, some people claim to be hostile to the aim of rationality when in fact their objection seems only to be to an exclusive preoccupation with rationality. It may very well be that an education that was solely concerned with promoting rationality would be wholly inadequate, since there may be many areas of human experience where rationality is irrelevant. It is not clear for instance, that rationality has much to do with appreciating art or falling in love, and yet these might both be areas of experience where education has some part to play. But to say that rationality is not the only important aim of education is obviously not the same thing as saying that it should not be an aim.

But suppose that neither of these two confusions is being made and that somebody none the less asks 'Why should I worry about having good reasons for my beliefs, my attitudes and the way I behave? Why shouldn't I simply act as the spirit moves me? After all, human reason is fallible, why should I not take the view of certain religious sects, such as the Baha'i faith, that my intuitive or inspired feeling is as good a guide as reason? What's so good about rationality?' The simple answer to such questions is that it may not be possible to show why the speaker ought to worry about having good reason, but he obviously does, otherwise he would not be asking for a good reason to worry about having good reasons for action and beliefs. More generally it may be pointed out that it is a presupposition of asking, in a serious frame of mind, such questions as 'What ought I to do in such and such a situation?' or 'What ought education be concerned to do?', that one is committed to the notion of giving good reasons. What is the point of asking such questions if one is uninterested in whether the reply is well-reasoned or not?

Of course this only shows that as a matter of fact most of us are committed to the idea of giving good reasons or to rationality as an ideal. It does not show that we ought only, or indeed ever, to act rationally, and it is not inconceivable that someone should claim to be totally uninterested in whether his own or anyone else's behaviour is explicable in terms of good reasons. All one can say to such a person, if he does exist, is that he is committing himself to an ideal in which anything goes (for it would not make sense to distinguish between sensible and foolish, acceptable and unacceptable behaviour, or defensible and indefensible conduct), and in which there is no room for meaningful communication. A world in which there was no respect for the notion of good reasons would be a world in which a remark such as 'I am going indoors because I am cold' would be no more sensible than 'I am going indoors because I ate a banana three weeks ago'. Furthermore, the man totally uninterested in reason could not make a meaningful objection to anything that happened to him, since there would be no such thing as a good reason for objecting (his objections would merely be subjective grunts of no interest to anyone else), and he could therefore hardly complain if we simply ignored him and his peculiar idea, which is presumably what, in the last resort, we should do. But I think it is clear that although such an individual is conceivable it is extremely unlikely that anyone should literally believe that the idea of having good reasons is of no importance whatsoever.

To deny the value of rationality is to do away with the importance of man's distinctive capacity for purposive action. To do away with the distinction between good and bad thinking is to deny the purpose of thinking.

Notes

1 Postman, N. and Weingartner, C., *Teaching as a Subversive Activity* (Harmondsworth, Penguin, 1971) p. 34.
2 See Barrow, R., *Radical Education: A Critique of Freeschooling and Deschooling* (Oxford, Martin Robertson, 1978) ch. 7.

Further reading

See at the end of chapter 8.

8 Self-determination

There are a number of terms that, in common with 'rationality', suggest that people should not be unthinking adherents of a code of conduct or of opinions and beliefs laid down by others. Examples of such terms are 'individuality', 'independence', 'self-determination', and 'self-direction'. These terms themselves may well not be synonymous but they have in common with each other the idea that what the individual does or thinks should be decided by himself. And this is so whether the notion of 'self' is explicit as in 'self-direction' or implicit as in 'individuality'. For the purposes of this chapter I shall assume that they are synonymous and shall concentrate on the concept of self-determination.

Self-determination involves the notion of thinking in the sense of reflecting, calculating, memorizing, predicting, judging, and deciding. To determine behaviour is to plan it or think about it in some sense. This is not to say that determined behaviour has to be entirely dictated by reason, and that emotions and feelings can play no part in it. A man might be said to be self-determining even though he acts in a certain way largely as a result of some desire. But he can only be said to be self-determining if his reason is also involved to some extent. If he simply responds automatically and directly to his desires, so that there is no attempt at conscious planning or decision-taking involved in his behaviour, it is difficult to see how one could regard him as *determining* his action in any sense at all. Provided however that his reason is involved to the extent of attempting to decide between conflicting desires, attempting to consider suitable means of achieving ends that may be dictated by his desires, and so on, it seems reasonable to regard his behaviour as determined.

Is there any further connection between the concept of self-determination and the concept of rationality in the sense outlined in the previous chapter, besides the fact that both involve the notion of thinking or reasoning? The answer surely is no. A man might be self-determining and either rational or irrational. Conversely a man might be rational and yet not self-determining, at least in respect of his actions, simply because he is not free to do as he decides. It is a necessary condition of a person's being self-determining that he should be free to act as he chooses, but this freedom is not a necessary condition of a person's being rational. To advocate rationality as an ideal is to advocate that people should have a certain attitude and certain standards of reasoning. To have this ideal does not in itself commit one to any partic-ular view about the extent to which people should be free from restraint or subject to rules. If one favours rationality as an aim then one will not favour situations in which people behave in certain ways simply because they have been told to do so by some authority figure. But the reason one will object to this state of affairs is that in itself the fact that somebody says 'do this' is not a good reason for doing this. There may none the less be very good reasons for doing what the authority figure demands and therefore one's commitment to rationality certainly does not commit one to the view that people ought not to abide by various rules and dictates from people in authoritative positions. It may sometimes commit one to the view that people positively ought to abide by such rules – if, that is to say, there is felt to be good reason for abiding by the rules in question.

In practice if people are to be encouraged to be rational then they will want to assess for themselves the arguments and dictates of others, and they will accept them or reject them in the light of their own reasoning. And therefore, given the undoubted difficulty of judging who is being more or less rational in particular situations, occasions will arise on which people will wish to reject the pronouncements of authority. There would be something suspect about claiming to be committed to rationality as an aim, and refusing to allow anybody any freedom to reject the status quo. But the fact remains that the concept of rationality puts the stress on the impersonal notion of reason and not on the independence of the individual agent.

By contrast the concept of self-determination involves the idea that the individual shall make his own decisions and says nothing about whether these decisions shall have been arrived at in a more or less coherent and consistent manner. I am self-determining if I do what I choose to do, whether my choice is sensible or not from my own or anybody else's point of view. So much is fairly straightforward. It is clear that one way in which an individual can fail to be self-determining is if he is subject to the control of other people or externally imposed rules that are backed by effective sanctions. But there are obviously other ways than this in which a man might fail to be self-determining. An alcoholic, for example, whose craving for drink is so strong as to dictate at least some of his actions (how he spends his money for a start), or simply a drunk, while he is under the influence of drink, could neither of them be said to be self-determining. In the same way a consuming passion for gambling, a consuming jealousy, or a consuming

love for someone may legitimately be said to interfere with a man's powers
of self-determination. Quite where one draws the line in practice between
the man whose love is effectively controlling him and determining his
actions, and the man, who, although deeply in love, remains self-determining,
may not be easy to say. All that we need note here is that passions and
emotions can in principle control people, and hence deny them the possibility
of self-determination, no less than physical addictions or other people.

Finally there is the important case of the indoctrinated individual. Clearly
it would be absurd to regard a man whose whole view of life is coloured by
what others have caused him to believe and who is unable to question this
view of life as self-determining. It might be true that formally such a man
decides what to do for himself, but his decisions will effectively be conditioned by the beliefs and assumptions with which he has been indoctrinated.
The 'he' or the 'self' that decides is itself the creation of other people who
are therefore in reality the ultimate determiners of his behaviour.

Now once it is admitted that the indoctrinated man is not self-determining
in any meaningful sense some would raise the question as to whether the
adult individual could ever be said to be truly self-determining. If a man is
self-determining then presumably he must have a 'self' that is not itself
determined in any way, runs the argument. We must be able to locate in him
some independent self that directs his behaviour. But can we in fact do this?
Common sense alone might suggest, even if the studies of psychologists,
geneticists, and sociologists did not make it clear, that we are all very much
the product of our environment and genetic makeup. The 'selves' that
control our behaviour are themselves, to some extent at least, formed by
external influences including the other people with whom we come into
contact as we develop. Such factors as the existence of peer-group pressure,
a dominant mother, advertisements, the character of teachers whom we
come across, or a broken home, influence and help to mould our characters.
And our character is part of the 'self' that may determine our behaviour.
Precisely *how* and to what extent various factors influence our development
may be a matter for a great deal of argument, but what cannot be doubted
is that it is the case that the 'self' referred to in the phrase self-determination
is itself originally determined by something other than itself. In which case,
it is concluded, it may well be that the individual who is free to do whatever
he chooses may in fact be no more self-determining than a man whose
freedom of choice is limited more obviously and directly.

This argument, although most of what it says about the way in which we
develop in response to environmental influences is obviously correct, does
not seem to me to be very significant. That is to say, although one must
concede that we are all to some extent the product of our environment and
genetic make-up, it is not going to get us far to suggest that consequently

none of us is self-determining. There is still a crucial distinction to be made between people who are free to question the assumptions, habits, attitudes, and beliefs that they may indeed have acquired unconsciously through the pressures of their environment and those who are not free to question them because they have been successfully indoctrinated. Surely we may quite reasonably regard the former as self-determining (provided that they are not coerced by others or dominated by some passion or craving), in contradistinction to the latter. However I have introduced this argument because it leads into an important digression that must be made at this point. Many of those who argue that, as things are, virtually none of us are truly self-determining, go on to conclude that the only way to realize the ideal of self-determining adults is to grant children self-determination from the beginning. In other words, self-determination must, if it is to be real, be preceded by self-development or self-regulation for children. We shall now look briefly at the concept of self-regulation.

Self-regulation

The term 'self-regulation' is used freely by A. S. Neill among others, so it will not be inappropriate to begin by considering what he means by it. He writes that 'self-regulation means the right of a baby to live freely without outside authority in things psychic and somatic. It means that the baby feeds when it is hungry; that it becomes clean in its habits only when it wants to; that it is never stormed at or spanked.'[1] This means, to take examples from Neill, that when his daughter went through a period of great interest in his glasses, snatching them off his nose to see what they looked like, he 'made no protest' and that she was allowed to play with breakable ornaments, that if children go through a period of stealing they should be 'free to live out this stage', and of course that they should be free to opt out of school lessons if they choose. 'To impose anything by authority is wrong. The child should not do anything until he comes to the opinion – his own opinion – that it should be done.'[2] The implication of such passages is clearly that Neill takes 'self-regulation' to mean complete freedom to direct one's own life and that he thinks that the concept can be meaningfully applied even to babies. There are just two things wrong with this: despite the quotations above, Neill does *not* take 'self-regulation' to mean this (alternatively he does, but he does not believe in children being self-regulating), and if this is what 'self-regulation' means it is surely absurd to claim that babies and young children can be self-regulating.

To take the latter point first: what exactly is a self-regulating baby? A self-regulating or self-determining adult, as we have seen, is one who makes his own choices and is not subject to any restrictions on his freedom to do so. But to make a choice in any meaningful sense, even to make a bad or foolish choice, involves by definition a degree of cognitive ability. To determine a course of action for oneself means to reflect upon the options available, to weigh these up and to select one. One is not regulating one's life if one simply drifts along responding automatically to various stimuli. To regulate one's life involves having a grasp of the notion of means to ends, having some knowledge about what will happen if one does this rather than that, consciously making decisions in the light of that knowledge and having some understanding of the idea that one *can* regulate one's own life. To talk in these terms of the baby or young child is just silly. The baby that is not fed until it cries out for food is not 'regulating' its life, it is responding automatically to the stimulus of hunger. Besides, what is this self? The concept of the adult self may be somewhat obscure, but what constitutes the self of the newborn baby? Is not the notion of the individual's self inextricably linked with such concepts as personality and character, and are not these things that develop, come into being or are acquired as one grows older? Does it make sense to talk of the 'self', 'character', or 'personality' of the newborn baby, or even of its potential 'self' or 'personality'? Isn't the whole point that whether one likes it or not, babies are born without identifiable selves and that the nature of the self and personality they will develop is inescapably bound up with the environment in which they grow up? (Note that to say this is not to deny considerable significance to the individual's genetic make-up. See Chapter 2.) While one is regulating the child's life for him (as of course one will to a greater or lesser extent whatever word one uses to describe the business), by feeding him, putting him to bed, and so on, one is imperceptibly – and no doubt to a great extent unpredictably – influencing the development of a particular kind of self. The mere fact that the mother breast-feeds rather than bottle-feeds, it has been suggested, may materially affect the nature of the self that will develop in the child in some way. Certainly factors such as the degree of security and love and the interests of parents and the other children in the local environment will act as influences towards the development of a particular kind of self. In short, a child cannot be literally self-regulating from birth, since his self is itself being formed and since he lacks the understanding, cognitive awareness, and knowledge that would be necessary for anything that could reasonably be termed 'regulation' or 'determining'.

But, as already suggested, despite careless remarks such as that 'the child should not do anything until he comes to the opinion that it should be done', Neill does not really believe that the child should be entirely self-regulating even if it were possible. Quite apart from the fact that once an adult has made himself responsible for providing and maintaining a particular kind of environment for the growing child – even if that environment is a relatively free or negative one – he has already begun to interfere with the development of the child, and quite apart from the fact that Neill's children are subject in large degree to the regulation of the majority will of other children, there are a number of examples to be found in Neill's writing that seem to indicate that he expects the adults to regulate the child's life to some extent directly. The seven-year-old child, for instance, who has decided to kick Neill's office door, will not find such behaviour tolerated. A three-year-old should not be allowed to paint the front door with red ink. A child should not be free to walk over the dining table, stand on a piano, play on the fire escape, take a wooden mallet to the keys of a piano, or leap onto a sofa with its shoes on. A child cannot be left to regulate for itself the clothes that it chooses to wear, for as Neill admits with reference to his own daughter, if they 'had allowed it, she would have run about naked all day in all weathers' and so they felt that they had to 'bully her into wearing what we think she ought to wear'.

Most of us may feel that the examples that Neill provides of instances in which the adult should interfere are eminently sensible. But the point is that once one has admitted that there are *any* such instances, the simple claim that children should be self-regulating (even if it made sense in reference to babies and young children) is obviously inadequate and it becomes blatantly contradictory to say that 'to impose anything by authority is wrong'. The term 'self-regulation', pregnant with desirable overtones and emotive force, is serving as a loose slogan to rally support for a particular point of view and obscuring what is really at issue. For what is really at issue is not whether the child should make his own decisions or have them made for him, but the degree to which and the areas in which he should be left to do what he feels like doing rather than being subject to the deliberate restraints of either other children or adults.

It would take us too far out of our way to give adequate treatment to the enormous and complex question of freedom, but I shall conclude this section by illustrating some of the problems involved, by reference to Neill. First it is important to distinguish two distinct questions which Neill does not always seem to do. They are: (i) What sorts of thing ought children be free to decide for themselves, or to do if they choose? (ii) What as a matter of fact is the best way to bring up children in such a way that they will behave in certain ways rather than others? The latter question is of course empirical and a great deal of the time Neill seems to be making the empirical claim that if you leave children free to do what they choose to do (or what they are free to do subject only to the pressure put upon them by other children), they will as a matter of fact in the long run make sound or sensible choices. Clearly his claim that children should never be 'stormed at or spanked' is just such an empirical claim, involving the belief that to intimidate the child by storming at him or spanking him is in the long run counter-productive. How true this is is not going to be decided by philosophical inquiry. Intuitively, and in the light of evidence produced by psychologists, one perhaps feels that Neill is right at least to the extent of arguing that 'storming and spanking' are not in general effective means to employ. One's attitude to the wider claim that without adult guidance or control children will make sound choices obviously depends to some extent on one's view of a sound choice. For instance we are told of the case of Mervyn, who 'between the ages of seven to seventeen...never attended a single class. At the age of seventeen he hardly knew how to read.'[3] Neill's point is that, though some might feel that here is an example of a less than sensible choice, 'when Mervyn left school and decided to become an instrument maker he quickly taught himself how to read and absorbed in a short time through self-study all the technical knowledge he needed'. In Neill's view the adult Mervyn was an admirable and successful man. But it would not be unduly cynical to wonder whether Mervyn might conceivably have done better, in his own judgement and on his own terms of course, if at an earlier age he had had more possibilities opened to him. And if that seems a groundless suggestion in relation to this particular individual, may one not legitimately wonder whether for every Mervyn there is not another child whose adult life is severely restricted by the choice he made as a child not to attend any lessons?

However, it must be stressed that these are empirical questions. From the philosophical angle the important question is how one decides at what point children's freedom should be limited, on the assumption that at least sometimes children will not make sensible decisions. What criteria does one use to distinguish between what people should be free to do if they choose to and what they should not be free to do whether they choose to or not? What criteria does Neill have in mind for distinguishing between the child who interferes with his work by playing with his glasses and the child who does the same thing by kicking his door?

Perhaps his most well-known answer to this question is his most inadequate. He refers to a distinction between 'freedom' and 'licence.' 'The whole freedom movement is marred and despised because so many advocates of freedom have not got their feet on the ground...It is this distinction between freedom and licence that many parents cannot grasp.'[4] But what is this distinction? This we are not told. All that we are given are a few examples (many of which have been quoted above) of either. But this simply means that 'freedom' is being used to refer to acceptable or desirable freedom and 'licence' is being used to refer to unacceptable or undesirable freedom. We are no nearer knowing what it is that makes some freedoms desirable (i.e. bona fide freedoms) and others undesirable (i.e. licence). What is the distinction between toilet training, which we should not indulge in, and regulating the child's sleeping habits, which we may? Why should the child be free to play with his mother's breakable ornaments and not to jump on her sofa?

The distinction between freedom and licence will not get us far, but Neill's other two answers will, at least in principle. They are respectively that children should be free to do whatever does not interfere with the freedom of others and that they should be free to do anything that does not harm themselves. These answers are comprehensible; they explain most of Neill's examples (e.g. the child should not play on the fire escape, wear no clothes, or have unbarred windows, because of the consideration of avoiding harm to himself. The child should not kick down the study door because that interferes with somebody else's freedom), and, in my view, they are in essence acceptable. But before leaving this topic we have to note two points. The first is rather trivial and is merely that, in the light of these criteria for restricting freedom, some of Neill's examples still appear contradictory. Surely the child who plays with my breakable ornaments, thereby breaking some of them, or who plays with my glasses while I am trying to work, interferes with my freedom no less than the child who kicks my door? The second is a related but important point. Though these criteria are comprehensible, they are not in fact easy to make use of in practice. For the real question is what one regards as constituting harm to the child, and what one regards as interference with the freedom of others. It would not be implausible to argue that children who make a lot of noise, who steal, who throw stones through other people's greenhouse windows, or even babies who are fed only and always when they cry for feeding, are interfering with the freedom of others, and that therefore they should be stopped from doing such things. (I am not suggesting that they necessarily should be. I am merely pointing out the complexities involved in the formula 'free to do what does not interfere with the freedom of others'.) Likewise – and this is really one of the important issues – an individual does not only harm himself by doing things like falling out of windows. Why should one not argue – as many would – that the child who is given the freedom to opt out of all lessons and who does so, may thereby harm himself in the long run? If we conceive of education as initiating people into worthwhile activities then, almost by definition, the child who opts out of education in this sense is harming himself.

I suggest, in conclusion, that precisely what children should be free to decide for themselves cannot finally be settled without reference to one's overall view of what education is and what it is for, and that is why the matter cannot be satifactorily concluded in a single chapter. If, simply by way of example, one believed that education was about filling children with information (and hence believed that it was valuable for the child to acquire such information), one would naturally conclude that it would be to the detriment of the child to opt out of this process. If one believed that it was worth while for the child to develop rational powers, one would likewise conclude that the child should not miss the opportunity to cultivate such powers. Conversely, to adopt the view that children should be free to opt out of lessons is implicitly to claim that this cannot harm them in any sense, which is evidently a large claim.

Conclusion

We have gone somewhat out of our way in the previous section because it transpired that the ideal of self-regulating children was a misnomer and that what was really at issue was the question of how one decides when it is legitimate to curb the freedom of children. But one thing is clear and that is that any attempt to suggest that only those who have been self-regulating or self-determining from birth can be truly described as self-determining adults must be rejected, since there is no such thing as a self-determining baby. The notion is a logical nonsense and, it is important to add, in practice not even avowed advocates of self-regulation have any intention of literally doing nothing to regulate the life of the growing child.

The question of the extent to which older children should be self-determining, that is to say the extent to which they should be free to do as they decide to do, has only been touched upon. It is an enormous and complex problem that can only be solved in the light of one's other values and educational objectives, for clearly one would not advocate the right of children to determine to do anything that one regarded as in some way unacceptable. Thus, purely by way of example, if one believed that people should show respect for other people, one would not approve of children being free to determine to show no respect for anyone else.

But suppose that it were to be argued not simply that children should be self-determining within broad limits, but that the overall objective of education should be to produce self-determining adults. That is to say, the claim would no longer be that on a number of issues – such as whether they attend lessons – children should make up their own minds, but that the supremely important thing was to bring children up in such a way that on all issues they were self-determining. The first point to note about this ideal is that it cannot be achieved by education alone. It is true that education could contribute to it: if people are to be self-determining then education will need to ensure that as they develop children do not succumb to the control of such things as drugs, drink, and distorted passions. It will also be necessary to ensure that education does not become indoctrination and that children acquire the habit of making their own decisions rather than meekly responding to the dictates of others. But these are only necessary conditions of self-determination. They are not sufficient to ensure that a man is self-determining, for he can only finally be self-determining if he has the freedom to do what he decides to do. And the question of what freedom he will in fact have as an adult is obviously a social or political question that has nothing to do with education. If our ideal is a community of self-determining adults, then, as opposed to the quite distinct educational aim of allowing children to be to some extent self-determining, there is very little beyond the negative point raised above that education can do about it.

But, just as it seemed far from clear that the idea of allowing children complete self-determination was acceptable, so it is questionable whether a community of self-determining adults is in itself a worthwhile ideal. What is the inherent value in people doing what they choose to do, regardless of what it is that they choose to do? Is it a good thing that I bite the heads of whippets, play video games all day, lie in the sun all day, or devote my life to the making of money, simply because I freely decide to do these things? If self-determination is our ideal, what happens when different individuals determine to behave in mutually exclusive ways? Are there not other considerations that must override or modify the claims of self-determination? Is our only concern, for instance, that the individual's allegiance to a particular political party shall be determined by himself? Is that *all* that matters? Are we not concerned about the reasons that he has for his allegiance?

It was pointed out above that the concept of self-determination has a certain amount in common with the concept of rationality: both put the stress on the individual's decision rather than the decision of others. What this and the previous chapter have really been about is the opposition between the view on the one hand that what matters is that the individual should ideally do what he chooses to do, and on the other hand the view that ideally he should do what there is good reason to do or that he should do what he chooses to do but that he should choose with rational understanding. In conclusion I wish to suggest that self-determination is an uninspiring ideal unless it is combined with rationality. This combination is essentially what is involved in the concept of autonomy. There is nothing particularly compelling about the ideal of a world in which nobody is answerable to anything or anybody except themselves. Whereas there is something very compelling about the ideal of a world in which people are concerned to be answerable only to the demands of rationality. It is the objective of bringing children to question and to think for themselves, provided that their questioning and thinking should be well-informed and ably performed rather than a matter of idle whim, that we should surely embrace. But, as already indicated, it is unlikely that this objective will be met unless a conscious and deliberate attempt is made by teachers to realize it.

Notes

1 Neill, A. S. *Summerhill* (Harmondsworth, Penguin, 1968), p. 104.
2 Ibid., p. 111. The examples cited occur, in the main, in the section entitled 'The Free Child'.
3 Ibid., p. 107.
4 Ibid., p. 105.

Further reading

For a collection of articles relating to the concepts of rationality and reasonableness the reader is referred to Part 2 of R. F. Dearden, P. H. Hirst, and R. S. Peters (eds), *Education and the Development of Reason* (London, Routledge & Kegan Paul, 1972). Attention may be drawn, in particular, to G. Ryle, 'A Rational Animal' and M. Black, 'Reasonableness' in that volume. A most useful book is John McPeck, *Critical Thinking and Education* (Oxford, Martin Robertson, 1981). See also Richard Tarnas, *The Passion of the Western Mind* (New York, Ballatine Books, 1991).

A. S. Neill is one of the most prominent advocates of self-regulation as an educational objective. His most accessible book is *Summerhill* (Harmondsworth, Penguin, 1968). For fuller critical attention to Neill see Robin Barrow, *Radical Education* (Oxford, Martin Robertson, 1978).

9   The postmodern challenge

The previous chapters have all emphasized reason and knowledge as key elements in the educational enterprise. Our selfhood is tied up with our minds; our ideal is individuals who can determine what to do for themselves in the light of good understanding and sound reasoning; education is the development of understanding of powerful and distinctive bodies or types of thought. The time has come to consider a potential challenge to this emphasis, represented by postmodernism.

Actually, it is not clear that the term 'postmodern' is in itself particularly helpful. It means different things to different people and in many cases it is not entirely clear what it does mean. The word seems to have been introduced in an architectural context in the 1930s, in order to differentiate a new contemporary style from the preceding 'modern' style. A similar attempt was then made to define some literature as postmodern in contrast to the fairly well-established notion of modernity in that field. However, it is already evident both that the dates that, broadly speaking, separate modern and postmodern architecture and literature, respectively, are different, and that the criteria that define postmodern architecture and literature are distinct. Even more confusing is the fact that some contemporary postmodernists claim that the very idea of definable periods or distinct epochs is modernist and there-fore incompatible with postmodernism. It comes as no great surprise, then, to find Lyotard (1984) defining the term obscurely as 'an incredulity towards meta-narratives' or that the *International Encyclopedia of Education* (1994) should suggest that 'it may be better to see postmodernism as a complex intellectual map of late twentieth century thought and practice rather than any clear-cut philosophic, political, and/or aesthetic movement'. It may indeed be better, in the sense of more accurate, to do this, but it is difficult to see it as better in the sense of any clearer. (It is also arguable that, whatever its origins, postmodernism has now evolved into a fairly rigid creed.)

The truth of the matter is that the word cannot be defined in a clear and consistent manner, given its history, its use in different contexts, and the opaque nature of the language of most self-styled postmodernists; and, that being the case, the word itself is not very useful. Despite the signs of orthodoxy among many who share an enthusiasm for the likes of Foucault, Lyotard, and Derrida, there are also signs of schism and heresy, not to mention the large number of people who nowadays almost unthinkingly characterize themselves and their thoughts as postmodern and who may mean almost anything by the claim. We therefore cannot talk of the post-modern agenda or even viewpoint. However, there are a number of claims that, rightly or wrongly, are commonly associated with postmodernism, and that, however they are labelled or classified, enjoy quite widespread favour today and that urgently need to be examined and evaluated. Chief among these are claims relating to truth and knowledge which, if shown to be correct, would substantially undermine the argument for education presented in this book. They are also, incidentally, despite their fashionableness and would be up-to-dateness, claims that have been familiar, argued about and for the most part rejected repeatedly throughout the recorded history of Western thought since Plato. We should therefore set aside at the outset any idea to the effect that these claims rest on recent advances or insights in thought.

The claims I have in mind are these: there is no truth; we cannot know anything; everything is as you see it; and what is taken to be knowledge is a cultural product. These are not all completely compatible, of course: if knowledge is a cultural product, then everything cannot simply be as the individual sees it. But any such incompatibilities are accounted for by a combination of classifying a diverse set of people and ideas as postmodern and the inconsistency in some specific thinkers and arguments. It should also be noted that some would appear to make these claims in reference to truth and knowledge generally, while others might qualify them arguing that they apply only in certain areas, such as values and politics. The latter view certainly has a greater *prima facie* plausibility, but it is far from clear that the claim can be substantiated even in a limited field, as we shall see. In the first instance, I shall consider the claims without reference to a restricted context.

The first point to make is a simple, but devastating, logical one: what would it mean to say that such claims as these are true? If there is no truth, how can this be true? If we cannot know anything, how can we know this? Simple as the point is, it is sufficient to awake us to the fact that there is something fundamentally ridiculous about such claims: to get away with credit for perceiving correctly that there is no such thing as being correct would certainly be to have one's cake and eat it too. Nonetheless, I shall proceed to give each claim in turn brief consideration. The reason for doing so, the reason for taking this challenge seriously, empty though I hope to show it to be, is that one should not underestimate the damage that such erroneous beliefs have done, are doing, and may in future do to our chances of making tolerable sense and taking appropriate control of our lives both individually and collectively. The malaise, the anomie, the ennui, the frustration, the anger that many people feel today are at least partly related to the insidious effects of these and similar beliefs; the prevalent lack of commitment and the unwillingness to praise or condemn, the assumption that 'realpolitik' rules the world and nothing can be done about it, and the retreat into materialism and instrumentalism can all, I believe, be traced in part to the effects of the common belief that nobody is in a position to say what is true and false, right and wrong. If the world is increasingly riven between indoctrinated and committed believers on the one hand, and cynical relativists, on the other, as there is a case for saying, it is not hard to see who will lose ground. That is fine, if we really have given up on the ideal of reason, truth, and knowledge. But have we? Should we? As Roger Scruton (1999) has written: 'even those enlightenment thinkers who distrusted reason, like Hume, and those who tried to circumscribe its powers, like Kant, never relinquished their confidence in rational argument...[Yet] reason is now on the retreat, both as an ideal and as a reality'. Consequently, as Wheen (2004) points out, Prime Minister Blair, while ceaselessly asserting his commitment to education, astonishingly defends the teaching of creationism rather than evolution as if it was equally valid. (It is true that the theory of evolution is just that, a theory, and as such not an incontrovertible demonstrated truth, but, unlike creationism, it is a rationally defensible theory).

Is there, then, truth? This is not the same question as Pilate's 'what is truth?', nor is it the same as 'what truths are there?'. The question is: is it the case that some things are true and some false (regardless of whether we know what they are)? To this question I respond with a few brief points that cumulatively will, I am confident, lead the reader to reply 'yes'. There are various claims that can be formulated in such a way that something must be true: 'either I am writing this at my desk in Vancouver or I am not' – that statement is itself true and one of the two claims within it must also be true. Even if we incline to the solipsistic view that we and the whole world are merely part of some dream, then the claim that that is so must be true (or false). It is true that nothing can be both a circle and a square at the same time. People occasionally try to argue against such an example, perhaps suggesting that magicians *can* square the circle or that these claims are somehow simply a function of our language which could have been different; but such responses invariably miss the point: yes, we can be made to think we are seeing a circle turn into a square or an actual circle can be turned into a square, but it cannot be square while remaining circular. Nor is this simply the consequence of our language: nothing that is simply what we call a square could at the same time simply be what we call a circle, and no language could be devised to alter that fact though one might be devised that ignored it, glossed over it, or gave some quite different sense to the utterance 'this is a square circle'. Not only is it clearly the case that there must be some truths, it is also surely evident that to deny this involves a degree of insincerity and bad faith. For who does (who could) live their life on the genuine presumption that there is no such thing as truth? Our daily life is predicated on the assumption that some things are true and others not; that is why we generally catch the bus, don't eat rat poison, and take some exercise. No philosopher who claims that he does not believe in truth is telling the truth.

There is truth: some things are the case, some are not. But how do we know what is the case? May the second claim, 'that we cannot know anything', perhaps be true? We should distinguish here between knowing something and knowing that we know something. If we define knowledge in a fairly conventional way as believing something that is true in the light of good reason, then surely we shall readily agree that knowledge is possible and, further, that we actually know some things. As in the case of truth, we certainly act as if this were so and it is inconceivable that we should do otherwise: it is because I know that the bus leaves at 3:10 pm that I am leaving the house now; it is because I know that roads can be dangerous that I worry about my young children running into the road. If one really and sincerely believed that no knowledge could be attained, one would inevitably be reduced to a state of existential angst that would be insupportable. Our lives reveal that we believe knowledge is possible and they also reveal a great deal of what we are confident that we know.

But can we ever know that we know? This question really boils down to the question of whether and how one can determine that the reason that supports one's true belief is good enough. I may be said to know that the sun will rise tomorrow, because the fact that it has done so everyday of my life so far represents pretty good reason to believe it. In fact, of course, it may not rise tomorrow, and strictly speaking I therefore shouldn't claim to know that it will. What about my claim to know that the theory of evolution is correct? This can be called knowledge because the reasoning in support of the theory is generally judged adequate, while, by contrast, any reasoning person (as distinct from one whose belief is based on faith) can see that creationism, though it *could* conceivably be true, is supported by no evidence and rendered implausible by other evidence. But it is of course the case that the theory of evolution (at least as currently understood) could be proved wrong (though only by the acquisition of further knowledge of the truth, it should be noted). It could be, in other words, that what is taken to be 'good reason' to support the belief turns out not to be. Do such examples imply that we cannot ever know that we know? No; they illustrate the fact that many of our claims to knowledge should be recognized as provisional – it is not that we necessarily don't know, but that we sometimes prove to be mistaken. But not all knowledge claims are provisional in this way: some are necessary truths or truths that are logically unassailable. We not only know that all triangles have angles that add up to 180°, but we also know that we know. Similarly we know that we know that it is true that if all men are mortal and Socrates is a man, then Socrates is mortal.

In practice, once the point is conceded that some knowledge is in principle possible and that there are some things that in sincerity we must acknowledge that we know that we know, the issue becomes one of distinguishing between knowledge claims that we have absolutely no reason to deny and others where we can only be cautious and provisional. In the field of medicine, for example, it is entirely appropriate to say that we know how to set a broken leg or that we know that aspirin, under certain specifiable conditions, reduces the likelihood of strokes, but it would be inappropriate to say that we know that an adult's insecurities stem from his toilet training.

In defending the idea that there is both truth and knowledge, there is no need to ignore some of the truth that is embedded in the argument of those who would deny it. It is true that different people perceive things differently; it is true that some of what we regard as true is so only because our culture made it so; it is true that some things are purely matters of individual opinion; it is true that our understanding develops over time (and sometimes regresses). Certainly there are distinctions such that different degrees of certainty are appropriate to different subject matters. That was part of the reasoning behind the argument for forms of knowledge: we can be more certain that we know that $2 + 2 = 4$ or that metals expand when heated than we can that God exists. As was noted in Chapter 4, it is not as clear and uncontentious what the appropriate way to test the latter proposition against experience is. But even in the spheres of religion or morality the difficulty of being sure that we know should not lead us to assume that there is no truth of any kind and therefore nothing to be known – only individual opinion. It is, for example, as obviously true that it is false to say that 'ugliness is wrong' as it is to say that $2 + 2 = 5$. Morality is about issues such as stealing and not about ugliness, and that is a fact.

The important conclusion is that it is not true that everything is as you see it. There are truths and falsehoods, correct and incorrect claims, and it is incumbent on us to use our reason to increase our understanding. The postmodernism of writers such as Lyotard confuses epistemological questions (questions about the nature of knowledge) with sociological questions: there are indeed ways in which what is taken to be knowledge is affected by such things as who has power, the nature of society, and the time and place in which we live. But what may have some influence on some of what we think we know is one thing (and even on a sociological level post-modernists tend to exaggerate the degree and extent of such influence). What knowledge is possible and what we do actually know are quite another thing. The essential point of education is to provide individuals with the understanding to make their own rational judgement as to what is known and what is not.

If the extreme relativistic claims commonly associated with postmodernism were true, it would have serious consequences for education. If everything is how the individual or a given society sees it and anything goes, then how does one begin to construct a coherent curriculum or a persuasive argument for any particular approach to schooling and teaching? How does one make any judgements in a world that denies distinctions of credibility or worth? It may be a bad thing to be too 'judgemental' in the sense of too 'inclined to pass judgements on others', but it is essential to our very way of life to make some judgements, if only between the edible and the poisonous. Fortunately, the postmodern challenge as interpreted here clearly fails.

Further reading

See further, Robin Barrow 'The need for philosophical analysis in a postmodern era', *Interchange*, vol. 30: 4, 1999. See also Daniel C. Dennett's *Freedom Evolves* (New York, Viking, 2003). The arguments about truth and knowledge considered in this chapter are as old as philosophy itself; among more recent books one of the most finely balanced is John Searle *The Construction of Social Reality* (London, Allen Lane, 1995). See also Simon Blackburn *Truth: A Guide* (Oxford University Press, 2005). On autonomy, see Eamon Callan *Autonomy and Schooling* (Ontario, McGill-Queen's University Press, 1993). Christopher Butler *Postmodernism* (Oxford University Press, 2002) is clear and concise. See also Raymond Gaita *Good and Evil* (Macmillan, 1991).

10 Needs, interests, and experience

There used to be considerable controversy as to whether the word 'education' was derived from the Latin word 'educere' or 'educare'. 'Educere' means 'to lead out', and those who saw this as the source of our word 'education' were anxious to appeal to the derivation as evidence that teachers, if they were truly educating, should seek to bring or lead out what was in some sense innate in the child, rather than to impose various preselected attitudes and characteristics on him. The teacher was to regard himself as a gardener tending a plant, rather than as a craftsman making a product. He should encourage the natural flowering or development of the individual, rather than attempt to mould him. This particular argument, conducted with reference to the supposed derivation of the word 'education', was more than usually silly. In the first place, the fact, if it were established as a fact, that the word 'education' is derived from a particular Latin word is not particularly compelling evidence to persuade one to teach in one way rather than another. In the second place, the Romans themselves used both 'educere' and 'educare' with reference to educating children, and it is therefore difficult to see how one can successfully establish one rather than the other as the source of our 'education'. In the third place, 'educere', besides meaning to lead out, was also used to mean to train, and 'educare', besides meaning to train, was used to mean to nourish, with reference to plants. In other words, either term could in fact be said to involve either of the contrasting views of education. One is glad therefore that this particular etymological game seems to be relatively out of favour at the moment.[1]

But although the attempt to carry the argument by reference to the derivation of 'education' is out of favour, the substance of the argument is very much alive. As we have already seen in considering the concept of self-regulation, there is a real difference of opinion between those who would put the emphasis on the idea of forming aspects of the child's personality through education, and those who would put it on the idea of the child being free to unfold his natural personality. There are a number of concepts and phrases, frequently to be found in current educational writings, which have in common the implication that the child's own point of view should take precedence over the teacher's, and that the child should himself dictate the scope and the direction of his education, rather than be educated in the light of the preconceived values and attitudes of adults. It is with some of these concepts that this chapter is concerned.

The most general of such phrases, and the one that may be said to summarize the view of those who are hostile to a notion of education that involves moulding or deliberately forming any aspects of the child's personality, is 'child-centred'. Any education that is not child-centred is not in fact education at all, according to P. S. Wilson.[2] In common with so much of educational jargon, the phrase 'child-centred education' has a built-in advantage for those who have a particular point of view to put forward, inasmuch as it seems self-evidently desirable. For who would want to deny the child himself any place at the centre of the idea of education? Presumably, very few. But then, if child-centred education is more or less desirable by definition, and if education cannot be education unless it is child-centred, we need to have a rather more precise idea of what is meant by the term. In what sense is the child to be central? Fairly obviously 'child-centred' is a portmanteau phrase that might reasonably carry many different meanings for different people. But if it is going to be of any use as an ideal, we need to have some agreement as to its meaning, and it is more than likely that the more precisely a meaning is delineated for the phrase, the less self-evident is the desirability of child-centred education going to appear. After all, when people have real differences of opinion as to what should take place in the name of education, it is seldom that these differences of opinion turn out to be merely verbal quibbles.

It seems clear that the very least that the term 'child-centred' must be taken to imply is that the child himself should be given consideration as a person in his own right. If one treats the child simply as a means to an end, or as a pawn to be manipulated to somebody else's advantage, then by no stretch of the imagination could one claim that the child himself was at the centre of one's educational scheme. To confine education to imparting skill in the three Rs simply so that the child, when adult, should be more serviceable as a clerk or secretary to other people, would not be providing child-centred education. It would involve a view of education that was centred on those who are expected to gain from the literacy and numeracy of the child at the end of the process. And it is precisely for having this view of education that the elementary school tradition of the nineteenth century, for example, has been frequently, and no doubt fairly, criticized. Children, it is argued, were sent to school not out of any concern for them, but out of concern for the employers who needed employees with particular rudimentary skills. This consideration rather than the advantage of the child as an individual dictated the nature of the education provided.

If education is to be regarded as child-centred, then, it must at least be concerned for the advantage of the child himself. It must regard him as an end in himself and not simply as a means to somebody else's advantage. The question as to whether it is desirable that this should be the case is, of course, distinct from the point that this is one basic criterion for regarding an educational scheme as child-centred. But that is not a question that I intend to pursue here, beyond remarking that it is difficult to see how anybody could justify the intention to use some other individual merely as a means (see Chapter 6). I shall therefore assume that, in so far as child-centred education simply means that the child should be regarded as an end in himself, it is desirable.

But although the implication that the child is an end in himself is an important gain for the notion of child-centred education, it is not in fact particularly helpful. For in principle a great variety of educational courses, content, and method would be compatible with the intention of treating the child as an end and not a means. One might instruct a child in the intricacies of Latin gerunds, or leave him to amuse himself in the playground, and reasonably claim in either case that the education one provided was child-centred in the sense that one was not treating the child as a means to somebody else's advantage. The gerund-grinding, one might claim, would develop the child's sense of accuracy and memorizing ability as well as enable him to read Latin literature, all of which would be to his personal advantage rather than anybody else's. We therefore have to consider whether any more can be said to tie down the concept of child-centred education.

So far the word 'child' has merely served to refer to the individual who receives attention in education and who happens, generally, to be a child. 'Child-centred' has been interpreted to mean at least that the individual who is receiving education should be regarded as an end in his own right. We should surely now add that the notion of child-centred education also implies that the child should be treated as a child, and not as a miniature adult.

It is Rousseau who is generally credited with being the first to recognize that children were not simply small adults and that their mental capacities, attitudes, feelings, and ways of looking at things were not simply relatively undeveloped, but were in many ways quite distinct from those of adults. However, who discovered it is unimportant, as indeed was the discovery itself until something more precise and positive was known about child psychology than was known to Rousseau. But this gap in our knowledge has now been considerably lessened by the advances made by psychologists, following on from the work of such men as Piaget. We are now in a better position, not simply to observe that the child is different, but to specify some of the respects in which he is different. Recognition of the child as a child must now involve recognition of such points as that before a certain age children do not have a grasp of the idea of volume, cannot be said to understand simple parables from the Bible, and more generally that they pass through stages of development such that what Piaget called a social stage can only follow on an egocentric stage.[3]

Although we shall not go into the details of child psychology here, it is obviously absurd to adopt a view of education without taking account of its findings. There is no point in saying that children ought to do this, that, and the other if they are psychologically incapable of doing so. On the grounds of efficiency and common sense alone, therefore, we should say that education should be child-centred with the addition of this second criterion: that the child should be treated as a child. Nor is there need for much argument over a third implication of the phrase 'child-centred', namely that individual differences between children should be taken account of. In other words it is not enough for education to recognize that a group of nine-year-olds are nine-year-olds and not adults, and to regard them as ends; ideally, education must also be concerned to recognize that each nine-year-old is a unique individual, and as such may need to be treated differently.

These three criteria may be said to constitute a minimum definition of the notion of child-centred education. If these conditions were not met, it would really seem most implausible to claim that one's view of education was child-centred in any sense. However these criteria will still not get us very far: they will rule out certain practices and procedures in education, but a great deal of room will still be left for very different kinds of education to count as child-centred. A very traditional manner of teaching, combined with a typical grammar school curriculum, could reasonably claim to be as child-centred as a very progressive situation in which children were left more or less free to do what they wanted to do. For both types of education might well take account of child psychology and individual differences, and both might claim to be concerned for the advantage of the individual children being taught. The difference between the two approaches would presumably arise from a very different view as to what ultimately was to the advantage of the children concerned.

Can one, then, say any more? Can one add any further criteria for the correct application of the term 'child-centred' to education, such as to make it more specific and hence more useful? A primary consideration of many of those who advocate child-centred education seems to be that the curriculum should be child-centred rather than subject-centred. Rather than the traditional pattern of a curriculum designed by adults in the light of an adult viewpoint, the curriculum should effectively centre on the individual children themselves. Instead of the curriculum consisting of such things as English, Latin, and maths, which the teacher feels are important, it should be constructed with reference to the child. We should teach children, not subjects, as the saying goes.

It is at this point that the concept of child-centred education becomes interesting. It is at this point that it becomes more specific and less self-evidently desirable. It also becomes rather complex. Granted that objection is being raised to a curriculum that is constructed by reference to what adults think important, what does it mean to say that the curriculum should be child-centred rather than subject-centred? Does it simply mean that children should do what they want to do? If it does mean that, a number of child-centred enthusiasts are very careful to veil their real meaning, for it is at this juncture, very often, that a number of further, attractive-sounding terms are introduced. The curriculum should meet children's 'needs' or children's 'interests', we are told; or the curriculum should be based on 'experience' or 'discovery'; or, less obscurely, but perhaps less convincingly, what is meant by a child-centred situation is one in which the 'subject matter and so on would be what was valued by the child'.[4]

Needs

The questions we have to ask are what precisely is meant by these phrases and are they commendable ideals. What, for instance, is an education or a curriculum constructed according to children's needs? Certainly, the suggestion that education should be according to children's needs seems *prima facie* unexceptionable. It would surely be very odd to say that education should *not* take account of children's needs. Furthermore, if one were to say that education should not take account of children's needs, one would effectively be opposing the notion of child-centred education in the minimal sense already outlined. If one deliberately took no account of children's needs then one could hardly claim to be concerned.with children as children and as ends in themselves. But is taking account of needs the same as educating according to needs? Are children's needs the only consideration in education? What are children's needs?

It is easy to talk as if there can really be no doubt as to what children's needs are, and as if, in order to identify them, we only have to conduct some empirical survey. But needs, whether children's or anybody else's, are by no means always obvious and indisputable. If somebody were to ask me what I need at this juncture of my life, I am not sure that I would be able to answer the question. I am not even sure that the question, put in this stark manner, would mean very much to me. Again, there are some things which presumably in some sense I do need, such as food and drink, which I am liable to forget that I need since I have them. I might think I need something and be mistaken, as, for example, a man might think that what he really needs is a wife, only to discover after some experience that it was the last thing he needed. I might need something and have absolutely no view on the matter as to whether I need it or not: for example, if I am unconscious, I may none the less need medical attention. Do I need to have a sense of humour in this day and age? Do I need a car? How much money do I need? Do I need to have access to libraries? And what about the question of the connection between wants and needs? Some seem to treat the two concepts as synonymous, which they are certainly not – I want an expensive compact disc player, but it is by no means clear that I need it. I might need something and not want it, for instance a penicillin injection – but what is the distinction between them?

These uses of 'need' make it clear that, although needs may be important, it is by no means clear what people's needs are, how one sets about assessing them, and therefore what education according to children's needs would actually consist of. They also make it clear that one point about the logic of the concept of need is that an objective is presupposed. One needs something *for* something, or one needs something given some prior assumption. One does not have needs in a vacuum. Even such needs as the need for food and water can only be regarded as needs on the prior assumption that one wishes to survive or that one ought to survive. One does not need food if one intends to starve oneself to death. Similarly, in so far as we take it for granted that we want everybody to survive without acute discomfort, then, in our society, we all need money since money is the means of obtaining various necessities for comfortable survival. But how much money we need is a difficult question to answer, since it depends on such factors as who we are, what we regard as comfortable survival, and various other objectives that we might have.

Wants and needs are to be distinguished essentially in that one may talk of wants without specifying any particular objective (although it may be true that in general we happen to want things for particular purposes), whereas to talk of needs necessarily implies some specific objective. I need a paintbrush rather than paper-hanging equipment, if my intention is to paint my room rather than paper it. If this specific objective is changed then I cease to need the paintbrush. In many cases the selection of an objective itself will be a matter of wants rather than needs. In general people do not need to paint their rooms rather than paper them, that is to say they do not have some further objective that necessitates paint rather than paper, they simply want one rather than the other. Our wants, then, become needs in the light of specific further objectives. I want an expensive car: it would give me pleasure to have one. But we do not start talking of my need for an expensive car unless specific objectives are brought into the matter, for instance that I have to drive a hundred miles every day.

The fact that a need logically implies some objective has two important consequences: first, it is not necessarily desirable to fulfil needs. Whether we think that a particular person's particular need at any given time ought to be satisfied, will depend on our evaluation of the objective at which this need is directed. A man who wants to commit murder needs the opportunity and the means to do so, but we should presumably not feel inclined to satisfy that need. A drug addict needs his drugs, but we might reasonably argue as to whether this is a need that should be satisfied. To put the same point another way, we may disagree as to whether a particular person does need something because we have different values. Some might argue that people need religion, because they value the objective of people having the sort of comfort and security that might be provided by a faith. Others, regarding other things as considerably more important than a comfortable faith, might respond by saying that people do not need religion. One important point that emerges from this is that assessing needs is not simply a matter of empirical research. Estimating children's needs requires consideration of evaluative assumptions as well as psychological and sociological data.

The second consequence of the fact that needs presuppose objectives is that, in order to assess needs, one also has to have knowledge about what is in fact required for a certain end. Before I can know that I need penicillin, I do not only have to assume the value of being healthy, I also have to know that penicillin will in fact restore my health. Furthermore, I have to recognize that I am sick. I have to have knowledge about myself as well as knowledge about means to ends. Just as I could not know whether my next door neighbour needs financial assistance without knowing what his financial resources are, so I cannot know whether I need to take a job as a teacher without knowing myself pretty well. I may want to be a teacher, I may feel that I need to be a teacher rather than an insurance clerk but, on the assumption that this need is related to the general objective of feeling self-fulfilled, I can only be right in claiming that I need to be a teacher if I am reading my own personality accurately. It may transpire that teaching makes me anxious and depressed, and that a job as a teacher was not what I needed for my fulfilment as an individual.

It follows that one may not be the best judge of one's own needs. Perhaps in general people are – that would be an empirical question – but it is not necessarily true that they will be: they may lack self-knowledge and consequently assess their own personality inaccurately, they may be mistaken about means to ends, or they may assume that certain ends would be desirable to them which turn out not to be when gained. There is then the further question of whether the ends that people set up for themselves, and therefore the needs that they have in relation to those ends, are morally desirable or more generally worth while.

It is at once clear that, whatever the case with adults, young children at any rate are very unlikely to be the best judge of their own needs – unless we assume some native intuition that cannot fail. In so far as they are not very self-aware, do not have a great deal of knowledge or experience about means to ends, do not tend to look into the future, and do not have the ability or experience to make an informed choice between ends, they are not likely to be very good judges of what they need, particularly if we assume that we are thinking of what they need from a long-term point of view. In many cases at least, what children think that they need will be indistinguishable from what they want. But, as we have seen, what people want or think they need is not necessarily what they do need. A child, for example, may feel that he does not need to learn to read. He is not necessarily wrong. We could only say that he was wrong if we could confidently predict that he will need it for some objective that at some stage he will embrace. But as a matter of fact, and despite the arguments of some deschoolers such as Goodman, it is highly likely that he is wrong.[5] In many ways life will be more difficult for him if he cannot read, and on the assumption, surely a reasonable one, that he will not want a difficult life then one thing that he does need to do is to learn to read – and that is all there is to it. (Goodman's argument is based upon the point that information can be gained through television and other aural and visual media. Allowing that this is so, and allowing that all education could be carried on through such aids as tape recorders and television, it should none the less be noted that to argue that children do not need to learn to read is to deny the objective of giving individuals the opportunity to pursue arguments and interests that go beyond and that may challenge the point of view of those who are responsible for programming television and audio-visual aids.)[6]

What then does the demand that education should be according to children's needs amount to? Very little. In the first place it is purely formal: it does not tell us what children's needs are. We might all agree with the demand in principle but disagree violently as to what children do need, for one's view of what children need is one and the same thing as one's view of child psychology, one's sociological knowledge, one's knowlege of means to ends, and one's view of what are desirable objectives all rolled into one. For example, if one held the view that traditional teaching techniques of drill and instruction were efficient and not harmful to the child's psychological makeup, if one believed in the value of reading Cicero in Latin (either for its own sake or for some further objective), if one believed that it was good to be cultured and that cultured people should have read Virgil, and if one believed in the value of going to a particular university that required a knowledge of Latin as an entrance requirement, then a most old-fashioned Latin course could be said to be part of an education according to children's needs. To convince a particular teacher that such a course did not meet children's needs one would have to convince him that what he valued was not valuable.

Secondly, as is clear from the previous paragraph, it is not going to be very easy to arrive at agreement on what children's needs are. There may well be agreement on certain basic needs simply because there is a degree of agreement on certain broad objectives and the means that are necessary to meet these objectives. For instance, we all agree that one objective is to provide children with the means and ability to survive. Children, like other people, therefore need food and shelter and certain basic skills. But even over the question of what basic skills they need there may be disagreement, as we have seen in the case of reading. Once we go beyond such an uncontentious objective we lose any kind of consensus of opinion as to what children's needs are. Even if we agreed that children should be enabled to flourish or thrive, rather than merely survive, in a complex industrial society, we should immediately open the door to rival views as to what 'flourishing' or 'thriving' actually involved, and hence as to what we needed to meet this objective. But to ask the sorts of question that one would need to ask to construct a curriculum according to children's needs – Do children need to study English literature? Do they need to do maths? Do they need to do what they feel like doing? – would simply be to open up the question of what should be done in the name of education.

Thirdly, talk of education according to children's needs is likely to obscure what might be an important distinction between what children need now for certain immediate objectives, and what they need for certain long-term objectives. Finally, although the phrase 'children's needs' may have the merit of reminding us that it is the child we are concerned with and what *he* needs rather than what we need for him, there is also the danger that we shall ignore the question of whether there are not other needs besides those of the child to be taken into account. In other words, is 'education according to children's needs' to be understood as meaning education *only* with reference to the needs of children, or does it mean with reference to the needs of children but also allowing consideration of the needs of society?

A word should be added about needs assessment. A number of programmes of, and strategies for, assessing the needs of various groups or individuals in various contexts have been developed and put into practice over the years. Because some means of assessing needs employ techniques that are familiar to social science research (such as the use of questionnaires and various types of observation), there is a tendency to think of assessing needs as a reasonably sophisticated technical business, such that experts in the field can furnish information that is fairly accurate and objective. In response it might be questioned whether the procedures in question really are reliable as means of getting at the truth. But the most important thing to appreciate is that such techniques of needs assessment, despite the words used, are not in fact even attempting to assess people's needs but rather people's opinions or views on people's needs (whether their own or others').

If, for example, we hear that a certain district in Northern Ontario wants to set up a new curriculum, suited to the particular needs of people in the area, we might welcome the additional news that what those needs are is going to be established by some rigorous and organized manner of assessing those needs. But, in fact, in nine cases out of ten, whether the researchers in question favour informal means of gathering information or formal means, the information will relate to what various people think are the needs that children in the locality have. Whether the children truly have the needs suggested is an entirely different kind of question. And, as we have already seen, to answer it requires sorting out and justifying various aims and values, as well as empirically establishing what the nature of life in the area may be, what people do lack and what are efficacious means to the chosen ends.

None of this is to say that education should not take account of, or even be for the most part based on, children's needs. It is simply to say that such talk does not really get us anywhere, nor does it help to clarify further the concept of child-centred education to say that it is education based on children's needs, since virtually any school from the most traditional to the most progressive could, given time, make out a reasonable case for saying that it was based on consideration of children's needs.

Interests

Unfortunately the idea of education according to children's interests is not much more helpful. Just as there is a distinction to be drawn between needs in the sense of felt needs and needs in the sense of objectively assessed needs (by which I do not mean the findings of needs assessment schedules), so there is an ambiguity between two possible senses of 'interest'. If I claim that my life is organized according to my interests, I might mean that it is organized in accordance with what interests me. That is to say I am interested in opera, Victorian literature, insurance, and swimming, perhaps, and my life is so organized as to give me scope to indulge these interests. Interests, in this sense, are those things with which I have a particular degree of interaction or engagement; things that provide satisfaction and pleasure for me. To claim an interest in something in this sense implies a degree of commitment and even liking for the business of thinking about it.

But I might also mean, by the claim that my life is organized according to my interests, that it is organized in accordance with what is good, desirable, or profitable for me. In this sense, a life organized according to my interests or in my interests, might, for example, mean such things as that I, rather than my wife, have the use of the car, that my next door neighbour rather than me is responsible for the upkeep of the partition fence between our gardens, and that in general my advantage is secured. Obviously what is in my interests and what interests me may happen to coincide: it is in my interests to write this book and it also interests me. But equally obviously the two may not coincide: it is in my interests to fill in my tax form, but it does not interest me at all. Conversely it interests me to study criminology, but it is difficult to see in what way it is in my interests to do so.

The question therefore is whether education according to children's interests is supposed to mean education in accordance with what as a matter of fact interests them or in accordance with what is in their interests. If we take the latter interpretation a situation arises similar to that which arose over the idea of education according to needs. Few would dispute that education should be in children's interests, and indeed once again the minimal definition of child-centred education that was outlined above (and which, it was suggested, was a desirable ideal) would seem to imply that education should be in the interests of the children, since otherwise one could hardly claim to be regarding them as ends in themselves. But agreeing that education should take account of children's interests in this sense would get us nowhere, for we should have the problem of deciding what *is* in children's interests still before us, and it is this problem on which there is so little agreement. Even those who propose what may seem *prima facie* to be the most bizarre or objectionable types of education seldom argue that they are unconcerned about what is in children's interests; they simply have their own view as to what it is that is in their interests. And, as with needs, to come to some conclusion as to what really is in children's interests would involve working through all the findings of educational psychology and sociology and working out one's overall philosophy of education. In other words the slogan 'education according to interest', if it means according to what is in the interests of children, would not constitute a helpful dictum for ending the debate about what form education should take and what content it should have. It would merely be another way of starting the debate. Instead of asking what is it desirable that children should gain through education, considering them as ends in themselves, we are asking 'What is in the interests of children?' The words are different, but the question is the same.

But suppose we interpret talk of interests in education to mean that education should be according to what does as a matter of fact interest children. Here the situation is very different, for although we cannot simply write down a list of what does interest children, since different children have different interests, there is not a great deal of room for meaningful disagreement as to what does interest particular children. Two teachers might debate for a very long time about what is in the interests of a particular child, even though they both know the child well, for they may disagree about the value of various objectives. But they would have little excuse for arguing deep into the night about what interests that same child. All they have to do to find out what interests him is to ask him. (Conceivably a person might make a mistake even as to what does interest him. He might claim to be interested in fishing on the strength of a one-day fishing excursion, which perhaps he enjoyed, without realizing it, for reasons that had little to do with fishing. A second outing might then cause him to realize that he was not interested in fishing. Allowing for this kind of mistake we should perhaps modify what was said above and say that the two teachers only have to give the child the opportunity to do various things and then ask him which interest him or alternatively observe which things he continues to do. For one indication that one is interested in doing something is that one freely chooses to do it when the opportunity arises.) The problem then with this view of education is not that it is unhelpful in practice, but that considerable disagreement will arise as to whether it is indeed desirable that education should be in accordance with what interests children.

An important point that would need clarification before many people would be prepared to commit themselves one way or the other would be what precisely is meant by 'according to' or 'in accordance with', and whether the interests of children are supposed to be the only determining factor in what goes on in schools or merely one determining factor. If the claim is simply that education should among other things take account of what interests children, perhaps more than it has sometimes done in the past, then many people with very different overall educational viewpoints might happily agree. For the claim would be so vague as to allow the support of all except a few extremists – if they exist – who held to the peculiar view that schools should positively avoid taking any notice of what interests children. One might for instance consider that children ought to learn mathematics, on grounds that have more to do with what is *in* children's interests than what actually interests them, but then, having decided that, go on to attempt to teach it in such a way as to interest them, specifically by starting from some point that does already interest them. To take another example, having decided that it is in children's interests to think critically about the institution of marriage one might choose to start from a consideration of some television programme that one happens to know interests them rather than from some serious novel which introduces the same theme but which does not interest them. The desirability of some such general concern for what does interest children already and for making what they are doing as interesting as possible seems hardly worth debating. That people should derive some enjoyment from their education is not a particularly contentious ideal, and people's interest is one of the most obvious and helpful forms of motivation. But of course, the suggestion that we should show some concern for interesting children is only uncontroversial because it avoids all the crucial questions, such as when should we ignore the fact that something does not interest the child very much? In what areas should we actually start from what already interests the child rather than simply attempt to interest him in what we insist that he does for other reasons? What are the other considerations that may conflict with and override the question of the child's interest?

But what finally of the view that education should be according to children's interests in the sense that the only determining factor in planning an education should be what as a matter of fact interests the child? The view, in other words, that stands in opposition to any attempt to reply to the question 'What should be the content of the education that we provide for our children?' that is couched in terms of what interests us, what we think they need, or what we think is in the interests of children or what we think it is good from society's point of view that children should do. Now this view of education *seems* to be a necessary condition of what some people mean by child-centred education. P. S. Wilson, for example, whose view that only child-centred education is education has already been mentioned, writes: 'The point of calling education "child-centred" lies in emphasising that even when a person who is being educated is a child, and even, therefore, when his interests often seem "childish" or silly or undesirable from the point of view of his adult teachers, nevertheless his education can only proceed through the pursuit of his interests, since it is these and only these which for him are of intrinsic value.'[7]

Wilson's position is both complex and, in my view, confused. But it deserves a brief mention since it is the only serious philosophical attempt to make sense of what I shall now call the extreme child-centred view (in order to distinguish it from the minimal and hopelessly vague definition provided earlier in the chapter). The reader is, however, referred to Wilson's book *Interest and Discipline in Education*, since the confusion may be mine rather than his. It should be stressed that Wilson does not commit himself to the view that the teacher should just stand back and *allow* children to pursue whatever interests come into their heads. In the first place the teacher has the positive task to perform of helping the child to see whatever may be of value in what interests him, and to develop in the child the inclination and the ability to pursue what is valued. All that Wilson is committed to is the view that the content of education has to be decided by reference solely to what individual children do as a matter of fact value. This, for Wilson, effectively means that what interests the child has to form the content since, as the quotation above indicates, the child can regard only what interests him as having intrinsic value.

Wilson might appear to gain some plausibility for his argument from such statements as 'There is always value, therefore, "in" my interest,'[8] for if one agreed that an individual's interests always had some value, one might at least begin to regard the notion of education according to children's interests, in this sense, as worthwhile. But the conclusion that there is always value in my interests, whatever they are, seems either badly phrased or simply mistaken. Wilson arrives at his conclusion by arguing that, since being interested in doing something can stand as a sufficient explanation of why one is doing it, a child's (or anyone else's) interest 'will always constitute a good reason for engaging in the activities which he sees as relevant'[9] to that interest. But this is either not true or else highly ambiguous. It is not true if by a 'good reason' we mean a reason that other people might regard as a sufficient justification, which is what we usually do mean. The fact that I am interested in torturing people does not constitute a good reason for doing so, in this sense of 'good reason.' What Wilson obviously means here by 'good reason' is simply an explanation or a motivation. It is true that my interest in torturing people will explain why I am doing so and serve as a motivation for my doing so. But then the fact that my interest will always constitute a good reason, in this peculiar sense of 'an explanation', does not lead to the conclusion that there is any value in my interest. At the very most one might say that people tend to see value in what interests them. But then why should we agree that education ought to consist simply of what children do as a matter of fact want to do, which is what all this talk of interest and value seems to amount to?

At this point we must note a second and most peculiar – in the circumstances – proviso laid down by Wilson. Not only should the teacher help the child to get something out of his interests, rather than simply allow him to indulge them, but he should also prevent the child indulging certain interests that are, perhaps, trivial or harmful. This seems at first sight a flat contradiction of the statement that education must proceed only through the child's interests. It turns out that it is not, because Wilson quite simply *defines* education with reference to interests. Anything else, such as imparting adult values, is to be called 'schooling'. But he agree that we ought to do some 'schooling' as well as some 'educating.' In other words, for practical purposes the whole argument seems to pivot on an arbitrary definition of 'education' and to give us virtually no indication of how we are to decide when to educate and when to school.

The thesis is therefore considerably less dramatic and considerably less revolutionary than Wilson seems willing to admit. He is arguing that, although there may be some adult values that we ought to bring children to hold, although there may be some children's interests that we ought not to encourage because they are trivial or harmful, none the less we ought to take good note of children's interests.

However, regardless of the logic of Wilson's argument, there is not much doubt that what he and some others in practice are advocating is that the school curriculum should be based on what does interest children and what they do value and want to do, rather than on what we regard as valuable. What are we to say about this view of a curriculum based on children's present interests?

If children's interests were to be the sole criterion of what went on in schools, then unless we believed that all children necessarily must have worthwhile interests if left to themselves, we commit ourselves to the view that there is no such thing as a distinction between worthwhile and non-worthwhile or between more and less worthwhile activities. We commit ourselves to the view that it does not matter what activities children engage in, provide that they are interested in whatever it is that they do. There can be no two ways about this: that is the necessary corollary of making children's interests the sole criterion of the content for education. (And at this point let us make a distinction between admitting, as many would, that establishing what activities are worthwhile may be very difficult and may invite considerable disagreement, and claiming that there is no such thing as a relatively worthwhile activity.)

Do we accept that if a child is interested in blowing up frogs with bicycle pumps or bullying smaller children the interest makes it an acceptable activity? These are examples in which the question of cruelty, or more generally moral considerations, might, for some of us, be thought to outweigh consideration of interests. Blowing up frogs might also be thought to be rather pointless. Do we accept that other examples of *prima facie* pointless activity, such as making paper darts, throwing stones in ponds and making mud pies, are worth pursuing in schools, just because they interest children? Do we accept the possible consequence that, at least in many cases, concentration on what does interest children now will deny them the opportunity of being introduced to activities which would interest them once they had been initiated into them? Jersild's empirical survey led him to the conclusion that 'the range of children's out-of-school interests' (i.e. of interests that arise without any deliberate attempt to create them) 'is quite restricted compared with children's potentialities'.[10] Do we accept that there is no point or good reason to develop, even create, potential interests? Is it a bad thing that I have an interest in the plays of Euripides, since I would never have developed this interest at a school that concentrated exclusively on the interests that I had acquired simply through my peer and social group? Why, in any case, are interests that arise out of my interaction with my peers – which is presumably how some children's interests arise – more hallowed than interests that arise out of my interaction with my teachers? Do we accept that they are? Even if we accept that the fact that the child values something or is interested in it makes it valuable, do we accept the possibility that some children's education will consist of exploring interests that they themselves will later lose interest in and regard as less than valuable? Do we, in other words, accept that there is not even to be a distinction between the present interests of children that are temporary and the present interests of children that will continue to interest them and seem valuable to them?

The reader must decide for himself. The point that is being made here is that if one or more of these conclusions seem unacceptable then children's interests cannot be the sole criterion for deciding the content of the curriculum. But if it is only one factor to be taken into account in constructing a curriculum, then talk of education according to children's interests has virtually no value until we have some more or less precise idea of what considerations are to override interests to what degree. Once we start to specify the considerations that might outweigh children's immediate interests – moral considerations, other value considerations, the adult's more experienced view of what will be of lasting interest and value (whether with Wilson we refer to these as schooling considerations or as educational considerations) – the stress on children's interests becomes meaningless, except as a general reminder to the effect that, as things are, a lot of what goes on in schools does not interest children, and that to gain their interest is to gain a most effective source of motivation. Only either by maintaining the thesis that the only criterion of value is what the individual of whatever age, experience or intelligence values, or by claiming it to be an empirical truth that children, given the freedom, select worthwhile interests, could the notion of education according to children's interests become more than a vague slogan that is useful only as a counterweight to the extreme view that whether children are interested or not in what goes on at school is unimportant.

None of this is to say that a curriculum that was drawn up with much greater reference to children's interests than has generally been the case hitherto and that did not start from the assumption that there were certain subjects that had to be taught, would necessarily be a bad or inferior curriculum. It might turn out to be an excellent curriculum, but to estimate whether it was one would have to do more than point out that it was based on children's interests. One would have to bring in other criteria to show why this curriculum based on children's interests was a good one.

Readiness

The concepts so far considered have been attempts to clarify the notion of child-centred education by providing a criterion for the content that would distinguish child-centred education from other types of education. The conclusion so far is that either the notion of child-centred education remains so vague as to mean all things to all teachers – this is the case if we take the minimal definition outlined or if we add that it involves education that takes account of needs or is in the interests of children – or else it gains precision at the price of becoming of dubious worth – this is the case if we interpret it as meaning education solely in accordance with the felt needs, expressed interests or actual values of children. It either amounts to a vague injunction to think of children or else to the specific demand that children should dictate the content of education. But there is another group of concepts that are often associated with the idea of child-centred education that in principle shift the emphasis from the content to the method. Child-centred education may be characterized not in terms of what is taught but in terms of various prescriptions as to how we should teach. Specifically it is associated with teaching according to readiness and through experience or discovery.

I say that 'in principle' these concepts provide prescriptions for method, but if one is not careful one can imperceptibly drift into the habit of using them as criteria for content. From the view that learning by discovery methods may be a valuable way of learning, some child-centred enthusiasts seem to come to the conclusion that whatever is learnt by discovery is worth learning, and that whatever is not learnt by discovery is not worth learning. Obviously the conclusion does not follow, and it is well to be on one's guard against this confusion at the outset.

The claim that teaching should proceed according to children's readiness seems unimpeachable. We may disagree to a great extent over a question such as is it or is it not in children's interest to study Shakespeare, but we surely have to agree that it is certainly not in their interests to be made to study Shakespeare when they are not ready to do so. But although we may all agree with this formal statement that does not mean that we are all going to agree as to when various children are ready to study Shakespeare (or pop music, social studies or anything else). What does it mean to say that somebody is ready for something or ready to do something? What does the concept of readiness involve?

To say that somebody is ready to do something is to say, if nothing else, that that person is able to do something or capable of doing something, and of doing it with some degree of success. It is not necessarily to say that he will do it extremely well, but it is to say that he will succeed in doing it. If a man is ready, in the sense under discussion, to begin building a house, then he is capable of building something that will serve as a house. If this house falls down the day after he has finished building, then in some respect he was not ready to build a house. If a person is ready for responsibility, he must be capable of exercising responsibility according to the criteria of success in exercising responsibility. A child who is ready to study Shakespeare must be able to study Shakespeare in such a way as to get something of whatever constitutes successful study of Shakespeare.

As already noted, findings of child psychology make it clear that children pass through various stages of mental development such that there will be certain ways of looking at things that they cannot achieve at particular stages, and hence certain types of things that they cannot do. For example, it is suggested, young children are not capable of understanding even simple parables as parables before what Piaget called the Formal Operations Phase (reached, generally, at about the age of eleven). Therefore, if our object in introducing parables to, say, six-year-olds is to impart the point of the parables, we are wasting our time. The children cannot assimilate the point of the parables *qua* parables. They are not ready for them. In addition, one can think of many thousands of things that children are not ready to do for many other reasons (besides psychological limitations), such as lack of knowledge and lack of physical strength.

Now it is plainly absurd to insist that children should do what they cannot do, and that is why we assent to the proposition that children must be ready for whatever we wish to introduce them to. But an emphasis on children's readiness in this sense is not going to be a great deal of practical help. First, besides the knowledge of child psychology, we should need to have a clear idea of what the study of Shakespeare involves before we could begin to assess whether particular individuals were capable of doing it. Secondly, it should be remembered that psychologists such as Piaget are talking in terms of stages: the ages produced to correspond with particular stages are merely generalizations. One cannot therefore conclude that because a particular child is only six years old it is impossible that he should be ready to understand parables as parables. Thirdly, and by far the most important point, the criterion of readiness will tell us what children cannot do but it will not help us to decide between the various things that they might do at any particular age. Let us assume, as experience would seem to indicate, that at the age of fourteen many children are capable of playing various card games, carrying out some kind of survey into the political allegiances of members of the local community, studying Shakespeare, studying pop music, studying maths, and so on. The notion of readiness is not going to help us decide which of these activities to encourage children to pursue.

Going beyond these considerations that limit the value of readiness as a significant criterion for making educational decisions lies an even more serious problem. How do we tell when a particular child is ready to do something? Rousseau wrote blandly of Emile not being allowed to read books (with the exception of *Robinson Crusoe*) until he was about fifteen and 'ready' to tackle literature; similarly, he was supposed to be 'ready' to undergo some elementary scientific training at the age of twelve. On what grounds does Rousseau claim, by implication, that children cannot be ready to read literature until the age of fifteen? We know that children can read – and understand – literature before that age. John Stuart Mill could read Greek by the age of four. What does it mean say that he was not ready to?

It is clear that what Rousseau is doing is extending the meaning of 'readiness'. For him an individual is only ready to do something when he has reached that stage which, in Rousseau's view, is the ideal point to undertake the task in question. On this view, to say that children are ready to read at the age of fifteen is a covert way of saying that in the speaker's opinion it is best that children should not learn to read until that age. There may be arguments to support this opinion, but if there are they need to be given and we have clearly passed a long way beyond the normal meaning of 'readiness'.[11]

No doubt it is because the concept of readiness, in the simple sense of 'having the ability to', is so unhelpful that many other educationalists besides Rousseau attempt to extend its meaning in one way or another and to write into its meaning further necessary conditions. Perhaps the most common tendency is to argue that 'to be ready' means to express an interest in as well as to be capable of. (Alternatively it may be argued that we can only know that a child is ready to do something, in the sense of capable of doing it, if he shows that he is ready by expressing an interest.)

One can think of examples involving the word 'ready' that do carry an implication of expressing interest. The scientist for instance who, flushed with the success of a moon-landing, says that he is now ready to send a rocket to Mars, clearly has an interest in doing so. And it may be the case that when we as individuals talk of our own readiness to do things, we generally imply also that we are not unwilling or uninterested in doing them. Certainly if we are referring to our own readiness we must obviously be conscious of our readiness. But this does not mean that interest or awareness are part of the concept of readiness. They are obviously not. Machines, that do not have interests or consciousness, can be ready to do things. Computers can be ready for programming. Buildings can be ready for habitation. A patient may be ready to leave hospital, although he is unaware of the fact and has no interest in doing so. A woman may be ready to take on the responsibility of motherhood although she has never even thought about the matter. Nor is expressing an interest the only clue as to whether somebody is ready to do something. It is certainly not a reliable guide since people may be interested in doing things which they are not ready to do. Expressing an interest is at best only a pointer to what somebody may be ready to do, and one can think of other equally effective pointers. For example, the mere fact that a child has successfully mastered various point of French grammar and can read simplified passages of French is a fair pointer to the fact that he is ready to tackle more complex passages.

However the important point with a word such as 'readiness' that different people are undoubtedly using in different senses is that we should be clear about the implications of the various uses. If, as I would argue, the concept cannot be more precisely delineated than as equivalent to 'capable of undertaking with a degree of success', it is of limited value in educational debate. If, on the other hand, it is taken to mean not only that a person has the ability but also that he is interested in exercising the ability or that he recognizes that he has the ability, then, as we have already seen in considering the notion of interests, it is very much an open question as to whether we wish to be entirely guided by readiness. It is one thing to say that we should not attempt to make children do what they cannot do, and quite another to say that we must not encourage them to start upon any activity until they express an interest in so doing or recognize that they are capable of so doing. When, therefore, we hear some specific claim such as that children should not start to learn to read until they are ready to, we need first of all to know precisely what is meant by 'ready to' in this context. Are we being advised to wait until children are capable of learning to read, in which case, presumably, we should agree and the phrase may have a certain value in reminding us that inasmuch as children differ there is no fixed age by which all children must be reading. Or are we being advised to wait until children show an interest in learning to read? If this is the case then surely, although we may agree that it is a factor to be taken into consideration (since if the interest is there the task will very likely be more pleasant and easier for the child, and hence the whole operation more successful) it is not the only consideration. There comes a point (assuming that one believes in the value of learning to read) at which if the child does not express a readiness the very least we should want to do is attempt to provoke his interest, and if that attempt gains no response we may even want to teach him to read despite his lack of interest. At what age such steps should be taken can only be decided by reference to the ability of the child and the degree of importance one attaches to reading both for its own sake and as a necessary means to further activities of educational value. What seems quite unacceptable is the view that nothing should be done in schools except what children express a readiness to do.

Discovery and experience

The view that education should proceed by means of discovery methods seems altogether more comprehensible. Here nothing is necessarily being said about what content of education is valuable. Rather the argument is that whether we are dealing with mathematics, Latin, or video games, it is preferable that children should find things out for themselves rather than be told everything. For example, rather than telling children a particular rule of mathematics and expecting them to learn it by rote (The square on the hypotenuse equals the sum of the squares on the other two sides), the teacher gives them certain data (in this simple case, perhaps, a triangle drawn to scale) and leaves them to discover the rule for themselves. In Latin, instead of beginning by learning how to decline a noun parrot-fashion, the child may be encouraged to read simplified passages of Latin, with aids to translation, from the beginning of his course, so that he comes to see for himself that a word that ends in '– um' generally stands as the object of the verb.

The claims for discovery methods involve the assertions that children learn better this way, are more interested, understand what they learn better, and in the process learn to think for themselves. These of course are empirical claims and can only be tested by experiment and observation. But despite one's intuitive feeling that the child who discovers the rule about the square on the hypotenuse for himself may have more understanding of that rule than the child who is simply told it, and hence in some sense may be said to have learnt it better, it is worth raising a few sceptical questions.

1 In what sense can the many thousands of people who learnt this and other mathematical rules by rote be said to have not learnt it very well? They acquired the rule, they used it, they understood it, and they know it still. Surely at the most the claim must be not that discovery methods are the most effective methods of learning, but that they are more effective for some children.

2 The general claim that an education based on discovery methods teaches people to think for themselves is rather obscure. In one sense of course it does so by definition. The child who works out the mathematical rule is thinking for himself. What is not clear is whether practice and skill at discovery or problem-solving in one area leads to proficiency at problem-solving in another area or whether such an education necessarily promotes good thinking or rationality. It must be

remembered that the child does not just discover a mathematical rule out of thin air; he is helped towards its discovery by the guidance of the teacher who selects and provides relevant data. What he is really gaining practice in is the art of drawing conclusions from selected data in a given field. This *may* promote a general skill at drawing conclusions, but clearly this skill can only be of use in situations where the individual has access to the relevant data. And even allowing for this it is difficult to see why the individual who is skilled at drawing conclusions in one area, such as mathematics, should necessarily be so in another area, such as politics, where the manner in which conclusions have to be assessed is entirely different. (This was part of the significance of the argument of Chapter 4 concerning forms of knowledge.)

3   Are there not various considerations that may count against an emphasis on discovery methods? For instance, do not considerations of time and the ability of children lead one to the conclusion that some things are better not left to discovery? Are there not some areas in which it is more important that children should have knowledge than it is to worry about how they acquire it, and are there not some areas of study that are less appropriate to discovery techniques than others?

These questions and observations do not amount to an attempt to discredit discovery methods in education. As already said, the value of such methods is in any case largely an empirical matter. The real point, that is brought out by the questions raised, is that there is a distinction between advocating discovery methods as the best way to gain certain objectives in particular areas of the curriculum and advocating discovery as an end in itself. The mere fact that a child discovers something for himself is not necessarily valuable.

Much the same may be said of the notion of educating through experience, if what is meant by this phrase is that experience can constitute a valuable way whereby children may learn. That is to say, one can see *prima facie* value in attempting to relate one's teaching to the child's actual experience, in attempting to give him experience of what he is learning, and in attempting to let some learning arise directly out of his experience. Understood in this way the demand that education should be through experience would amount to the general injunction that what goes on in schools should be made to seem relevant to the child, and the injunction could be defended on the grounds that the child will gain more and learn more effectively if he does feel that what he is doing is of some relevance to him.

But once again there is a great difference between arguing that as a matter of fact a great deal of what goes on in schools is ineffective, in terms of its own objectives, because it is irrelevant to the experience of children or because they do not see the relevance to their present or future experience, and arguing that the child's experiences can serve as the criterion whereby to assess what ought to be taught in schools. Imagine that a class of fifteen-year-old boys from homes in which books are scarcely read are due to read a book during the course of the term. If the teacher has any choice in the matter one can at once see a case for him selecting a book such as Barry Hines' *Kes* rather than Jane Austen's *Pride and Prejudice*. The former is likely to have a much more immediate impact on them, since it relates much more to their experience, and to be as useful in terms of the desired objectives as *Pride and Prejudice*. (I am assuming that the objective is not simply to acquaint the students with great literature, and therefore we can ignore the question of which of the books is better as literature.) But it would be a different matter entirely to argue that, since these particular boys come from homes where reading is confined to a cursory glance at the sports pages of the newspapers, reading books does not relate to their experience and they should not therefore be encouraged to read books at all.

One is therefore a little chary of phrases such as 'education through experience' or 'education is growth' since they are so ambiguous. The last phrase is Dewey's and he characterizes education in terms of experience. But it is symptomatic of the danger inherent in using such slogans that Dewey seems to have been misunderstood by many who regard themselves as his followers. For many take him to have advocated the view that education is taking place (i.e. that desirable education is taking place) provided that the child is provided with an environment in which he is free to grow or in which a sequence of experiences can arise out of the child's original experience, without any imposition or control on the part of the teacher. In other words the view seems to be attributed to Dewey that the mere fact of growing or developing, in the sense of changing from a child to an adult, could somehow constitute becoming educated.

In fact Dewey offered a rather more plausible view than this. In the first place he took for granted certain objectives which were, broadly speaking, based on the ideal of a democratic state. These objectives were that children should become tolerant and rational adults, able to cope with a relatively high degree of social freedom without abusing that freedom to interfere with the freedom or well-being of others. Given these objectives, Dewey argued, education must avoid stultifying the individual's capacity to think for himself and promoting in him the idea that for every question there was only one right answer which was the answer handed out by those in authority. Therefore education should not proceed by a series of dogmatic answers, rules, and fiats from the teacher. The school should order the child's development through experiences, in a small-scale social setting that mirrored the democratic world. But the experiences in the school situation were not to be selected solely with reference to the children's actual present experience. They were to be selected by the teacher and the teacher was to select with reference to two criteria: first any experience which the children were to have must have an immediate appeal to them (in Dewey's terminology, 'interaction'), but secondly it must also have a propensity for leading on to further experiences that would also provide interaction. And no experience that involved anti-social tendencies would at any stage be selected.[12]

It is at once apparent that, for Dewey at least, behind the casual and careless slogans about growth and experience lie strong qualifications. To say that the school should provide opportunities for children to experience situations or activities that are not anti-social, that are appealing to the child, and that will lead on to further experiences, is very different from saying that experience should be the sole criterion of education. One might still object to Dewey's view on the grounds that teachers should not only start from experiences that already appeal to the child but that they should also create or promote interest in experiences that do not have an immediate appeal to the child (as I have been suggesting throughout this chapter); furthermore, even accepting Dewey's position, there is room for a great deal of argument as to which experiences measure up to his conditions. But our concern here is to question the view that experience alone can provide a sufficient criterion for deciding what ought to go on in schools. I suggest that it cannot. For the claim that the teacher is doing all that he needs to do and all that he ought to do if he helps the child to explore his present experiences, involves the claim that there is no distinction between worthwhile and non-worthwhile experiences and that it is in some way improper for the teacher to enlarge the horizons of the child and to initiate him into experiences that he would never have come across if education were confined to an exploration of his experience.

Our conclusion must be that although much of what passes for child-centred education may be extremely valuable and although there may be points of importance embedded in various child-centred theories, the term 'child-centred' itself is too obscure to be of much practical benefit. It may be taken to imply one or more of a variety of points, some relating to the content and some to the methods of education, as we have seen. The term 'child-centred' itself has a limited value in that it draws our attention to the importance of the child himself as an end and as a child, and in the same way talk of children's needs, interests, readiness, and of educating through their experience or by discovery have a certain value in indicating a desire on the part of the speaker to let the child be himself, enjoy himself and think for himself. This may be an emphasis worth stressing in opposition to an emphasis on the idea of schools as places in which children are ruthlessly initiated into the grim realities of life.

But these phrases are of very little practical help since all of them seem capable of more than one interpretation. In the case of needs, interests and readiness it seems that either they are of little use as guides (What do children need? What is in their interests?) or else, on a different interpretation, it seems highly questionable that they are desirable guides (Should we really only educate in accordance with what children want to do?). In the case of discovery and experience there is the ever-present danger of confusing an effective technique with an end in itself, and so far as the question of technique goes it is perhaps a more open – empirical – question than some would admit as to how far and in what circumstances and for what purposes they are effective. It may be suggested that a great deal more empirical research is needed into the efficacy of various types of education than is in fact yet available. But this research cannot begin until it is clear precisely what claims we are supposed to be researching into.[13] When a teacher says that discovery methods are best, what is he claiming that they are best for? If he gives a specific reply, such as that discovery methods in mathematics produce adults who are better mathematicians, and remember more of what they learnt in school or find it easier to apply their mathematical skill to new problems as they confront them, does he actually have any evidence to support this claim? (Not that a lack of evidence would necessarily prove his claim to be false. But it would be nice to have a clearer picture of what we do know and what we merely believe.) In relation to this point it may also be suggested that there is a certain lack of clarity in a great deal of educational theory as to whether various arguments are supposed to be empirical or evaluative. Whether we are talking about deschoolers, free-schoolers, child-centred theorists, or traditionalists it is often unclear whether they are claiming that their approach and their methods will achieve better results in terms of certain broadly agreed objectives, or whether they are arguing for an entirely new set of objectives. In most cases, no doubt, a little bit of both is going on, but it is vital to keep the two types of argument distinct since they have to be assessed in entirely different ways: the former type of claim can ultimately only be tested by empirical means, the latter by philosophical.

It should be stressed that the argument in respect of all the concepts considered in this chapter (interests, needs, readiness, experience, and relevance) is not that they are undesirable or valueless, but that they cannot serve as criteria either for curriculum selection or to define successful education.

Finally, let it be noted that nothing that has been said in this chapter can stop an individual taking up the extreme position that education should consist simply of children doing what they choose to do, provided that he is prepared to accept the possible consequences of that view. But what we can say is that we should not be lulled into acceptance of this view by the claim that this is what 'child-centred' means and our feeling that education should be child-centred. Child-centred education does not necessarily mean what the extreme advocate of *laissez-faire* wants it to mean. It can mean a great variety of things. That is why it is not a very helpful term.

Notes

1 Note however a variant of this game in Postman, N. and Weingartner, C., *Teaching as a Subversive Activity*. The authors claim (p. 67) that 'the word "educate" is closely related to the word "educe"', evidently with the object of adducing this point as evidence in favour of their particular view of education.

   The idea of education as a process of 'leading out' what is already innate in the child can be traced back at least as far as Plato, who illustrates the contention vividly in his dialogue the *Meno*. But then Plato believed in reincarnation!

2 Wilson, P. S. See, in particular, 'Child-centred education' in *The Philosophy of Education Society of Great Britain, Proceedings of the Annual Conference*, January, 1969, p. 120: 'unless actual situations involving children can become child-centred they cannot become educational', and, p. 124, 'traditional practices are not educational at all, to the extent that they are not child-centred'.

3 See Brearley, M. and Hitchfield, E., *A Teacher's Guide to Reading Piaget* (London, Routledge & Kegan Paul). For a simpler and brief introduction to Piaget's works and ideas see Morrish, I., *Disciplines of Education* (London, Allen & Unwin, 1967) chapter 8. The text stresses that we must take note of what we can discover about child psychology. For reasons to do with the scope and nature of this book it does not suggest that there is anything problematic in psychological research in theory. For the view that there is, see Egan, K., *Education and Psychology (New York, Teachers College Press, 1983)* and Barrow, R., *Giving Teaching Back to Teachers* (Brighton, Wheatsheaf, 1984). On the concept of childhood, see Aries, P., *Centuries of Childhood* (Harmondsworth, Peregrine, 1986).

4 Wilson, P. S., 'Child-centred education,' op. cit., p. 106.

5 Goodman, P., *Compulsory Miseducation* (Harmondsworth, Penguin, 1971).

6 It is also to ignore the important question of the relationships between thought and language, and language and reading/writing. See Barrow, R., *Language, Intelligence and Thought* (Aldershot, Edward Elgar, 1993).

7 Wilson, P. S., *Interest and Discipline in Education* (London, Routledge & Kegan Paul, 1971) p. 66.

8 Ibid.

9 Ibid., p. 63.

10 Jersild, A. T., *Children's Interests* (Teachers' College Publications, Columbia University, New York, 1949).

11 For a detailed study of Rousseau's educational views, see Barrow, R., *Radical Education* (Oxford, Martin Robertson, 1978) chapters 2 and 3.

12 See Peters, R. S. (ed.), *John Dewey Reconsidered* (London, Routledge & Kegan Paul, 1977).

13 Sadly the warning implicit in this sentence has not been heeded. See Chapter 13. See also Barrow, R., *Giving Teaching Back to Teachers* (Brighton, Wheatsheaf, 1984).

Further reading

H. Entwistle, *Child-Centred Education* (London, Methuen, 1970) provides a cool and moderate survey of the field. P. S. Wilson, *Interest and Discipline in Education* (London, Routledge & Kegan Paul, 1971), notwithstanding my criticisms in the text, is both a fuller and better argument for what I have termed the extreme child-centred view than his article 'Child-Centred Education' in the Philosophy of Education Society of Great Britain's *Proceedings of the Annual Conference*, January 1969.

R. F. Dearden, *The Philosophy of Primary Education* (London, Routledge & Kegan Paul, 1968) includes a chapter on 'needs' and 'interests'. See also his article ' "Needs" in Education' in R. F. Dearden, P. H. Hirst, and R. S. Peters (eds), *Education and the Development of Reason* (London, Routledge & Kegan Paul, 1972).

11 Creativity

Nearly forty years ago the Plowden report argued that the primary school should lay special stress 'on discovery, on first-hand experience, and on opportunities for creative work'.[1] Following that, it was not uncommon to see advertisements for college of education lecturers inviting applicants whose teaching 'would offer those taught opportunities for creative activity'. Despite the blatant overworking of the term, and consequent attempts by philosophers to elucidate and pin down a variety of distinct species of creativity, it is still frequently encountered and it still, more often than not, has no clear or precise meaning. Giftedness, for example, itself one of the most confused concepts to have emerged in educational discourse, is often taken to incorporate creativity. Similarly, research into effective teaching (see Chapter 13), will often refer to students' creativity as an index of success. But in both cases, usually, no attempt is made to analyse the concept. Instead, uncritical reliance is placed on some standard creativity test. It seems, as was once too truly remarked of IQ tests, that creativity is what creativity tests test.

In what sense of 'creative', for instance, would it be true to say, as Lytton does, that 'we cannot...deny the epithet "creative" to the five-year-old child who produces a picture of square cows and peopled with round-bellied neckless mums and dads'?[2] Surely the sense of 'creative' as used here bears little relation to its use in the suggestion that Shakes-peare can be picked out as a creative playwright or Einstein as a creative scientist.

We are not concerned, presumably, with the use of the term 'creative' in a neutral descriptive way as equivalent to 'productive' where nothing is implied about the quality of what is produced or the conditions under which it is produced. A mother might refer to her child as creative simply because he is continually making things such as model aeroplanes, buildings of toy bricks and meccano models. If pressed on the point as to why she calls this kind of activity creative, she might reply, simply enough, that to create something is to make or produce it – to create a fuss is to make a fuss, to create the world is to produce the world – and that therefore, since her son is creating things, he is obviously creative. But this use of creative carries with it no necessary overtones of approval or disapproval. It is not necessarily either desirable or undesirable to be creative in the sense merely of a producer or a maker.

Our concern must be with the normative use of the term, that is to say with a sense of 'creativity' that is taken to be desirable by definition. One would not attempt to defend a French course as part of the curriculum if one did not believe in its value in some respect. No more would people advocate creativity lessons unless they assumed that creativity was valuable in some respect. Clearly the mere business of making something, without any reference to what is made or produced, how it is made or why it is made, is not necessarily valuable. The normative sense of 'creative' must therefore have certain other conditions written into it, besides the mere condition of producing. What are these further conditions?

One fairly obvious condition is that what the creative person produces should be his own. In one sense, of course, anything that anybody produces is his own. If I offer an opinion it is my opinion. If I write a book it is my book, and if I build a house it is my building. But what is meant here is that whatever is produced, be it a building or an idea, must be the agent's own in the sense that it must be the outcome of his reasoning, planning or working out: it must represent his way of looking at whatever it is he produces. What a creative person produces cannot simply be a copy, an imitation or a representation of somebody else's work. An argument or theory is not my own, in this sense, if I simply regurgitate somebody else's. To be a creative thinker I must do my own thinking and not simply parrot the thinking of others. It follows from this that a skilled forger or skilled craftsman, whose sole concern is to make reproductions of antique furniture, cannot be called creative. They may be highly skilled and deserving of great admiration. One may feel that those forgers who have reproduced the paintings of great masters, sometimes even reproducing their techniques as well as their products, deserve greater credit as painters than they have usually received. But they are not creative artists.

But these two conditions alone (that one should produce and that it should be one's own) are surely not sufficient to characterize a creative person. If they were, then all builders, all novelists, all architects, all hairdressers, all scientists, and all painters provided that they worked with some understanding of what they were doing so that their products were the outcome of their way of looking at things, would be creative. But if virtually everybody is by definition creative, the term ceases to pick out anything of significance.

A third necessary condition, I suggest, is that what one produces should be original in the sense that it breaks new ground. Thus Einstein would not be regarded as a creative scientist if, besides producing theories of his own (in the sense outlined above), he had not also produced theories that broke new ground in the scientific sphere. A man is not a creative mathematician just because he is good at maths and can therefore, as a result of his understanding, produce theories that are his own rather than regurgitations of the theories of others. But this criterion of originality is not to be understood as necessarily demanding a break with the traditional ways of proceeding in a sphere, as the Impressionist school may be said to have evolved a new approach to painting and not simply original paintings, as Wagner may be said to have conceived a new kind of opera or music-drama, and non-Euclidean geometry may be said to have involved a new kind of mathematics. Obviously such originality of form or technique is not a necessary condition of creativity. If it were composers such as Mozart and Haydn, novelists such as Dickens and painters such as Constable could not be called creative.

What is meant by saying that a creative person must be original or break new ground is that what he produces must be distinctive in some way. The distinctive element that makes the work original may be very slight in terms of the measure of difference between it and other works. For instance a creative photographer may concentrate on often photographed and familiar scenes, and the originality of his work may depend entirely on the angle from which he takes his shots. Or a composer may produce a piece of music that substantially consists of quotations from other composers: the originality in this case may lie entirely in the selection, arrangement, or juxtaposition of the quotations. But however slight the measurable difference, it is that originality which is one crucial factor in a creative work.

According to Dostoevski, to say that man is a creative animal is to say that he is 'predestined to strive consciously for an object and to engage in engineering – that is incessantly to make new roads'. This quotation introduces the possibility of a fourth necessary condition of creativity. To be creative does one have to have the intention of producing creative work? Could a man be creative by accident? This question has become of particular interest in view of the fact that inanimate computers might be programmed to produce works such as Virgil's *Aeneid*, with the suggestion that given enough time monkeys provided with keyboards might bash out works that *prima facie* stand as works of art, and with the knowledge that many works of art exhibited in recent years, particularly in the sphere of painting, are produced by random means (e.g. simply upsetting various tins of paint on a canvas).

We have to distinguish here between a creative person and creative work. We are familiar with the idea that the two are inseparable: creative work is the work of creative people and creative people produce creative work. However beautiful we find some natural scene we do not think of it as a creative work of art (unless we specifically think of it as the work of God, perhaps). It is precisely the fact that computers and keyboards, which provide the means for monkeys to write, are relatively recent discoveries that raises the possibility of creative work that is not the product of humans. Work can now be produced that is neither directly the product of humans nor simply the product of nature. If, then, a computer or a monkey could produce a work that was, let us say, comparable with a Shakespeare play there seems no reason why we should not call it a creative work. But it would none the less seem very odd to describe the monkey or the computer as creative, except in the purely descriptive sense of productive. The condition that a creative person should produce work that is his own already implies that a creative person must be conscious of what he is doing. For if an argument, a theory, a play, or a painting is really my own, this is to say that it is a genuine product of my way of looking at things, and my way of looking at things presupposes consciousness. Monkeys and computers do not have their ways of looking at things, they do not produce their work in response to a conscious process, their work cannot be their own in the sense intended, and therefore they cannot be creative.

To say that a creative person must be conscious of what he is doing is not to say that if Shakespeare was creative then he must have intended to write *Hamlet* in the way that *Hamlet* turned out before he started. It is to say that *Hamlet* must have arisen as the result of a deliberate intention to produce a play on a certain broad theme. As far as this condition goes, therefore, there is no reason to deny that the painter who drops tins of paint at random on to a canvas is creative. The painting that results is not a painting designed and planned in the manner that the Mona Lisa was planned. But it is a painting that is the outcome of a deliberate plan none the less. Had the painter accidentally spilt his paint then the case would be different – the product might be regarded as a creative work, but the artist could not claim to be a creative artist on the strength of this accidental product.

There is another reason why we should hesitate to call monkeys creative. To call somebody creative is to attribute a tendency to him. One can imagine a situation in which one would describe somebody as creative on the strength of one work – 'Did James really write this? I had no idea he was creative' – but none the less the implication of calling someone creative is that he is more than a one-shot artist. Shakespeare differs from the monkey not only in that he had some idea of what he was doing, but also in that whereas with the monkey we await the statistical probability that given time his random tapping of the keyboard will produce a coherent poem or whatever, with Shakespeare, precisely because he did know what he was doing, we may expect all of his attempts at play-writing to result in plays. We obviously cannot tie creativity directly to output. We cannot say that the more one produces the more creative one is. Haydn was not more creative than Brahms because he composed a great deal more. And some creative people have in fact produced very little. None the less we should generally expect a creative person to give evidence of his creativity consistently. The fact that I produce an original thought that is my own does not make me a creative thinker if every other thought that I produce is unoriginal and taken over from somebody else.

We thus arrive at the view that a creative person in any sphere is one who tends to produce original work that represents his own way of looking at things in that sphere. The obvious and crucial question now arises as to whether that is all that there is to being creative, or whether we have to add some reference to the quality of the work produced. If we do not add reference to quality as another condition of creativity certain consequences have to be accepted. First, virtually anybody who had a spark of independence in him (so that his way of looking at things could indeed be said to be his own) could be said to be creative. The very fact that I know very little about painting, with the result that any daub I produce on a canvas is very much my own, would paradoxically make me a creative painter. The mere fact of my sitting down to write a novel would turn me into a creative novelist. For what I wrote would be a product that was my own and was original in some degree; it would be consciously produced and there need be no problem about tendency, since presumably I could then write another novel. This consequence, I suggest, is quite unacceptable. I do not know how to paint, my novels have no merit whatsoever: I am neither a creative painter nor a creative novelist.

Secondly, though obviously related to the first point, if any distinctive product consciously produced is evidence of creativity then the assumption from which we started – that it is desirable that people should be creative – is thrown right open to question. It is one thing to say that it is desirable to produce creative writers and scientists if we have in mind examples such as Shakespeare and Einstein (examples which carry the implication of quality), quite another if we have in mind virtually anybody who puts pen to paper or has an idea. The only way in which one could defend the thesis, that creativity without reference to standards or quality was a normative concept or a desirable quality, would be to argue that the mere fact that somebody produces something original is a praiseworthy feature of that individual. The reader must decide whether a scientist who produces a theory that is absurd but original (because nobody else would countenance such absurdity) is to be praised on that account, whether an artist who produces a smashed pane of glass, smashed in a subtly distinctive way, is therefore to be admired, or whether a photographer who takes a series of photographs without removing the cover from the camera lens is on that account alone to be revered. For myself, I claim emphatically that none of these three people are *necessarily* to be admired, and that therefore either we cannot necessarily attribute creativity to them, or else 'creative' must be understood as a purely descriptive value-free term, and it is a separate question as to whether we wish to promote such creativity.

Thirdly, if we do not write into the concept of creativity some reference to quality, then the word is in fact redundant. All novelists would be creative, since no two novelists have ever written the same book and no novelists (or at any rate very few) have ever written books that are not their own work. All people who thought at all would have a claim to be creative thinkers, since despite the fact that we may group ourselves in broad categories (e.g. some of us are socialists, some liberals, some conservatives) no two people think exactly alike; every individual, by the mere fact of being a unique personality, is in some respect a distinctive or original thinker. If the word 'creative' were redundant, it would make no sense to talk of promoting creativity. The demand for creative persons would simply be a demand for novelists, scientists, mathematicians, and so on.

We therefore have to add as another necessary condition of being creative that the individual should produce good work. And this is where the problem really starts, because in some spheres at least it raises the fundamental question of what the criteria are for good work. In the sphere of science and mathematics the problem is less great: a creative scientist is one who makes advances in scientific knowledge which are genuine advances in knowledge. One can judge that the Russian scientists who produced the sputnik were creative because the sputnik, to put it crudely, worked. But in the sphere of art assessing creativity will involve reference to aesthetic criteria which are notoriously difficult to assess. This is why in the example of the photographer who does not remove his lens cover I had to write that he was not 'necessarily' creative. My point there was that the fact that he was being original would not alone make him creative. But some people might accept that, and go on to argue that he was none the less creative because his blank photographs were works of art. If that seems preposterous to some readers one has only to think of John Cage's *4'33"*, heralded by many as an artistic work of quality, which consists of a pianist sitting at a piano with the lid down over the keys and playing not a note. We cannot, unfortunately, go into the question of aesthetic standards here. The point to be stressed is that given that there are some standards, that there is a distinction between good art and bad art, then the mere fact that I produce a colour pattern that nobody else has done does not make me creative: the pattern must have some quality; it must come up to certain standards.

If the analysis of creativity given above is acceptable, then certain things follow from it. The first point is that one part of what it means to be a creative artist, scientist, or whatever, is that one is a good artist, a good scientist, or whatever. The converse of course is not true: I may be a good mathematician without being a creative one, because I may not produce any original work in mathematics. But if I am a creative mathematician then I shall both produce original work and work that is good work according to the standards of mathematics. It follows from this that in order to assess whether a man is a creative scientist we shall need to refer to different criteria than those that we shall need to refer to assess whether he is a creative photographer. Maths, science, novel writing, photography, and so on are distinct activities and to be good at any one of them requires distinct talents and reference to distinct standards and ways of proceeding. And it follows from this that there is no necessary reason why an individual who is creative in one respect or sphere should be creative in any other. It there-fore does not make much sense to refer to one individual simply as creative or more creative than another. When we do pick out an individual such as Leonardo da Vinci as creative, without specific reference as to what spheres he is creative in, we mean not that he had some quality (creativity) that, say, Beethoven lacked, but that he showed himself to be creative in many spheres. Da Vinci was not more creative than Beethoven, as one might say he was more good-tempered. He was creative in more spheres.

How do these points affect the stress on creativity in education? Before going any further we may as well face the fact that despite the impression one may get from some educational writings, virtually nothing is known about what as a matter of empirical fact produces creative people in various spheres. That is to say virtually nothing is known about how one may best hope to produce a Shakespeare or an Orton, a Mozart or a Cage, a Darwin or an Einstein. It well may be that such people are born and not made at all. There is, of course, a certain amount of evidence (though not a great deal even here) to suggest that where children are given a certain amount of scope for free expression in the art room they grow up less restricted in their artistic expression than those who are not given such freedom. Or that chil-dren who are encouraged to partake in problem-solving situations are less ill at ease as adults in problematic situations. Such considerations may be very important from an educational point of view, but it should now be clear that to make either of these assertions is not really to say anything about creativity. One is hardly surprised at the suggestion that those who are brought up to express themselves freely in paint or to take a delight in problem-solving should tend, as adults, to feel free to express themselves in paint and enjoy problem-solving. But the questions still remain as to how important these things are, as to whether there are not other things equally important even in the sphere of painting, and as to whether such children can be called creative. To express oneself is not to be creative, despite the fact that to be creative involves among other things expressing oneself. To solve problems seems an admirable thing to do, but practice in solving problems in school does not automatically mean that one will be able to solve any problem as an adult.

If our intention is to promote creativity then clearly we have to meet the following requirements: (i) We have to avoid instilling in children the idea that everything is known and determined, and that they must observe the acknowledged experts in any field and cannot follow their own distinctive way of looking at things. (ii) We have to promote ingenuity and imagination so that individuals are capable of making the imaginative leaps necessary for breaking new ground in any sphere. (iii) We have to produce skill and understanding in any given sphere, for without these how, except by chance, is the individual going to be a good scientist, artist, or whatever; how is he going to have the excellence that is a part of creativity?

Once these considerations are spelt out one immediately has grave doubts about a lot of so-called creative activity in schools, for it neither is creative nor is there any reason to suppose that in isolation it will promote creativity. What, for instance, could be meant by a 'creativity hour' or a lesson simply entitled 'creative activity'? As we have seen, it does not make sense to talk of creativity in a vacuum: individuals can only display creativity in various spheres of activity. The idea of children being creative, as opposed to having a creative maths lesson or a creative writing lesson and so on, is a simple nonsense. This is a small point, of course, since presumably what is meant by a creativity hour, in most cases, is that it is an hour in which children may practise being creative in various spheres, or, perhaps specifically the implication is that they are doing art and craft as opposed to maths and science. But small though the point may be it is symptomatic of the confusion that seems to surround the notion of creativity in schools. In order to avoid that confusion let us proceed by considering creativity in respect of various spheres one by one.

What are we to say in respect of artistic creativity when, for example, Anderson remarks that 'the creative environment must provide freedom for each person to respond truthfully with his whole person as he sees and understands the truth'?[3] Clearly the reply must be that this is indeed one thing that the creative environment must provide, but it is not all that it must provide. If children are simply given access to the materials for painting and left to respond truthfully with their whole person (the very idea of which, incidentally, I find perplexing in reference to *young* children: does not a truthful response involve the idea of considerable self-awareness?) they are not necessarily being creative. What is happening in such a situation is that the first of the three requirements outlined in the last paragraph but one is being met: the children are being encouraged to paint as they feel inclined and not in response to the instructions of others. It is possible that they are being imaginative and that therefore the second requirement is being met, although in terms of promoting creativity it is not at all clear how one does best promote ingenuity and imagination; obviously not by restricting the free expression of the child completely, and that is why one accepts a degree of freedom as a necessary part of the creative environment. But placing all the stress on a complete freedom of expression would seem to be self-defeating. For in these circumstances how is one to judge between the imaginative and the unimaginative piece of work? Either one argues that any sincere expression of oneself is imaginative, or one has criteria for distinguishing between imaginative self-expression and unimaginative self-expression. And if there are criteria for imaginative work, there seems no reason to suppose that children will necessarily become imaginative simply because they are free to express themselves. But it is the third requirement that is all-important and *that* requirement is not being met at all. How are children expected to become creative artists if they are brought up under the impression that anything they do with their heart in it is creative? How does one expect to produce a creative composer or painter if one does not teach the child how to compose and how to paint and if one does not familiarize him with what has already been done in those fields and with what at the present time counts as music or painting?

Much the same may be said of 'creative writing'. In so far as an emphasis on creative writing means that there is a case for suggesting that repeated corrections of stories, on the grounds that they are mispunctuated or misspelt, may stunt the child's enthusiasm and spontaneity, it obviously cannot be dismissed as an absurd idea. But it is not true that any spontaneous writing is creative writing, and it therefore does not follow that a systematic acceptance of anything the child writes promotes creativity. It is no doubt true that spelling and the accepted rules of grammar have got very little to do with being creative. It is probably also true that some creative artists have not been particularly gifted as spellers and grammarians. It is certainly true that some creative writers, such as Joyce, have deliberately abandoned conventional rules of grammar and spelling to a large extent. But it is equally true that many creative artists have emerged from a schooling that taught them to spell and punctuate, that much creative work has been written according to such rules, and that there is a limit beyond which not even a Joyce can go if his work is to be read by others. Certainly if one wants to produce creative writers one does not want to curb their spontaneity. All that is being said here is that it is not in fact clear that some concern with such things as spelling and grammar need curb spontaneity, that, more importantly, spontaneity alone does not produce creative writing, and that treating children's writing uncritically and undiscriminatingly as creative cannot help to promote creativity in that sphere in that child. To become a creative writer he needs to acquire skills, understanding of other creative works, and familiarity with what has been written. He needs knowledge and critical standards, neither of which are promoted by creative writing lessons understood as spontaneous writing lessons. The only way out of this impasse is to argue, as Britton has done, that the definition of literature is a piece of writing that is written for its own sake and involves the writer in reflecting on his own past experience.[4] If that is what literature is, then children may be said to be writing literature. The reply to this is that this is not in fact what most of us mean by literature, but that if we accept the definition it becomes, as White has pointed out, an open question as to whether there is necessarily any value in people writing literature.[5]

Even more obviously if we wish to produce creative mathematicians or scientists, it is insufficient simply to leave children to proceed as they see fit. What usually seem to be meant by creative maths lessons are lessons in which the child is encouraged to discover for himself from certain data certain solutions rather than being simply given the answer (with or without the explanation). Now there may be very good grounds for advocating this discovery method (see Chapter 10), but the fact remains that such a procedure does not mean that the child is being a creative mathematician, that such a procedure alone cannot produce creative mathematicians, and that, for what it is worth, creative mathematicians can, as they have done throughout history, arise without having had the benefit of such teaching methods. The situation is quite simple: to be a creative mathematician is to be a good mathematician and to have the ability and the originality to go beyond the current bounds of mathematical knowledge. If all we wanted from maths lessons was a host of creative mathematicians it would still be an open empirical question as to how much one needed to instil mathematical knowledge in order to cover the ground and to what extent one could do this without stunting the originality and questing frame of mind that are also necessary for creativity.

It seems fairly clear that the term 'creativity' is currently being used in a variety of senses and that it covers a number of different ideas that are not all equally valuable. When a course, such as the Cambridge Schools Classics Project, is advertised as a course that will promote creativity one simply does not know which way to turn. What kind of creativity and creativity in what sense? Will it produce creative classicists? There is absolutely no reason to suppose that it will, since it is a two-year foundation course and at the end of it the pupils' knowledge will simply be insufficient to allow for any creative contribution to classics. Will it produce creative artists or creative thinkers? This one suspects is the sort of direction in which the course is aimed, since it consists largely of exercises in free drawing and expressive writing as well as providing the opportunity for argumentative pieces of writing. But here we have a perfect example of the muddle that we are in. The course, like so many others, does provide the opportunity for spontaneous self-expression and for a degree of argumentative writing. It suggests, for instance, that the child might draw a picture of the goddess Athene or write a newspaper obituary on the death of Achilles. But the value of the argumentative piece must be very slight if the child's work is not corrected according to some standards (this point of course is outside the control of the originators of the course) and in view of the fact that the child knows very little about the historical figure of Achilles. Unless one adds to the course some reference to standards in the work children produce and a concerted attempt to provide information, it is difficult to see any value in it at all except as a relaxation period. But more to the point, even with those additions there is nothing necessarily creative or contributory to the development of creativity about the course.

We must distinguish clearly between spontaneous self-expression, ingenuity, problem-solving, and creativity. When Wyn Williams argues that an emphasis on discovery methods is 'vital because it emphasises the need for children to be creative',[6] he is confusing the issue. It does not necessarily do any such thing, nor is there any obvious reason to accept the assumption that we need creative people. Creative scientists have an obvious utilitarian value, but why in point of fact do we need to be so concerned about producing creative artists?

The situation, then, is this. To be creative in any specific sphere demands knowledge and understanding of that sphere. Any education that ignores this point is not making a realistic effort to promote creativity in various spheres. Originality is also a necessity, and it well may be that the American educational situation prior to the launching of the Russian sputnik was such as to curb originality and the tendency to attempt to break new ground in the scientific sphere. It may also be that discovery techniques and problem-solving activity will sharpen the tendency towards originality, or at least avoid the stultifying effect that traditional inculcation of information may have. All that can be said here is that these are empirical points and there is not as yet any convincing evidence that such teaching techniques make a material difference in terms of producing creative scientists. Such techniques may of course be advocated for reasons that have nothing to do with creativity (e.g. that the child understands better what he sees for himself, that his interest is sustained, that he thinks for himself) but that is a separate question.

So far as creativity in the arts goes there is no evidence to support the view that an individual who is a creative writer will also be a creative scientist, even supposing that he is a good scientist. Creativity in the arts therefore has to be defended on its own terms. It has already been suggested that much of what passes for creative art in schools is not creative, does not necessarily produce creative artists, and that it raises the question of the need for creative artists. The question that really has to be asked here is what is the value of self-expression in art.

Self-expression is a necessary condition of creativity and therefore if creativity is our goal self-expression must play a part. But, since it is not a sufficient condition, it cannot be our sole consideration and since it is unrealistic to pretend that we even want all our children to be creative writers, let alone that they will be, we have to ask whether the emphasis on self-expression can be justified without reference to creativity. Presumably it may be defended to some extent on therapeutic or psychological grounds. That is to say it would not be implausible to suggest that some opportunity for self-expression without reference to critical standards may be educationally valuable in that it provides relaxation and promotes self-confidence in children. Further than this, it may lead children to reveal more of their inner-self which may have psychological value. For example, a child with a troubled home background might derive some benefit from writing freely about this. But clearly not all children are in need of such therapy and even for those who are, there are other things to be done in schools besides provide it. If all writing lessons become exercises in self-expression they cease to provide relaxation, and if all writing is self-expression only it ceases to promote self-confidence. For why should being able to do what anybody can do promote self-confidence?

The conclusion that seems inescapable is that self-expression in the artistic sphere has a part to play both because it can be educationally valuable and because it is one necessary part of artistic creativity. But self-expression alone is not sufficient to warrant talk of creativity. Finally, then, what can be said of the five-year-old child who produces 'an image of the world as he sees it, littered with square cows and peopled with round-bellied, neckless mums and dads'. Lytton, it will be remembered, claims that we cannot deny the epithet 'creative' to such a child. Now certainly Lytton may use the term in such a way that it makes sense to regard the child as 'creative', which is precisely what he does. For him the term can be understood to indicate that someone has had a subjective feeling of 'effective surprise' in producing a work, and therefore the child may have been creative. As against this strange view it may be pointed out that

(i) it *is* a strange use of the term: when people call Shakespeare a creative writer they simply do *not mean* that he had a feeling of effective surprise when he wrote *Hamlet*; (ii) it is not really a definition that serves any useful purpose, since the notion of effective surprise is at least as obscure as creativity itself (What *counts* as effective surprise?); (iii) little use could be made of such a definition, since it is entirely unclear how the teacher is supposed to know whether the child has indeed experienced effective surprise; (iv) and, above all, if this is what creativity is taken to involve, it is difficult to see why one should regard it as valuable.

It is difficult to avoid the conclusion that Lytton has offered us a persuasive definition of the term. That is to say, conscious of the fact that creativity has overtones of desirability for most of us, he has defined it in terms of what he thinks desirable. But there seems no obvious reason to agree with his judgement that this sense of 'creativity' is in itself desirable, and there are many reasons such as those outlined in this chapter for claiming that to feel effective surprise is not in itself to be creative.

Notes

1 Plowden, Lady, 1967, vol. 1, p. 187.
2 Lytton, H., *Creativity and Education* (London, Routledge & Kegan Paul, 1973) p. 3.
3 Anderson, H. H., 'Creativity in Perspective' in Anderson, H. H. (ed.), *Creativity and its Cultivation* (New York, Harper, 1959) p. 253.
4 Britton, J., 'Literature' in *The Arts and Current Tendencies in Education* (University of London Institute of Education, 1963) p. 42.
5 White, J. P., 'Creativity and Education' in Hirst, P. H. and Peters, R. S. (eds), *Education and the Development of Reason* (London, Routledge & Kegan Paul, 1972).
6 Williams, W., 'The Proper Concerns of Education' in Rubinstein, D. and Stoneman, C. (eds), *Education for Democracy* (Harmondsworth, Penguin) p. 163.

Further reading

See at the end of chapter 12.

12 Culture

The cultural élitists

There are a number of educationalists, sometimes loosely and perjoratively referred to as cultural élitists, who are primarily concerned with the appreciation rather than the production of art. The cultural élitist view may be said to stem from the work of Matthew Arnold and T. S. Eliot in particular, and perhaps one of its most well-known representatives was G. H. Bantock. The view is such that it may be taken to involve hostility to much of what in fact goes on in schools in the name of creativity, precisely because it is feared that the disregard for standards in the work that children produce, that frequently characterizes creativity lessons, renders the work something other than genuinely creative. This partially explains Bantock's dictum that 'too much freedom is incompatible with education'.[1] Education, for Bantock, must include some reference to the notion of appreciating excellence, and this appreciation, it is claimed, will not be promoted by a situation in which children are free even from the controls and limitations provided by the standards of excellence in any sphere. To put it crudely, if a child's writing does not have to meet any standards of coherence or quality, if his freedom is not even limited by such considerations as these, then he is not being introduced to even the idea of excellence, and therefore he will be in no position to appreciate it. By definition, then, he will not be being educated. Bantock is not necessarily opposed to the aim of promoting artistic creativity, provided that it is genuine creativity, but it may none the less be thought that the stress of his view lies with the notion of appreciation rather than production.

Despite close affinities in their views, Arnold, Eliot, and Bantock cannot be lumped together without qualification, but all three, I think, would have accepted the broad outline of a thesis such as the following.

There is a body of art that consists of works (whether music, literature, painting, sculpture, etc.) that are manifestly superior to other works. They are superior to other works in the same sphere and they also have an importance that renders them more valuable than works or products of other spheres of human activity. Two points are being made; not only are some books better than other books, as Shakespeare is superior to what Bantock calls 'the ephemeral offerings of railway bookstalls',[2] but also good literature in general is more valuable than such things as Bingo. The cultural élitists are hostile both to popular culture (pop music, television, thrillers, etc.) and to the utilitarian dictum of Bentham that, provided people derive the same amount of pleasure from either, pushpin is as good as poetry. The body of superior works of art referred to is, in Eliot's terminology, high culture. (I shall refer to it as Culture, with a capital C.) Society should be concerned to maintain the production of Culture and also to promote appreciation of it. But to appreciate Culture requires a developed sensitivity and a disciplined understanding of what is involved in the various works. Understanding, in turn, involves knowledge and intelligence. People do not generally simply pick up a play by Shakespeare and appreciate it. The thesis is prepared to accept the possibility that it is not possible for all individuals to attain the degree of sensitivity, knowledge, and intelligence requisite for true appreciation of these Cultural works; and it is therefore prepared to accept as an unfortunate fact as things are, that, in so far as education is to be concerned with initiating people into the high culture, it will have to do so with a minority. It seems to be essentially for this reason that those who hold this view have acquired the title of 'élitists'.

Before considering the problems in this view and the elaborations and modifications proposed by Bantock, it is necessary to distinguish two uses of the word 'culture', which, if not distinguished, can lead to considerable confusion. Generally when one refers to various cultures in a society, and often even when one refers to the culture of a society, one is using the word 'culture' as an anthropologist might (or as a sociologist might use the term 'sub-culture'). This use is quite distinct from the use of the term to denote what Eliot calls a high culture or what I mean by Culture, which implies reference to works of a high aesthetic standard. When the anthropologist refers to the culture of a society, or the sub-culture of a group within a society, he means to pick out a way of life or a code of living that is distinctive of that society or group. Thus he can talk of the Innuit culture, meaning simply to refer to the behavioural customs, the manners, the interests and so on of the Innuit. Likewise he can contrast the aborigine culture with that of a sophisticated modern society, or pick out the distinctive features of the way of life of a commune and refer to it as commune culture. In theory this use of 'culture' is purely descriptive; it contains no implications about the value or otherwise of any culture referred to. Furthermore there is no particular stress on the sphere of art. In the anthropological sense of the term we may say that it is a feature of our culture that men wear trousers, that there is a monogamous institution of marriage, that we often eat boiled cabbage, that pubs usually have dart boards, and so on.

When we talk of Culture, we are not simply using the term in a neutral descriptive sense. Culture is a normative notion. Culture, though we may disagree as to what constitutes it, is in some sense desirable. A man is not Cultured simply because he belongs to a group with an identifiable culture in the sociological sense. The sociologist may tell us that there is a rock culture, and he may tell us what it consists of, but we do not therefore conclude that a rock enthusiast is a Cultured man. A Cultured man is not simply a man who abides by any code of living. Only a particular kind of code of living, a particular kind of way of life, will count as a Cultured way of life in the non-sociological sense. And one aspect of the Cultured man's way of life, at least, must have some reference to the sphere of art. A man who has absolutely no interest in and no knowledge of any kind of art may be a number of admirable things, but he is not even a serious contender for the title of 'Cultured'. In the same way, whereas initiation into the culture of a society in an anthropological sense means initiation into the way of life of that community, initiation into Culture must involve, perhaps among other things, introduction to what are regarded as works of some artistic quality.

The importance of being aware of these distinct uses of the term 'culture', and the dangers of not being clear about them, can be illustrated by reference to Eliot (although it is only fair to add that there is room for considerable argument over the correct interpretation of Eliot). For despite the title *Notes Towards the Definition of Culture* and a chapter entitled 'The Three Senses of "Culture" ', Eliot does not offer a clear and coherent definition of the term and he seems to equivocate between its various senses. Eliot argued that in any society there were a number of cultures ranging from high to low. He added that all these cultures were valuable in that their coexistence promoted friction, which in turn kept things alive and productive and prevented a static apathy taking over. Although all cultures have their value, however, it seems that the high culture is in some sense superior. That, at any rate, would seem to be the implication of the term itself and of remarks such as that there are different levels of culture and that, ideally, 'the individual shall...take his place at the highest cultural level for which his natural aptitudes qualify him'.[3] It is difficult to see how the notion of striving to attain the 'highest cultural level' possible for the individual can avoid being interpreted as involving the claim that 'high' is being used to some extent evaluatively. But what is not clear is what makes a culture a high culture, and whether it is not in fact contradictory to talk of a low culture (which, by implication at least, Eliot does), unless Eliot is confusing the two uses of 'culture'. For if we are talking about Culture, and if Culture by definition involves superior works of art, how can there be a low or inferior culture in this sense? How can one say that Culture consists of a body of superior works of art, but that some Culture may consist of inferior works of art? It looks very much as if Eliot has confused the two uses of the term and that what he means by high culture is Culture, whereas what he means by lower levels of culture are various codes of living or life-styles, as he clearly does in a celebrated passage in which he remarks that: '[culture] includes all the characteristic activities and interests of a people: Derby Day, Henley Regatta, Cowes, the twelfth of August, a cup final, the dog races, the pin table, the dart board, Wensleydale cheese, boiled cabbage cut into sections, beetroot in vinegar, nineteenth-century Gothic churches and the music of Elgar.'[4] In other words Eliot would seem to be saying that there are various cultures or sub-cultures in the anthropological sense in any given society, and that the friction between them is valuable, but there are only certain specific works that constitute Culture. The best culture, in the anthropological sense, is that which has regard for Culture, in the non-anthropological sense.

Whether this is fair to Eliot or not, Bantock is at any rate well aware of the problem and of the danger of confusing two senses of 'culture', and in order to clarify what in his view is really Eliot's position, he introduces a third sense of 'culture'. This sense of 'culture' lies midway between the anthropologist's use of the term and Culture.

> It is applied selectively to important areas of human thought and action. But in itself it is not intended to imply anything about the quality or value of these activities and thoughts. In my meaning of the term, a folk song, a 'pop' song, and a Beethoven symphony are similarly representative of culture.
>
> ... To speak of '*a* culture', then, in this usage, will be simply to refer to a number of important forms of human thought and behaviour without any distinction of value as between one manifestation and another, and to the pattern of their interrelationship.[5]

This is clear, but the question is whether the introduction of this sense of 'culture' will solve the problem that some find in the cultural élitist thesis as developed by Bantock.

According to Bantock, in the pre-industrial past there were essentially two cultures in our society – the bookish culture or the culture of the literate minority, and the folk culture or the culture of the non-literate majority. Industrialization has killed the folk culture and we have in its place, for the majority, a commercial and industrial pseudo-culture. Education should be concerned to preserve the bookish culture for those to whom it is suited, but it also needs to find and promote a new folk culture for the majority – a culture that may be on a different level from high culture, but which will none the less have value as being a genuine culture.

But something surely is wrong with this argument. For on the one hand we are told that 'culture' is being used without respect to notions of quality or value and that it may include pop songs, for example. On the other hand we are told that the culture of the majority today is not really a culture at all because it lacks what we may broadly call any artistic merit. The fact is that in Bantock's neutral sense of the term the industrial culture, with its detective novels, television and rock music is as much a culture as the folk culture (consisting of folk lore, tales, folk songs, maypole dances, and so on) that we may imagine belonged to the world of George Eliot's *Adam Bede*. In order to argue that the industrial culture is in some sense undesirable or inadequate compared to the folk culture it has replaced we must in fact drop Bantock's sense of the term 'culture' and revert to the notion of culture as involving something of value, and argue that the folk songs and dances of the past, though they were not high culture, none the less had a quality that their modern equivalents lack. This is precisely what Bantock would claim (as a generalization) but it raises the fundamental question of how one recognizes either high culture or different levels of culture (in Bantock's third sense) as opposed to the products of a culture in the anthropological sense.

At any rate it seems important to distinguish the two separate theses that Bantock is putting forward: (i) that the way of life of pre-industrial society, including such things as its music and other art forms, has gone and been replaced with a way of life, including its art forms, that is unsatisfactory in a number of ways, with the result that one task of education is to promote a new culture, that has some quality, for the majority; (ii) that Culture, or high culture, which happens to have been the interest, historically speaking, of a literate minority, is today in danger of being ignored in society, and in particular in education. Far from an increased emphasis on education and the spread of literacy having spread Culture to the majority 'a diffusion of education seems to have had a deleterious effect on the highest cultural standards'.[6] Instead of more people having access to Culture, more people seem to be less interested in Culture, and the work that is being produced in the sphere of art is coming up to lower Cultural standards. A vulgar commercialism and a lack of discrimination and taste is in danger of engulfing what Arnold called 'the sweetness and light' that is inherent in great art. The widespread abolition of the grammar schools, which for a long time had been concerned to maintain the highest cultural standards, was just one more step towards the denigration of Culture.

It is with this second thesis that the remainder of this chapter will be concerned (since the problem of how one evaluates different levels of

Culture is no different in kind to the problem of how one evaluates high culture). In general terms the argument is clear, but not without its problems. First we have to distinguish between what is essentially involved in it and what are merely contingent points. The most obvious contingent point is the whole business of whether this initiation into high culture must in practice be reserved for a few. It is not part of the cultural élitist view that only a select minority are *entitled* to this distinctive kind of education, although critics of it have sometimes written as if it were. Nor, as is absolutely clear from Bantock's preoccupation with the whole question of the folk culture, is there any suggestion that the majority do not matter. All that the cultural élitists are in fact committed to is the claim that high culture is extremely important and the conditional claim that its importance is such that, if as a matter of fact it has to figure predominantly in the education of only some, it should do so.

Some have attempted to dismiss this thesis on the grounds that it is inegalitarian and it is therefore necessary to give brief consideration to that objection. An egalitarian society is one in which all members of the society receive equal treatment; an egalitarian educational system is one in which all children are treated equally. But equal treatment clearly does not necessarily imply the same treatment; it does not *mean* identical treatment. Or perhaps I should say, more cautiously, that if anyone does mean by equal treatment literally the same treatment for all, regardless of differences between them, it is difficult to see why we should be in favour of equal treatment for all. For although there may well be good reason for demanding that people should receive identical treatment in a great many more areas than they in fact do receive it in any particular society, it is difficult to accept that treatment should be the same for all in every respect. To advocate such would involve, among other things, a denial of special medical provision for the sick and disabled, a denial of pensions for the elderly, an insistence on identical amounts of food being provided for every individual from the newborn baby to the wrestling champion, and exactly the same education for everybody from the mentally defective to the child prodigy. If we wish to avoid this absurd conclusion then we cannot say that equal treatment *means* the same treatment. And in reply to the question 'What *does* the claim that everybody ought to be treated equally mean, then?' it is difficult to see how one can do more than follow those philosophers who have argued that the principle of equality is a formal principle that demands that people should be treated the same except where there are differences between them that constitute relevant reasons for treating them differently in particular respects. In other words the principle of equality is one and the same thing as the principle of impartiality.

Impartiality means treating people in the same way in identical circumstances. It does not mean simply treating people in the same way, which would involve being indiscriminate. An impartial person is one who discriminates only with good reason. An indiscriminate magazine editor would be one who accepted anything that was sent in as a contribution for publication; the notion that there might be reasons relevant to the judging of the relative suitability of various submissions, such as the quality of the contributions or their relevance to the purpose of his magazine, would mean nothing to him. A partial editor would be one who had his reasons for discriminating between contributions, but whose reasons were bad reasons or reasons that were irrelevant to the purpose of his job. He might, for example, accept a series of bad and unsuitable articles because they were written by his brother. An impartial editor would be one who did the job of distinguishing between submissions for publications, accepting some and rejecting others, on good grounds, that is on grounds that were relevant to the nature of the task he is supposed to be performing.

The demand that people should be impartial is therefore the demand that people should not treat people differently unless good reasons can be given for so doing. But in calling this principle formal we draw attention to the fact that it only tells us the sort of way in which we should proceed. It does not in itself help us to decide what reasons constitute good reasons for differential treatment in particular cases. But if we accept this identification of the principle of equality with the principle of impartiality, it does follow that there is nothing *necessarily* inegalitarian about proposing different kinds of education for different children.

But, it may be argued, surely to advocate elites is by definition inegalitarian? The answer to this question would seem to depend on which of two senses of the term 'élite' one has in mind. Consider the following examples of *prima facie* legitimate uses of the term:

1 The élite of the Russian nobility.
2 The élite of the motor industry are the Ford workers.
3 The élite of society.
4 The scientific/artistic élite.
5 Pop singers are the élite of the younger generation.
6 The rugby fifteen/the prefects form the élite of our school.
7 Grammar schools preserve an élite.

Two things are immediately clear about the concept of an élite from these examples. First, élites do not necessarily have anything to do with social class. Obviously a particular social class may happen to form an élite, but if it does it is not simply because it is a definable class. As the examples indicate, one can refer to élites within classes (1), to élites that bear no relation to classes (4, 5, 6) to élites that perhaps coincidentally involve reference to class (2), as well as to classes as élites. It is not inconceivable that the élite of a particular society should turn out to be more or less any of the élites referred to in the examples. That is to say the élite of society might be the élite of the nobility, but it might in principle equally well be the elite of the motor industry or the scientific élite. (In footnote 7 to this chapter, in the third edition, I added the comment that I was no longer sure that it was true that Ford workers were the elite of the motor industry. It is now quite evident that it is not true; furthermore, it is questionable whether the motor or any other part of industry can any longer be said to have an elite. Despite that, I have retained the example and need only stress that its hypothetical nature does not prevent it serving as an example to illustrate the conceptual and logical points that need to be made.)

Secondly, it is clear that part of the meaning of an élite is that it is an identifiable group within a larger group. The notion of an élite in vacuo is meaningless. To pick out an élite necessarily involves distinguishing between the élite and other people within a definable group, as the Ford workers are an identifiable group within the larger group of workers in the motor industry. But it is equally clear that this is only a necessary condition and not a sufficient condition of picking out an élite. We can pick out the group of window-cleaners, Catholics, short people, Marxists, and so on within our society, but we should not want to describe any of these groups as elites. What are the criteria whereby we distinguish between an élite and any other definable part of a larger whole? Why is it that it is the Ford workers who are generally referred to as the élite of the motor industry and not, say, the men who attach wing-mirrors to cars in whatever plant they work?

The answer to this last question is fairly obvious and is contained within the dictionary definition of an élite as 'the choice part of society', 'the best part of anything', or 'a select group of people'. Those who attach wing-mirrors to cars are not singled out as an elite because there is nothing remarkable about them as a group in relation to other workers in the motor industry. In no sense are they 'select' or the 'choice part' of the community of workers in the motor industry, whereas, *prima facie*, the Ford workers are a 'select group' if only in that they are better paid than their fellow workers in other parts of the industry.[7] But although better pay may provide the reason why Ford workers are regarded as an élite, it is clear that 'élite' does not *mean* 'a better paid group'. If the prefects form the elite of a school that is not because they are better paid. The élite of any group or community is the select part of that group or community and it is a further question as to what are the criteria for regarding part of a group as 'select' or 'choice'.

It is at this point that we see the emergence of two quite distinct senses of 'élite'. For the terms 'select', 'best', or 'choice part' are ambiguous. What might be meant is either the best part in the sense of the most advantaged, privileged, or best treated part, or the best part in the sense of the most able or competent part. If the former sense is intended there remains the question of whether anything further can be said about the nature of the advantage. As we have seen in the case of the Ford workers it may very likely in practice be an advantage in financial terms, but it does not necessarily have to be. What seems to be very often implied, particularly by those who regard themselves as anti-élitist, is that élites are groups that are privileged in respect of influence which in practical and political terms may very often become power. Thus the prefects of a school or the members of the rugby fifteen might be said to form an élite in so far as they are the influential or powerful members of the school community, as well as, more simply, in so far as they are granted various privileges. Now whether élites, in this sense, are anti-egalitarian or objectionable, obviously boils down to the question of whether one believes that there can be differences between people of any sort such that they constitute relevant reasons for preferential treatment in certain respects. But this is not the sense of élite that seems to be intended by the cultural élitists. What they are anxious to preserve are élites in the sense of groups of particularly able or competent people in various spheres. Thus Eliot writes that the doctrine of élites 'appears to aim at no more than what we must all desire – that all positions in society should be occupied by those who are best fitted to exercise the functions of the positions'.[8] It is obviously true that in some societies those who form élites in this sense may also form élites in the other sense of being relatively privileged, and it well may be that some cultural élitists regard this as justifiable (as may a number of other people who have never come across the terms 'cultural élitist'). But that would be a separate question. All that is inherent in the cultural élitist thesis is the claim that individual children have different capabilities and that it is important for education to take account of these differences and to foster and preserve élites, in the sense of highly competent groups, in various spheres of human activity including the Cultural sphere. To regard this élitist theory as necessarily inegalitarian would amount to saying that there cannot be relevant reasons for regarding children as being variously suited to different kinds of education and that it is an offence to the principle of equality to acknowledge that some are more competent scientists, artists, or whatever than others.

It must be stressed that the purpose of the above paragraphs is very limited in scope. It is simply to suggest that it is unconvincing and inadequate to dismiss the cultural élitist theory simply by deploying slogans such as 'inegalitarian' or 'élitist' against it. It is not obviously inegalitarian or élitist in any objectionable sense. But this is not to say anything about the practical question of comprehensive schools to which the cultural élitists are hostile, or about the suggestion that concern for the promotion of élites in the sense of highly competent groups leads in our society to élites in the sense of privileged groups who perhaps do not deserve their privileges.

The latter criticism involves raising three questions of great complexity in themselves, which it is beyond the scope of this book to do more than point to: (i) Are there any criteria, such as ability, responsibility, hard work, or intelligence, which justify preferential treatment in any respect? (ii) Ought education to be used as a means for dealing with what are essentially social or political issues? That is to say, ought one to do away with educational distinctions in order to alleviate social distinctions? (iii) *Can* education be effectively used as such a means? To put the point in crude terms: will refusing to treat certain children as a group whose superiority in a specific area is acknowledged, necessarily lead to a social situation in which there are no groups that are distinctive in terms of preferential treatment?

The former issue (that of comprehensive education) is beyond the scope of this book because it is ultimately an empirical question. Once it is clear what is meant by a comprehensive system of education (which, it must be admitted, is *not* always clear), then it is a matter for experiment and research as to whether such a system will or will not be more or less successful than various other systems at maintaining standards of competence and excellence in various spheres, or as to whether it will be relatively successful at achieving other objectives (such as breaking down social barriers) that may be regarded as equally or more important.

On the assumption that the aim of maintaining standards of excellence in various spheres is in itself generally desirable, the question we are concerned with here is the specific question of the desirability of promoting Culture and maintaining cultural standards. And this question obviously cannot be answered until we have a clearer idea of what constitutes Culture.

The concept of culture

What, then, is Culture? Why is it important? And what precisely is meant by the claim that appreciation of Culture demands a disciplined understanding? Does this necessarily imply a disciplined education in the more general sense of an education in which children are for the most part subject to the authority of the teacher? These questions have a particular interest, because what we are face to face with here is a specific example of the conflict in education between those who think that some activities just are more worth while than others, and that education should initiate children into such activities, and those who deny this, or, alternatively, argue that anything is worth while if people like doing it.

What sort of things would we expect of a Cultured man? Certain ways of behaving, perhaps, certain interests, certain information? Approaching the matter in this way, Schofield came to the conclusion that a man was Cultured in so far as he did 'the done thing'.[9] For example, in educated circles the done thing is to open doors for ladies, blow one's nose with a handkerchief rather than one's sleeve and be familiar with Shakespeare rather than Mickey Spillane and Bach rather than Bruce Springsteen. Now of course in any society there will be a close link between the society's view of a Cultured man, and doing the done thing in that society. But this definition of a Cultured man is plainly unsatisfactory. For who is to decide what is the done thing? Suppose, as seems to some extent to be the case in our society, there is a great divergence of opinion as to what is the done thing. Could one be considered a Cultured man in our society if one never read any books, disliked Bach intensely, but appreciated Madonna greatly? Certainly one could be said to be conforming to the done thing in some quarters on these conditions. Is a Cultured man simply a man who does the done thing according to the majority view in society? But the majority might be quite uninterested in art. It seems that once again we are quietly shifting from one sense of 'culture' to another: to do the done thing is to conform to the culture of one's group and one could therefore be said to be cultured, in the anthropological sense. But in general the phrase 'Cultured man' does not have the two uses that the word 'culture' does. A Cultured man is one who has some smattering of Culture and, although our view of what constitutes Culture will obviously be closely linked to what we value, Culture is not synonymous with what the majority value. The fact that many million more people read and like Agatha Christie than read and like Elizabeth Gaskell does not turn *Murder on the Orient Express* into a work that belongs to our Cultural heritage. (It does of course belong to our culture in the other sense.)

Eliot offered two attempts at a definition of Culture (or high culture, in his terms). 'Culture may even be described simply as that which makes life worth living. And it is what justifies other peoples and other generations in saying...that it was worthwhile for that civilisation to have existed.'[10] And elsewhere in talking of the need for European men of letters to preserve and transmit their 'common culture' he expands the phrase into 'those excellent works which mark a superior civilisation'.[11]

It is indisputable, I think, that, as Eliot says, what we mean by 'Culture' and what we mean by 'those excellent works which mark a superior civilisation' are one and the same thing. Our Cultural heritage consists of those works that are deemed to be admirable. But this kind of definition is not going to help us at all, given that we live in a society and in an age where there is a great divergence of opinion as to what works, past or present, are the marks of a 'superior civilisation' (whatever that means). What are these excellent works? Who is to decide and how does one decide? Eliot's plea amounts to the injunction that we should be concerned about valuing the works of art that we value. Who could deny that? The problem is that the works that Eliot and Bantock value are not valued by those who object to their view.

Much the same has to be said of Arnold's view that education should be concerned to introduce children to 'the best that has been thought and spoken in the past'. Once again this may serve as an equivalent of what we mean by 'Culture', but it does not help us decide what is the best that has been spoken or thought in the past. (It is also open to the objection that the best from the past *may* be inferior to much of the present. This is not a view that I personally hold, but until we have some criteria for distinguishing good from bad or Culture from chaff there is nothing much that one can say to those who maintain that education should be concerned exclusively with the present, if it is to be concerned with works of art at all.) Arnold did go on to attempt to delineate qualities that go to make the best that has been thought and spoken. He refers to high ideals, high tone, sweetness and light and the Grand Style, for instance. These tantalizing phrases are themselves elaborated on. The Grand Style, we are told, is 'the result when a noble nature, poetically gifted, treats with simplicity and severity a serious subject'. But the problem is that these qualities are themselves value judgements couched in obscurity: What is a noble nature? Why is simplicity valuable? Do we agree that a good play must present high ideals? When Arnold explains what he means by the Grand Style, he has in mind Milton as a master of it. But it would not be absurd to claim that Bob Dylan was an example of a noble nature, poetically gifted, who treats serious subjects with simplicity. It would not be absurd, but one feels that Arnold would not accept the example.

The truth is that any attempt to define the qualities that produce a work that belongs to the category of Culture runs up against one of the most perplexing of philosophical problems: how to arrive at criteria for aesthetic excellence. In the previous chapter (Creativity) the view that there are no standards, or that self-expression is the only one, was treated rather scornfully. But here is the other side of the coin, and the point that lends some plausibility to that view: if there are standards, what are they and who is entitled to determine them? It is not altogether surprising that Arnold finally observes that one must *feel* the quality of, say, Milton in order to know it. But this capitulation to an intuitive view suffers the defect that intuitive views in other areas do: if it is all a matter of intuition, who are we to tell anybody else what they ought to intuit? In other words, if the cultural élitists were to adopt an intuitionist position, they would automatically defeat their own argument that there are some excellent works, by objective standards, that children ought to be encouraged to come into contact with.

Just as the term 'creative' is complex and in practice misleading, since it implies standards when there is often very little agreement as to what the standards are, so 'Culture' is in practice not a particularly helpful term. The important question to ask of an advocate of Culture is what works he regards as culturally significant and why he does so. Here the cultural élitists do provide some help. Between them they produce a list of examples which contains such figures as Aeschylus, Shakespeare. Milton, Eliot himself, Yeats, Bach, and Beethoven.[12] It is at once apparent, even from this selective list, that their view of excellent works is more or less equivalent to the list of works that have traditionally been admired by those concerned with education. But whereas Arnold would have found few schoolmasters who would dispute his examples, it is precisely because many teachers today either dispute the value of such works, or at least dispute that they are so valuable as to warrant educational time being spent on them, unless children happen to show an interest in them, that it is incumbent on those who wish to maintain the practice of initiation into the appreciation of such works to explain why this is important. Obviously it will not do to argue simply that they are great works of art. For it is the question as to whether they are, and if they are whether that is important, that is at issue.

Bantock argues as follows: 'Some human activities are of greater importance than others because they represent a more deliberate, refined and sophisticated exploitation of human potentiality, as poetry is superior to pushpin'.[13] 'It is not difficult to show that the study of poetry involves a higher and more deliberate degree of brain organisation, affects more aspects of the personality and produces more valuable consequences – the utilitarian criterion – than the study of pushpin.'[14]

He seems to be producing three reasons for encouraging the study of a Shakespeare play, rather than leaving the children free to do what they want or to study various other human pursuits: that it requires, and therefore the study gradually promotes, greater intelligence, greater sensibility or sensitivity, and that it has other valuable consequences. But it is difficult to see what these other consequences are supposed to be. One point that Bantock does not mention, which could be another consequence, is that great pleasure might be derived from reading Shakespeare, but then great pleasure might be derived by some from playing video games or reading comics. What are the 'more valuable consequences' that studying poetry may have than playing video games? Surely the only consequences that studying poetry can have (or indeed studying anything else) are the consequences that the study has for the individual in terms of affecting his mental and his emotional development and his enjoyment. In other words Bantock is only making two points: that the study of poetry involves greater intellectual ability and greater emotional sensitivity than the study of a good number of other things. To this may be added the claim that it may provide a rich source of enjoyment.

Without going into the problem of what precisely constitutes intellectual ability or what intelligence is, we should surely agree that reading a poem with understanding requires greater intelligence than playing Bingo. Bingo is a game of chance and it is frankly difficult to see what P. S. Wilson can possibly mean when he writes: 'I am fairly sure that some do, and quite certain that one could…benefit educationally from Bingo', unless he intends to define educational benefit simply in terms of enjoyment. When he adds the more specific claim that Bingo 'can be done "seriously" and results, then, in the development of "conceptual schemes and forms of appraisal which transform everything else" '[15] one is not clear what one can say in reply, except that he is obviously wrong.

Straightaway, then, we may say that the study of literature may be regarded as more worth while than *some* other activities on the grounds that it involves things that they do not. It is open to anybody to say that in his opinion intellectual ability and emotional sensitivity are unimportant. But few of us would. We would be much more likely to question the extent to which literature is one of the best vehicles for the transmission of these qualities. For instance, it might be argued that although *playing* Bingo could not possibly be said to involve or develop intellectual ability, some kind of study of the social phenomenon of Bingo would involve no less intellectual ability than the study of literature. Going on from there it might be suggested that, given a shortage of curriculum time, it would be more profitable to study such things as detective novels or pop song lyrics than what are conventionally regarded as great works of literature, since such study would hold children's interest more and hence stimulate greater effort and enthusiasm, while at the same time making intellectual demands on the pupils. In reply to this Bantock would seem to be saying that the sort of intelligence required to analyse and understand a Shakespeare play is in some sense superior to the sort of intelligence required to analyse and understand pop lyrics or the changing fashions in pop music over a period of years.

I do not see how one could deny that a Shakespeare play (or a Dickens novel or an Eliot poem) is more complex than the average pop lyric or detective novel. But that is not quite the same thing as saying that the study of one requires a higher and more refined degree of intelligence than the study of the other. The assumption seems to be that those who do study, understand, and appreciate great works of literature, will therefore be more intelligent in some general sense or have a superior kind of intelligence to those who do not. The problem here is that the notion of a superior kind of intelligence is frankly mystifying. How is this special kind of intelligence to be defined except in terms of the fact that it is related to understanding literature? And to say that that is a superior kind of intelligence would seem to beg the question. If on the other hand we just say that people who appreciate literature are more intelligent this raises the simple question of whether it is actually true. Is there any evidence to support the claim that those who have whatever is involved in an intelligent understanding for poetry necessarily have greater intelligence in respect of other aspects of human life and activity? The answer is that there is no evidence at all to support this claim: a man might display considerable intelligence in Shakespearean criticism and prove relatively incompetent in all other spheres of his life. Thus, although one could hardly deny that it requires intelligence to study and understand poetry or literature, it is not clear that this amounts to a very strong argument in favour of promoting the study of literature in schools, since there are a great many other activities that also require intelligence.

The strong card in the cultural élitist hand, therefore, is surely the reference to the development of emotional sensitivity or the schooling of feelings. Despite what has been said in the previous paragraph we surely accept that some intelligence is required for the study of literature, and even perhaps the empirical generalization that people who have such intelligence are unlikely to be devoid of sense in other spheres. The weakness of the argument so far has been that so many other areas of study, which might be selected for quite different kinds of reason, also demand and promote intelligence. But whereas a sociological study of the rise of Bingo, or the shifting patterns of pop music, or a purely scientific education, would involve intelligence they would not have much to do with the development of feelings. The real case for concern with Culture in education is surely that the study of Culture involves both the intellect *and* the emotions. Besides the fact that the study of literature makes intellectual demands on us, through it 'we can become more aware of the feelings we have and we may also be able to develop new sorts of feeling'.[16] Understanding Othello involves appreciating that Othello is jealous. One might say that to understand Othello properly, one would have to have experienced jealousy, but conversely that to introduce children to the character of Othello is a way of introducing them to the concept of jealousy or of sharpening their perception of it and some of its implications.

Of course, just as it was not clear that an individual who had an intellectual grasp of such a play would necessarily display a great deal of intelligence in other spheres of his life, so it seems implausible to suggest that it is a necessary truth that those who have emotional sensitivity in the sense that they can put themselves imaginatively in Othello's position and feel what he feels, will have or display such sensitivity outside the theatre. We are familiar with the example of the Nazi leaders who apparently had a deep appreciation of various cultural works, but on whose sensitivity as human beings this had very little effect. One way to dismiss such examples is to argue that the fact that the Nazis were so lacking in sensitivity as human beings is merely proof that their appreciation of Culture was only apparent and not genuine. The trouble with this line of argument is that it makes its conclusion true by definition: appreciation of Culture must involve a high degree of sensibility in the individual in other aspects of his life, because anyone who clearly lacks such sensibility will be said to lack a true appreciation of Culture. Since this is plainly unsatisfactory, it seems to me to be preferable to concede what in any case one would have thought was obviously true: there can be a divorce between the individual's capacity to feel or experience certain emotions and his actual tendency to do so in specific situations. One can feel with the characters of a play, but for some reason fail to feel with one's neighbours. But to admit this is merely to admit that concern for the study of Culture is not a panacea for all our ills – a point that few, if any, would deny. The basic claim may still stand, and that is that in so far as literature is predominantly concerned with human emotions and feelings, it is obviously true that to appreciate literature involves understanding and recognizing those emotions and feelings. Through literature we may initiate the child into experiences that might otherwise lie outside his sphere of awareness. What is finally significant about a Shakespeare play, from the educational viewpoint, is not so much that it is a relatively complex structure and therefore undoubtedly requires some intelligence to grasp its structure, nor the claim that it requires some special type or high degree of intelligence to understand, but rather the nature of it. For a Shakespeare play, whichever one you choose, treats of people, their feelings, their relations with one another, their responses to situations, the way in which they act, the reasons why they do so and the consequences of those actions. It introduces the reader to some of the complexities of people and behaviour and thereby may develop the imaginative sensitivity of the reader beyond the limits set by his own experience.

Throughout the above paragraphs it will be noted that I have unquestioningly used Shakespeare as an example of a writer of quality and his plays as examples of works of art or works that belong to high culture. I have done this simply in order to have some example whereby to bring out the sorts of claim that the cultural élitists are making. A Shakespeare play fairly uncontentiously may be said to demand intellectual and emotional maturity for its appreciation as well as being a potential source of enjoyment. It is therefore clear, in broad terms, why the cultural élitists are anxious to promote the study of such works. What however still remains unclear is how one sets about selecting specific works, how one distinguishes between better and worse works of literature, and how one distinguishes between different levels of culture. What, in other words, are the criteria of excellence within the broad spectrum of works that demand an intellectual and emotional response? Surely a popular novel such as Mary Stewart's *My Brother Michael*, being as it is a love story set against a background of wartime Greek resistance to the German occupation, demands an intellectual and emotional response for its appreciation, and yet, one presumes, it is not part of high culture. Why is it not? To this Bantock would reply, as he does in reference to the superiority of Donne's love lyrics over modern pop lyrics, that a Shakespeare play is 'more complex, more varied',[17] and 'truer' to the complexities of the various emotions portrayed than a Mary Stewart novel.

Now although there may be dangers in introducing these criteria (Is complexity necessarily a virtue and simplicity never? – Arnold, as we have seen, certainly valued simplicity; Is not the criterion of 'truth' going to be very hard to handle in reference to the portrayal of emotions?), none the less this would seem to me to be essentially fair comment. The simple and romantic conception of love in many pop songs does not do justice to the reality and complexity of love as it is actually experienced by most of us: to some extent therefore it misleads and distorts rather than develops and expands our sensibility in respect of the business of falling in love and understanding the complexities of our own feelings and those of others. What I confess to feeling very uneasy about is not the distinction between high culture and popular works of literature, poetry, or songs, but the claim that there can be levels of culture and that the folk culture of the past was of value, whereas the popular culture of today is not. For if complexity, variety, and true representation of the 'multi-faceted character of the emotion'[18] in question are criteria for pinpointing work of cultural value, it is very difficult to see why 'Greensleeves' should rank as culturally valuable, whereas modern pop songs, by and large, do not. To this Bantock would reply by reference to the commercial inspiration and 'the emotional falseness of popular culture'[19] today. But the motives or inspirational source of the composer would seem to me to have very little to do with the value of the work produced (after all, the Homeric poems were composed for the price of a meal by wandering bards, and Mozart was commissioned to write a number of his symphonies). It may well be true that today's pop culture is by and large produced and marketed by hard-headed businessmen, but there is no obvious reason why what they produce should not be as true a representation of some emotion, on the same simple level, as 'Greensleeves'.

There are a number of other interesting questions that one might raise in relation to the cultural élitists: even if we were to grant that adults who appreciate literature are in some general sense likely to be more intelligent and more sensitive than those who do not, does it follow that the *best* way to develop intelligence and sensitivity in children is through study of such works? Might there not be other and better ways of developing these qualities, which would none the less result in individuals being able to appreciate such works as adults? Is the suggestion of the cultural élitists only that individuals who can take on such an education benefit as individuals or that the community also benefits from the existence of such individuals? Is there supposed to be something inherently good about the existence of great works of art, or are they valuable for the pleasure they give and their educative value? What would it mean to say that the Parthenon was inherently valuable?

But we must call a halt somewhere. It is undeniable that the selection of general criteria for aesthetic excellence is one of the most tantalizing of philosophical problems, and that the cultural élitist position is vulnerable on this point of how one selects great works of literature. Perhaps in practice there is no alternative but to consider specific works and attempt to make specific comments about them, which I take to be what we generally mean by literary criticism. Of course, as we know well, literary critics have to make value judgements as well as draw out what the features of various works are, and they do not by any means always agree in their evaluation. The view that there just are certain great works and we all know what they are is too simple and too naive to be acceptable. On the other hand, we must not confuse the fact that cultural standards are hard to determine and sometimes difficult to reach agreement on, with the assumption that anything between hard covers is as good as anything else between hard covers.

Notes

1 Bantock, G. H., *Education and Values* (London, Faber, 1965).
2 Bantock, G. H., *Culture, Industrialisation and Education* (London, Routledge & Kegan Paul, 1968) p. 15.
3 Eliot, T. S., *Notes Towards the Definition of Culture* (London, Faber, 1948; rev. ed., 1962) p. 25.
4 Ibid., p. 31.
5 Bantock, G. H., *Culture, Industrialisation and Education*, p. 2.
6 Bantock, G. H., *Education in an Industrial Society* (London, Faber, 1963) p. 71.
7 [I do not know whether this is true anymore. But it may none the less continue to serve as an example to make the conceptual and logical points I am concerned with here.] See comment on page 162.
8 Eliot, T. S., op. cit., p. 37.
9 Schofield, H., *The Philosophy of Education* (London, Allen & Unwin, 1972).
10 Eliot, T. S., op. cit., p. 27.
11 Ibid., p. 124.
12 It is incidentally noteworthy that there are still proponents of the 'list' of great works and that the lists continue to refer to the familiar examples.

See, e.g., Bloom, A., *The Western Canon*, (New York, Harcourt Brace and Company, 1994), and Murray, C., *Human Accomplishment*, (New York, HarperCollins, 2003).
13 Bantock, G. H., *Education in an Industrial Society*, p. 201.
14 Ibid., p. 94.
15 Wilson, P. S., 'In Defence of Bingo' in *British Journal of Educational Studies*, vol. XV, no. 1.
16 Bantock, G. H., *Culture, Industrialisation and Education*, p. 77.
17 Ibid., p. 76.
18 Ibid., p. 76.
19 Ibid., p. 83.

Further reading

For a general survey of creativity tests from the psychologist's point of view see H. Lytton, *Creativity and Education* (London, Routledge & Kegan Paul, 1971).

For philosophical approaches to the concept see, in particular, J. P. White, 'Creativity and Education' in R. F. Dearden, P. H. Hirst and R. S. Peters (eds), *Education and the Development of Reason*. See also R. K. Elliot, 'Versions of Creativity' in *Philosophy of Education Society of Great Britain, Annual Proceedings, July 1971* vol. v, 2. Most recently, see Sharon Bailin's lucid *Achieving Extraordinary Ends* (Boston, Kluwer, 1988).

The concept of Culture has not yet been adequately dealt with from a philosophical angle, but for the cultural elitist view see T. S. Eliot, *Notes Towards the Definition of Culture* (London, Faber, 1948) and G. H. Bantock, *Education in an Industrial Society* (London, Faber, 1963) or *Culture, Industrialisation and Education* (London, Routledge & Kegan Paul, 1968). A valuable recent volume is John Gingell and Edwin Brandon, *In Defence of High Culture* (Oxford, Blackwell, 2000).

13 Research into teaching

Teaching is not perhaps a very philosophically interesting concept, but it is obviously central to the educational enterprise and there are some very interesting questions to be raised about the empirical research that is conducted into and around it. When I say 'not philosophically interesting' it will be remembered that I mean that it is not an idea that perplexes one, leaves one boggle-eyed or bewildered, or that stands in obvious need of delicate and intricate teasing out. To be sure, one can observe that it is a polymorphous term (that is to say, it takes many forms so that instruction and discussion might equally count as examples of teaching), that the verb 'to teach' takes two accusatives (so that one teaches somebody something, and the old adage 'I teach children not subjects' is rather robbed of its force), and question whether it is an achievement or task word and how it is conceptually tied to learning. (Am I teaching you, for instance, if you are learning nothing?) But one surely does not lie awake at night despairing of getting an adequately clear idea of teaching, as one might in respect of love, justice, happiness, or indeed education. In general, it may take one's fancy, but it's not a great mystery. We know well enough what teaching is.

What is a bit of a mystery is what enables some people to do it well and others not. There is of course a conceptual question here: what counts as doing it well? But that is not what I want to concentrate on. We can reasonably enough say that teaching well means teaching by whatever morally acceptable means will promote and achieve the educational aims that have been discussed throughout this book. That still leaves the question, when we see individuals obviously teaching well, how do they achieve what they achieve? By virtue of what are they successful, and what are the best ways for teachers to proceed? Now, on the face of it these are not conceptual questions, but questions to be inquired into empirically. One needs to observe, to look, see, taste, or assess by means of one or more of the senses, in some organized kind of way, what actually goes on when successful teachers (or indeed unsuccessful ones) are in action. But how is one to accomplish this?

Styles of research

A popular pastime amongst empirical educational researchers is to contrast, discuss, and argue about the rival merits of what may loosely be termed quantitative and qualitative research methods. (Many are unhappy with the implications of these, and indeed the many other terms sometimes used in the debate, such as formal, informal, systematic, and ethnographic. The main line of demarcation is between those who wish to organize their research more or less exclusively around what can be measured, and those who wish to organize it around what can be assessed, the latter allowing of impressionistic judgement and other relatively individual modes of evaluating.) But such debate seems to me largely wasted.

In the first place, as already suggested, in many cases the distinctions are not even clear (there is even something called quasi-experimental research, which a cynic might allege to be a cover up for what is essentially clearly non-experimental). Until it is absolutely clear what, if anything, the difference is between, say, formal, systematic, and quantitative research and precisely how they are to be contrasted, if they are, with informal, ethnographic, or qualitative approaches, we cannot have a coherent debate about their relative merits. If, as sometimes seems to be the case, there is some degree of overlap between various purportedly distinct methodologies, the situation becomes even more confused. In the second place this is surely not an argument that makes sense in the abstract, because what is at issue is not some inherent quality in one type of research or another, but the appropriateness of particular modes of research to particular issues. Since educational issues are of many different kinds and logical types, it is to be expected that quite different types of research should be brought into play on different occasions. The question therefore is not whether research into teaching should be conducted by means of quantitative measures (on some such grounds as that they are more 'objective') or qualitative measures (on some such grounds as that they are more 'insightful'), but what kind of research can sensibly be utilized to look into this particular aspect of teaching as opposed to that. That is to say, the form or type of research (the research model, as they like to say) that should be adopted must be decided by reference to precisely what kind of thing (or, in most cases, what different kinds of thing) are being inquired into.

Furthermore, much of the argument amongst researchers themselves is of a technical nature. It is about whether research is being properly conducted on its own terms (e.g. was the sample truly random, the sample size adequate, the reliability rating significant?) rather than about the terms on which it is being conducted. This is rather like the distinction between discussing whether a poem is well written in respect of observing the iambic metre, and discussing whether the iambic metre is well chosen.

The questionable and misleading nature of this debate (misleading because it wrongly suggests that those involved are being self-critical and analytic at a fundamental level) is intensified by the tendency to misuse or unconsciously take advantage of the ambiguity of some of the terms involved. Here we do run into some genuinely conceptual difficulties. What, for example, is objectivity? We all have a broad and hazy idea of what is meant by the word, but what precisely is meant and how is it related to subjectivity? Are they opposites, incompatible or what? Some say that systematic observation and other quantitative means of research are to be preferred in that they are more objective. But are they more objective in some way that matters? Perhaps calling such methods objective is just another way of saying what the mode of research is (for instance that it concentrates exclusively on the readily observable and pre-specified, at fixed intervals). The question of importance, however, is whether the attempt to understand something such as my marriage by categorizing my wife's and my own behaviour at thirty-second intervals, in terms of some seventy pre-specified observable behaviours, is likely to reveal more of the truth, more accurately, than various other approaches. Calling it 'objective', if that merely draws attention to the mode of observation, does not represent an argument; but if 'objective' is taken to mean something like 'a dispassionate record of the truth', then it is absurd to assume that this method is necessarily more objective than, say, the impressions of an experienced observer. No doubt, in the latter case, one places a lot of trust in the competence and judgement of an individual. and there are many other equally obvious dangers to watch out for, but none of this shows that in principle it is not a better way to investigate such a question, whether it is more or less objective in some technical sense. And if it is a more appropriate way to investigate a particular problem, the fact that it does not involve the kinds of procedure that allow of high validity and reliability scores is neither here nor there.

In far too many textbooks and courses on research methods the cart is placed before the horse: we are invited to become thoroughly immersed in and to perfect our understanding of one or more approaches to research and to consider their technical strengths and weaknesses, *before* we have given consideration to the particular kinds and nature of problems that arise in the context of education and teaching, before indeed we have given thought to what teaching and education are, and, consequently, before we have faced the question of what kind of research would be appropriate to this particular enterprise. It is rather like perfecting striking skills without giving much thought to whether we are going to play baseball, cricket, or hockey. (I need hardly add that very often the question of appropriateness is not faced at all, even after the technical aspects have been dealt with.)

In addition, in the realm of methodological discourse, we are commonly faced with ambiguous and confused concepts and a marked absence of any attempt to get to grips directly with conceptual issues. There is also a virginal refusal to come face to face with judgements of value. Questions such as: 'Is it morally acceptable to teach in this way?' 'Is this practice of educational value?' 'Is this leading to something worthwhile?' as well as the above-mentioned 'Is this an appropriate way to look into this matter?' are resolutely avoided in standard research methodology textbooks and courses. Answers are provided neatly, impersonally, sanitized, and indirectly by adopting the methodology of one's choice. In committing myself to, say, systematic observation as a style of research, I no longer have to face up directly to questions such as 'Does it make sense to inquire into whether this practice is a useful one when teaching maths to twelve year olds?' but can hide instead behind generalities of the type 'This mode of research is more objective' 'Our validity rating is high in this kind of research' or 'Our criteria (of observation) are public and unequivocal'. No doubt in some sense, at least some such claims are true as far as they go. But these are not the points that ought to be at issue. The main issue ought to be what is the most appropriate way to examine this particular question, and if the question is such that the most appropriate way will have to be acknowledged to be unlikely to yield a definitive, unquestionable, answer, then we have to live with that fact.

Conceptual issues

During the last fifty years or so there has been an amazing amount of research conducted into teaching, or particular aspects of it, and it continues unabated. There are a number of books that conveniently summarize some of the research (see for example Dunkin and Biddle, Good and Brophy, and the *Handbook of Research on Teaching*). But, in the light of what has already been said, the philosophical reader is forewarned to expect a lack of real critical consideration. There is criticism, but it is mainly of the technical and rival methodological type just referred to. Whereas, the main problem with the bulk of the research is conceptual, and, although this is formally acknowledged by some, the nature, limits, and difficulty of conceptualization are evidently not familiar to many people working in the field. Conceptualization, as I hope by now readers will appreciate, cannot be equated with definition, if that means providing a verbal synonym. It is no good saying that 'love' is 'having deep feelings for another', and thinking one has now analysed the concept. One hasn't. What feelings? How deep is deep? What does 'having' feelings entail? Such questions are real, difficult, and the sort that need answering if we are truly concerned with analysing the concept of love. Nor does one truly explain a mysterious, unobservable, concept such as love by operationally defining it in simple observable terms. One simply distorts it. (Here again, note that behavioural definitions are not inherently objectionable. It depends on the concept. A behavioural definition of something that is essentially to be characterized in terms of behaviours, such as physical strength, is fine; it is appropriate. A behavioural definition of love is, on the face of it, madly inappropriate, because love isn't that kind of thing.)

The conceptual weakness of research into teaching is to be found primarily in three areas; perhaps paradoxically the issue is not about the concept of teaching itself which, as I said above, is relatively unproblematic. The first and most important thing that one needs to have a sure and clear conceptual grasp of is the educational enterprise itself; the second is the concept or concepts directly at issue (e.g. we may be inquiring into the effects of the teacher's sense of humour in teaching or the student's degree of home support, in which case we need an adequate conceptualization of humour and support respectively); and the third is what may be called the particularities of local content or local conditions, by which I mean to refer to such things as what subject is being taught and what group of people we are studying. If we are studying the effects of humour in a Latin lesson, then we need to understand what counts as a good Latin lesson, which may very probably differ in important respects from what counts as a good PE lesson or a good social studies lesson. If we are studying the effects of humour on gifted children, then we need a clear and coherent conceptualization of giftedness, such as is not currently readily apparent in books on gifted children.

Elsewhere I have criticized examples of research for failing to conceptualize adequately any of the above three areas, and I maintain the strong thesis that the bulk of such research is meaningless in view of its logical and conceptual shortcomings.[1] However, here I want only to make the point generally – as befits a philosophical textbook concerned with principles rather than particulars. Whether particular pieces of empirical work, and if so how many and to what extent, are guilty of the errors and confusion that I claim they are, the reader can judge for himself at another time. The question here and now is whether it is correct to argue that conceptualization, in the sense that we are concerned with, is vitally important in the three areas mentioned.

The case for insisting on the need for an adequate conceptualization of the educational enterprise seems to me as good an instance of logical necessity as one is likely to come across. It just does not make sense to conduct empirical research into teaching, in any manner or mode, without a clearly articulated conception of the educational enterprise. For research into effective teaching requires criteria of success. (That is to say, we need to know what criteria have to be met for something to count as an instance of successful teaching.) But the success that we are supposed to be and claim to be interested in is educational success. A good teacher is, by definition, one who contributes to the successful education of his students. Therefore, in order to judge whether someone is a good teacher, you have to have a very clear idea of what counts as being successfully educated.

This is so obvious a point that one may briefly inquire why it needs to be stated so bluntly, and why it is not acknowledged or lived up to in practice, as I maintain it is not. There seem to be three rather similar and closely related explanations of why people do not proceed in ways that show that they appreciate the need for a clear conceptualization of the educational enterprise. The first is that they do in fact have such a conceptualization, but have not chosen to articulate it. But, in so far as this is the case, it is unsatisfactory. It is not sufficient that the researcher should have an adequate conception. We, the public, need to know what a particular researcher understands the educational enterprise to involve and in what he considers educational success to consist, in order to be able to judge for ourselves the plausibility of his research. If he says that his research leads him to the conclusion that x is a good teaching technique, even if we trust his research so far as methodology goes, we need to know to what sort of educational ends this technique is a good means. If we do not know his ends, we are in no position to decide whether we too approve the means or teaching technique.

Secondly, and I believe that this is the most usual explanation, the researcher may see the need for sound conceptualization of the educational enterprise, and try to meet it, but fall short because he is not really sure what is involved in the clear analysis and articulation of a concept. Here we run, once again, into the difference between analysing a concept and providing various other types of definition. I hope that it is clear from the course of this book that analysis is to be distinguished carefully from a whole host of more or less similar, but none the less quite distinct, activities, such as engaging in or providing metaphors, verbal synonyms, similes, and various other things. The fact is that analytic skills have to be cultivated, and, if research programmes are going to be improved at the level of conceptualization, researchers are either going to have to become philosophers or philosophers become researchers.

Thirdly, sometimes there is a view of the educational enterprise implicit in research that is clear enough, but is highly questionable. (There is, of course, always some idea implicit, since, if nothing else, the researcher's idea of educational success can be identified with success in respect of the instruments and measures used. But the idea implicit is by no means always clear or coherent; nor is it always recognized, even by the researchers themselves.) What I am getting at here is the extent to which, if certain educational research is to be taken seriously, we would have to assume that being well educated consists of things such as being able to draw facile pictures, to solve artificial and sometimes trivial puzzles, to recognize various sounds, and to look attentive. For many research programmes into teaching estimate student achievement largely or solely by reference to performance at such tasks and to other equally banal standardized tests of achievement.

It is equally evident that the particular object of one's research interest must be conceptualized properly, and the same rules of proper analysis apply: giving examples must not be confused with providing criteria, nor must any other substitute for proper analysis be accepted. It is also necessary to establish that what one is interested in can be meaningfully, and in some appropriate manner, monitored. It is not necessary that it should be directly observable, but it is necessary that whether we choose to rely on direct sightings, indirect indices, or judgement, is decided by the nature of the concept rather than the methodological orientation of the researcher. To take but one example: if I want to inquire into the effects of the teacher's sensitivity, I need to make it quite clear what criteria have to be met for something to count as an instance of being sensitive. Establishing the criteria, formulating the conditions, necessary and sufficient, or, conceivably, rolling, for determining instances of sensitivity is *not* to be confused with giving examples of sensitivity, paraphrasing what it is to be sensitive by recourse to a thesaurus, defining it in the manner of a dictionary as 'keenly perceptive; reacting to stimuli', likening it to something else, or describing it metaphorically. Then, having established exactly what it is, I need to note precisely what kind of thing it is. Is it, for example, such a thing as can, by definition, be directly observed or its presence equated with directly observable behaviour? Is there a good argument to show that while it is not to be identified with any set of directly observable phenomena. its presence may be inferred from directly observable evidence? Is it, rather, the sort of thing that can only reasonably be detected by the judgement of the well-practised observer? (If so, how does one recognize or develop the 'well-practised observer'?) Is it the kind of quality that individuals can reliably recognize in themselves or others, so that questionnaires of various sorts might be appropriately used? Having sorted that issue out, I am in a position to recognize or work out whether it would be appropriate to conduct my research by means of, say, systematic observation, or participatory observation, or whatever, in this particular case. Prior to coming up with an analysis of the right kind (and note that paradoxically the issue is not so much whether my account of sensitivity is correct or true, but whether I provide a clear account of it in the right terms), I am in no position to formulate a research methodology on rational grounds.

The requirement that the local content be adequately conceptualized is partly a technical matter of variables; if we do not specifically take account of the fact that we are studying a history lesson and gifted children, then we may fail to see that our conclusions are based on data that are significantly attributable to the fact that it was history and not physics, and that the students were gifted. In order to take account of such variables, we need a clear definition of them. But it also arises partly out of a belief that the idea of there being generic teaching skills (at any rate of significance and rarity) is questionable. In other words, if I am researching into the effects of, say, writing on the blackboard, it is partly a matter of technical competence that I take account of the fact that my sample are learning Latin rather than geography (since what counts as success will differ); but it is also important because, on the face of it, and contrary to the un-thought-out premise of much research, it is highly unlikely that writing on the blackboard is either desirable or undesirable *in general*. It is likely to depend on what you want to achieve, and that may vary from subject to subject, if not from class to class.

If we bear the above points in mind, we can reasonably proceed to undertake empirical inquiry into some aspects of teaching. But it may be worth suggesting, if only as a counter-balance to the current fashion for trusting to empirical inquiry in everything: (i) that a lot of questions about teaching, though undoubtedly empirical in some degree, just don't lend themselves to empirical research, and certainly not to research of the formal, systematic variety; (ii) that folk wisdom to the effect that good teachers are, if not born, at any rate educated rather than trained or made, is true, and that there is no appreciable set of techniques or skills that will make a poor teacher good or prove necessary to a good teacher. It may, more plausibly, be suggested that there are some rules of thumb that will prevent a poor teacher from being a disaster. Indeed it may be that this is the truth that explains the long life of otherwise ridiculous research in this area: we have such a distorted conception of education and so many poor teachers, that it probably does pay to discover, laboriously, ways of controlling largely disaffected classes; and (iii) that one can come to recognize a lot about good teaching by a process of reasoning. If you know what you are trying to achieve, in what context, with what subject matter, and you know something about yourself and your students, then you ought to be able to work out some sensible and desirable ways to conduct yourself.

In my most pessimistic moments I imagine a school founded on the claims of empirical research into teaching in terms such as the following. (The reader should note the implied qualification: what follows is an extreme characterization, drawn in order to highlight the dangers.) It would consist of teachers adopting a number of specific techniques and tactics, behaviour and organizational ploys, routines, and rules. They would proceed to a considerable extent formulaically rather than by intelligent response to situations. They would, so to speak, be playing American football rather than soccer, the former consisting of a variety of set plays determined by the coach, the latter leaving far more to the individual and the autonomy of the team as a whole. Paradoxically, given the heavy emphasis on the scientific objectivity of such research, what particular techniques teachers selected would be largely a matter of chance. This is because, as it happens, if we take the research of the last fifty years seriously at all, there is a great deal of contradictory evidence on a number of specific issues. So in the end, when deciding, for example, to adopt this or that approach to the teaching of reading, you pays your money and you takes your choice. Some of the rules of thumb adopted will on the face of it be trivial. (Although one must be careful here not to beg the question, I admit. In so far as my general line of criticism in this chapter were to be without foundation, then I could not reasonably assert that a claim such as that the teacher should always use students' first names is trivial. For the research asserts that it is not trivial.) Some of the rules will be very difficult to interpret: for example, be 'with it', show warmth, and be considerate, may be good advice, but it is far from clear what counts as being 'with it', warm, and considerate (the conceptual issue again). Some principles appear to be logically necessary truths dressed up as empirical findings, as for example, when teachers are told that they should be interesting or clear. The bulk of them, because of the nature of the research that lies behind them, will enjoin discrete, fairly mechanical behaviours of the type 'look people in the eye', 'do not lecture or instruct', 'ask five different kinds of question in equal proportions', 'recapitulate the work of the previous class at the beginning of the following one', 'require students to follow five or six specific steps when they are going to write an essay'.

Not only do the majority of such principles seem to me to miss altogether the essence of what teaching is about and requires, and to be in themselves somewhat 'poor things', but there is also the added fear that, since, by and large, the research is conducted in such a way as to assume that these skills are generic and these rules of universal application, teachers in this imaginary high school will adopt them routinely in every class, without any thought for what is being taught to whom and why. (Good heavens, shouldn't one sometimes stand on one's head just because it's a hot Friday afternoon?) Furthermore, because this school with its endless repetition of lessons that start with recapitulation, then move through five types of questioning, with a great deal of eye contact, minimal instruction, and so forth, has, by definition, bought into the empirical research paradigm, it follows that questions such as 'What is education?' will not be on its mind. The 'education' it provides will be the skill-training, information-processing kind of enterprise, that suits the industrial, military, and management models from which much of the research is derived, rather better than it suits the kind of education that we have argued for in this book. Nor are teachers of this type likely to be the sort of people who, throwing caution to the wind, capitalize on particular situations, doing what they see an opportunity to do rather than what they have been prepared to do by rote. Putting it very plainly, there is not, so far as I know, a shred of evidence in the world that doing any of the things enjoined by empirical research (that are truly empirical claims and that involve specific behaviours) *as a matter of routine* will be in any way advantageous, if our ideal is to produce educated people of the type formally characterized in Chapter 3 – or, to lapse for once into the easier realm of examples, if we intend to produce the likes of Pierre Trudeau, Winston Churchill, H. G. Wells, Margaret Drabble, Harold Macmillan, Robertson Davies, Jacques Barzun, or Leonard Bernstein, persons who for all their faults at least approximate to what we are after in the name of education.[2] (I should stress again that I have depicted an extreme possibility. I do not deny that there are various useful rules of thumb, principles, and precepts to be offered nor that it is possible for individuals to make intelligent and flexible use of rules and routines. My point is that the dominance of the idea of a science of teaching militates against such intelligent and flexible use.)

But, of the two broad divisions of research referred to above, and notwithstanding what was said there about the folly of judging in the abstract, I wish that there were rather more of the informal variety, because I think it more appropriate a mode of research for a greater number of more important and worthwhile educational questions. Whether, for example, a teacher is being humorous, is being taken to be humorous by his students, and is consequently being paid attention to, seems to me more plausibly answered on the strength of the judgement of one who, in the light of experience and understanding, has watched and come away with a feeling, than by any measure of humour that I am familiar with.

However, neither that example nor any other single instance is of particular interest to me in this context. My concern is with the spirit of the age (particularly as it affects education), which I take to be anti-philosophical at a time when what it most clearly needs is more competent philosophizing. Whether empirical research into teaching can in principle yield much information of importance may be open to doubt, in the light of the three points made above. But it is certain that we cannot reasonably rely on such research so long as it falls as short conceptually as it has done heretofore.

Notes

1 See, in particular, Barrow, R., *Giving Teaching Back to Teachers* (Brighton, Wheatsheaf, 1984).
2 Note that in at least one case the person in question was not considered a successful student in conventional academic terms; that, however, does not mean that he (Churchill) may not be regarded as well educated.

Further reading

See Robin Barrow, *Giving Teaching Back to Teachers* (Brighton, Wheatsheaf, 1984) or appropriate entries in Robin Barrow and Geoffrey Milburn *A Critical Dictionary of Educational Concepts* (Brighton, Wheatsheaf, 1986). For a broad estimate of the field, see *A Handbook of Teacher Education*. See also Barrow, R., and Foreman-Peck, L., *What Use is Educational Research? A Debate* IMPACT. No. 12, Philosophy of Education Society of Great Britain.

A useful summary of research, though no longer up to date, is provided by M. J. Dunkin and B. J. Biddle, *The Study of Teaching* (New York, Holt Rinehart & Winston, 1974).

14 Conclusion
Theory and practice

J. L. Austin once remarked that philosophers tend to succumb to the temptation of oversimplification. In their search for rounded, coherent, all-embracing 'theories' they often limit their investigations to a few well-worn concepts and to a few facts. The net result is that the history of philosophy is littered with 'tidy-looking dichotomies'[1] and the student is under the mistaken impression that, if he is to make progress in philosophy, he has to embrace one half of a given dichotomy – he has to produce arguments to show that man is free or that man is not free, he has to take a view on the reality of the material world or its unreality, and so on.

Austin need not have restricted his remarks to philosophers. Many people besides philosophers readily fall foul of the 'either/or' dichotomy and teachers in particular tend to fall foul of a particular manifestation of it, namely the 'educational theory/educational practice' dichotomy. Theory and practice, in the educational context, are often dramatically opposed: 'It may be all right in theory, but it won't work in practice', 'I've got no time for all this theory, I'm a practical man', 'Theory gets you nowhere'. The implication of such remarks is that theory is one thing and practice another, totally different thing, that theory is essentially a useless activity carried on by starry-eyed dreamers who have no knowledge of, and no interest in, practical realities.

But to what extent is this true? Let us begin by clarifying what is meant by 'theory'. It is clear that there are different kinds of theory, or different senses of the word 'theory'. Thus there are (i) mathematical theories. In pure mathematics one encounters the theory of equations, the theory of probability, the theory of numbers, and so on. Such theories exhibit a number of theorems (or results) derived from certain basic premises or postulates and the kind of derivation is usually described as deduction. Thus 'a is greater than b' and 'b is greater than c' yield the deduction, 'therefore a is greater than c'. Generally speaking, pure mathematicians are not concerned that their highly organized, tightly welded abstract theories find practical application; indeed, very often they betray lordly indifference to the possibility. But this fact does not cause the 'practical' man, or the 'practical' teacher, much worry. Mathematical theory is not what he has in mind when he inveighs against theory, and he would not regard the pure mathematician's disregard for practical application as an example of his thesis that theory and practice are poles apart and utterly unrelated. Like a great many other people he probably thinks that pure mathematicians are a highly respectable group of people *usefully* employed in that, whether they like it or not, their theories *do* find application in the 'real world' via the (ii) theories of the well-developed natural sciences of which physics is, perhaps, the paradigm.

With respect to theories of type (ii) it is once more manifest that the slogan 'Theory gets you nowhere' is not directed against these. For it is clear that the theories of natural science *have* got us somewhere if not where all of us want to be. Controlled experiment forms an integral part of the natural scientist's procedures and the possibility of his researches finding technological application is, therefore, always present. The breathtaking technological advances of the last few decades serve as dramatic reminder of the successful marriage of theory and practice as far as natural science is concerned.

Not surprisingly, the success story of natural science inspires others working in different fields. If there can be a science of nature, why should there not be a science of man? And if it is possible to adapt the methods of natural science to the science of man – the human, or social, sciences – will not the success achieved by natural scientists attend the efforts of the social scientists? So we get (iii) social scientific theories deserving of separate classification because of their inbuilt methodological deficiencies – for example, the fact that they treat of human beings and not of inert matter, and the fact that moral considerations act as a restraint on 'experimentation'. And, lastly, we have (iv) the kind of theorizing undertaken in this book, differentiated from (iii) in that whereas psychologists and sociologists, say, undertake empirical investigation in the form of surveys and experiments we, as philosophers, do not. Theorizing for us consists in no more than a sustained attempt to 'think things through' with particular regard for the meanings of words as the principal medium of thought. Our kind of theorizing harks back to one of the senses of the Greek word from which 'theory' is derived, namely contemplation.

It is theories of types (iii) and (iv) that attract the 'practical' teacher's scorn, for sociologists and psychologists and philosophers, unlike mathematicians and natural scientists, treat specifically of educational matters. I shall not attempt to defend type (iii) theorizing against the practical man's strictures – sociologists and psychologists are well able to look after themselves – and I shall concentrate on the defence of the 'thinking things through' kind of theorizing as exemplified in the preceding chapters of this book.

First, then, let us consider the objection to the effect that theory is unrelated to practice or, in the specific terms of the preceding paragraph, the objection that thinking things through in philosophic fashion is unrelated to what people *do*. Taken at its face value this is surely an untenable position. Suppose, for example, a teacher said, 'I don't get my children to learn their tables by heart because I don't want to indoctrinate them', and suppose that the teacher then gave thought to the notion of indoctrination and came to the conclusion that getting children to learn their tables by heart did not constitute indoctrinating them, would we not now expect a change in that teacher's *action* in the classroom? Again, suppose a teacher held the belief that the purpose of education is to get children through examinations but that thinking about the concept of education brought about a change in his belief about its purpose, would we not now expect to find changes in what he actually did in the classroom? Or suppose that this teacher abandoned, as a broad guide to action, the precept 'Get them through their examinations' and substituted the precept 'See that they develop'. Would we not feel justified in asking what is involved in seeing that children develop, and if it were the case that the teacher could not tell us, would we not now counsel further thought on his or her part about the concept of development? Far from theory being unrelated to practice we have here an instance of theory – thinking about what it is to develop – being a necessary prerequisite to action. Until the practical consequences of acting in accord with the precept 'See that they develop' are spelled out there can be *no* action in accord with it.

I once went into a primary school to look at a music lesson being given by a young teacher. The children, aged about eight or nine years, were learning a new song. I noticed that most of the children were grunting tunelessly and I said, in all innocence, to the teacher after the lesson, 'Oughtn't you to be getting them to sing in tune?' She was taken aback, not because my suggestion of a teaching objective ran counter to one of her own objectives, but because, as it turned out, she had no idea as to what it was she ought to be doing. I did not press home my questioning, although I suppose I could have asked why they were singing at all. Why weren't they tearing up newspapers or playing snakes and ladders or just being left to their own devices? How can there be *selection* of activities to be carried on in schools without prior thought being given to the question of what ought to be done and what ought not to be done, and why?

Often those who denigrate theorizing of the type (iv) kind show themselves to be inconsistent. This is the case, for example, when the objection to theory is expressed in some such way as, 'You get on with your philosophizing and leave me to get on with educating'. For, presumably, he who makes a remark such as this either must have some conception of what it is to educate, in which case he must have done some thinking, or else he has done no thinking at all, in which case it is difficult to see what he wants to be left to get on with. A last-ditch defender of the anti-theory thesis might claim that his is a consistent line in that he doesn't have to think at all about education in order to 'get on with educating' – he simply does what other people tell him to do. It's true that a claim like this would remove inconsistency, but at what cost? For the picture with which we are now faced is of a man content to serve as a mere agent, a mere tool of others, content to carry out to the letter instructions emanating from superiors in the institutional educational hierarchy. And even then hated theory will not have been disposed of; theorizing will now be carried on by the superiors, and, of course, it may be of a most unpalatable kind.

There are two main clusters of educational problems that await 'thinking through' and the basis of the division is made in accordance with the relative remoteness and relative nearness of the problems to classroom concerns. Thus, problems to do with equality of educational opportunity, the future of the public schools, the rights of parents as far as the education of their children are concerned, the place and relative importance of vocational education, and so on are examples that would figure in the first cluster. It is unlikely that a teacher of chemistry or of history would find that thinking about problems like these affects in any significant way his teaching of chemistry or history, his principal classroom concern. Now, in spite of this relative remoteness of such problems a strong case could surely be made for saying that all teachers *ought* to be aware of them, to have thought about them, and to be prepared to take an informed view on them. It is at least arguable that this is a duty incumbent upon any person who would count himself a member of a profession, apart from the fact that if educators are not prepared to think about such problems other people will and, further, will *act* on the basis of their conclusions.

The second cluster of problems has, in general, to do with the classroom. Some of them we have already considered in evaluation of the 'theory is unrelated to practice' thesis. But this thesis often takes the more precise form of 'Theory doesn't help me in the classroom'. As far as this cluster of problems is concerned, it has already been suggested that it's a very odd teacher indeed who can get by without any kind of thinking designed to illuminate day-to-day teaching – the teacher as mere agent. But now let us examine the more specific objection to theory in greater detail. Consider one or two examples of everyday classroom actions involving what is done and how it is done. Teachers of young children often read stories to them and often these stories have a moral point or punchline; some teachers favour the asking of questions by pupils, others tend to regard questions as no more than pointless interruptions to the free flow of exposition; different teachers operate different kinds of sanctions – punishment for essentially the same type of misdemeanour takes diverse forms; some teachers set great store by 'creative' activities (free expression in painting, writing, etc.), others set greater store by the mechanics of an activity (spelling and punc- tuation in the case, say, of writing). Examples like these could be multiplied almost indefinitely. Now, how can it be that thinking about these activities and techniques is of no assistance? Thus, suppose I ask a teacher who does not favour questions, 'Why don't you allow questions to be asked?', eliciting the reply, 'Because they learn more if I don't allow questions'. I then say, 'Do they understand what they learn?' and a dialogue then ensues about what it is to understand – and what it is to learn – the upshot of which is that the teacher is prepared to take a somewhat different approach and finds, perhaps, that there is a more precise definition of what he or she is doing, or ought to be doing. Again, with respect to the telling of stories, per- haps a teacher chose stories with a moral punchline in accord with a desire to do something in the way of moral education. Would not thinking about the whole notion of moral education help to suggest other techniques that might be tried, serve to render more clear what it *is* to educate morally? It is very difficult to believe that reflection on curriculum and teaching techniques does not provide, and never will provide, assistance to a serious-minded teacher intent on doing a good job.

So it should be unnecessary to say, 'Teachers ought to think about the why and wherefores of their everyday classroom practices' for the simple reason that such thinking is part of what is meant by 'teacher', not in the sense of 'child minder' or in the institutional sense of 'one whose job consists in going daily to a school', but in the normative sense of 'good teacher'.

There is one other point to be made about theory and practice in the classroom. It is that, at this level, theory and practice are intimately inter- connected and that the rigid dichotomy between them finding expression in 'Theory is one thing, practice another' is a false dichotomy. Obviously theory will modify practice and practice will modify theory. The notion of theorizing about classroom activities if one is not going to *try out* the theory and refine and modify it in the light of practice makes no kind of sense, or, at the very least, it is difficult to see what the point of the theorizing is meant to be. As a matter of fact teachers' objections to theory of the kind under discussion are usually objections to failure on the part of theorists to have sufficient regard to the practical side of the equation. The familiar complaint runs along the lines of arguing that lecturers in education have never known what classrooms and children are like, or have forgotten what they are like. Objections of this kind are not in reality objections to theory *per se* but the danger is that they will be mistakenly seen as such and result in decrying, not the present arrangements relating to, say, teaching practice, but the very act of thinking about teaching.

There is an even more specific interpretation of the 'theory is unrelated to practice' thesis. Someone might accept all that has been said so far but go on to observe that I have missed the point, which is that what is wanted from theory is a set of directions enabling all teachers to control their children, to keep discipline, a set of directions telling teachers what to do with youngsters who don't want to learn anything, are rebellious, and so on. Clearly, philosophical theorizing alone cannot provide direct, detailed specifications of this kind. I simply cannot see theory providing someone equipped with all the personality defects ever unearthed by psychologists with foolproof means of controlling and stimulating the interest of recalcitrant pupils. Nevertheless, careful thinking might ameliorate the conditions under which some teachers operate. Consider, for example, some of our practical arrangements governing the young probationer teacher. As far as one can judge it seems to be the case that a number of schools still operate in accordance with the principle that the new entrant to the profession has to prove his worth by showing that he can handle the roughest, toughest classes there happen to be. Either he cracks under the strain or, if he survives, he is eventually rewarded by being assigned to some of the 'A' forms when another unfortunate arrives. Is such practice justified? Is it not the case that questions of control and discipline ought not to be left to inexperienced young teachers to work out alone but that staffs as a whole should deal with them in concert, taking care that new members are shielded to some extent from direct confrontation with very difficult children and certainly supported if they run into difficulties? And is it not the case that teachers as a body ought to bring before society as a whole awareness of the disciplinary problems that exist in some schools as a reminder that the onus is not upon teachers alone to resolve these problems? Surely these are questions that need to be *thought* about.

Finally, there is a general objection to theory of type (iv) and, for that matter, to theory of type (iii). This general objection consists in pointing out that such theories do not provide *certainty*. They are grievously deficient in this respect compared with mathematical and scientific theories. Thus, it might be said that we have not provided *proof* that education is this rather than that, or ought to be concerned with this rather than that. Just as psychologists have not *demonstrated* that non-streaming is a more efficient way of organizing for teaching and learning than streaming, or that learning by discovery is more effective than learning by instruction. This is quite true. We have not provided proofs of the mathematical variety – the paradigm of proof – but could we, in logic, do so? It has to be recognized and faced up to that the matters of which we have treated involving, as was pointed out in the Introduction, fundamental questions of value at every turn, are not matters which can be treated mathematically or in accord with the procedures of natural science. Proof in the sense of mathematical demonstration, the QED of Euclid, is not to be had here and in its place, as was argued in the chapter on rationality, we can only offer *reasons* for thinking this rather than that. As Aristotle observed: 'for the man of education will seek exactness so far in each subject as the nature of the thing admits, it being plainly much the same absurdity to put up with a mathematician who tries to persuade instead of proving, and to demand strict demonstrative reasoning of a public speaker.'[2]

Because of this methodological fact – that mathematical proof is not to be had in all spheres – it must be the case that there will be differences of opinion on educational issues. In this book we have sought to show that people who are prepared to exercise their reason and powers of critical thought, and who are prepared to work to sharpen them, may come to firmly based opinions of their own – may, indeed, come to agree about some of those issues. And if they find agreement on some other issues hard to achieve they may come to accept the inevitability of disagreement and learn to live with it. Speaking to the Commonwealth Universities Congress about, *inter alia*, the idea that universities were seeking to restore a common culture, Sir Alan Bullock said, 'I don't believe that it existed in the past and I do not think it is desirable; it would be stifling, claustrophobic. I believe there have always been differences of opinion and cultural splits. The problems discussed in our universities are open-ended. There are no definite answers. If you do not like this pluralism you should not have been born; because it is what life is about.'[3]

Notes

1 Austin, J. L., *Sense and Sensibilia* (Oxford University Press, 1962) p. 3.
2 Aristotle, *The Nicomachean Ethics*, I (iii), 4.
3 Bullock, A., reported in *The Times*, 15 August 1973.

Further reading

See chapter 6, by Harold Entwistle, of J. W. Tibble (ed.), *An Introduction to the Study of Education* (London, Routledge & Kegan Paul, 1971), chapter 7 of *Introduction to Philosophy of Education* by J. Gribble (Boston, Allyn & Bacon, 1969) and P. H. Hirst's paper 'Educational Theory' in J. W. Tibble (ed.), *The Study of Education* (London, Routledge & Kegan Paul, 1966).

For a full list of the many useful articles published in the Journal of Philosophy of Education (previously *Proceedings of the Annual Conference of the Philosophy of Education Society of Great Britain*) see vol. 15, no. 2, 1981, and indices published in subsequent volumes.

Bibliography

Annis, David B. (1974), *Techniques of Critical Reasoning*, Columbus, Charles E. Merrill.

Archambault, R. (ed.) (1965), *Philosophical Analysis and Education*, London, Routledge & Kegan Paul.

Aries, Philippe (1986), *Centuries of Childhood*, Harmondsworth, Peregrine.

Austin, J. L. (1962), *Sense and Sensibilia*, Oxford, Oxford University Press.

Ayer, A. J. (1971), *Language, Truth and Logic*, Harmondsworth, Penguin.

Bailey, Charles (1984), *Beyond the Present and the Particular*, London, Routledge & Kegan Paul.

Bailin, S. (1988), *Achieving Extraordinary Ends*, Boston, MA, Kluwer.

Bantock, G. H. (1963), *Education in an Industrial Society*, London, Faber.

——(1968), *Culture, Industrialisation and Education*, London, Routledge & Kegan Paul.

——(1981), *Dilemmas of the Curriculum*, Oxford, Martin Robertson.

Barrow, Robin (1975), *Moral Philosophy for Education* London, Allen & Unwin.

——(1976), *Common Sense and the Curriculum*, London, Allen & Unwin.

——(1978), *Radical Education*, Oxford, Martin Robertson.

——(1981), *The Philosophy of Schooling*, Brighton, Wheatsheaf.

——(1982), *Injustice, Inequality and Ethics*, Brighton, Wheatsheaf.

——(1984), *Giving Teaching Back to Teachers*, Brighton, Wheatsheaf.

——(1990), *Understanding Skills: Thinking, Feeling and Caring*. London: Ontario, Althouse.

——(1993), *Language, Intelligence and Thought*, Aldershot, Hants, Edward Elgar.

——(2006), *Plato: His Precursors, Educational Thought and Legacy*, London, Continuum.

Barrow, Robin and Milburn, Geoffrey (1986), *A Critical Dictionary of Educational Concepts*, Brighton, Wheatsheaf.

Benn, S. I. and Peters, R. S. (1959), *Social Principles and the Democratic State*, London, Allen & Unwin.

Best, David (1978), *Philosophy and Human Movement*, London, Allen & Unwin.

Blackburn, Simon (2005), *Truth: A Guide*, Oxford, Oxford University Press.

Bloom, A. (1994), *The Western Canon*, New York, Harcourt Brace and Company.

Born, Rainer (ed.) (1987), *Artificial Intelligence: The Case Against*, London, Croom Helm.

Brent, A. (1978), *Philosophical Foundation for the Curriculum*, London, Allen & Unwin.

Bridges, David (1979), *Education, Democracy and Discussion*, London, NFER.

Bridges, David and Scrimhaw, Peter (eds) (1975), *Values and Authority in Schools*, London, Hodder & Stoughton.

Broks, Paul (2003), *Into the Silent Land*, New York, Atlantic Monthly Press.

Butler, Christopher (2002), *Postmodernism*, Oxford, Oxford University Press.

Callan, Eamonn (1993), *Autonomy and Schooling*, Ontario, McGill-Queen's University Press.

Carr, David (2003), *Making Sense of Education*, London, Routledge.

Cavalieri, P. and Singer, P. (eds) (1993), *The Great Ape Project*, London, Fourth Estate.

Chomsky, Noam (1967), *Syntactic Structures*, New York, Mouton.

Cohen, Brenda (1981), *Education and the Individual*, London, Allen & Unwin.

——(1982), *Means and Ends in Education*, London, Allen & Unwin.

Cooper, David E. (1980), *Illusions of Equality*, London, Routledge & Kegan Paul.

——(1983), *Authenticity and Learning*, London, Routledge & Kegan Paul.

——(ed.) (1986), *Education, Values and Mind*, London, Routledge & Kegan Paul.

Cotterill, Rodney (1989), *No Ghost in the Machine*, London, Heinemann.

Damasio, Antonio (2003), *Looking for Spinoza*, Toronto, Harcourt.

Dearden, R. F. (1968), *The Philosophy of Primary Education*, London, Routledge & Kegan Paul.

——(1976), *Problems in Primary Education*, London, Routledge & Kegan Paul.

——(1984), *Theory and Practice in Education*, London, Routledge & Kegan Paul.

Dearden, R. F., Hirst, P. H., and Peters, R. S. (eds) (1972) *Education and the Development of Reason*, London, Routledge & Kegan Paul.

Degenhardt, M. A. B. (1984), *Education and the Value of Knowledge*, London, Allen & Unwin.

Dennett, Daniel C. (2003), *Freedom Evolves*, New York, Viking.

Doyle, J. (1973), *Educational Judgments*, London, Routledge & Kegan Paul.

Dunkin, M. J. and Biddle, B. J. (1974), *The Study of Teaching*, New York, Holt Rinehart & Winston.

Dunlop, Francis (1984), *The Education of Feeling and Emotion*, London, Allen & Unwin.

Egan, Kieran (1979), *Educational Development*, New York, Oxford University Press.

——(1983), *Education and Psychology*, New York, Teachers College Press.

Eliot, T. S. (1962), *Notes Towards the Definition of Culture*, London, Faber.

Entwistle, H. (1970), *Education, Work and Leisure*, London, Routledge.

——(1970), *Child Centred Education*, London, Methuen.

——(1978), *Class, Culture and Education*, London, Methuen.

Flanagan, Owen (2002), *The Problem of the Soul*, New York, Basic Books.

Flew, Antony (ed.) (1956), *Essays in Conceptual Analysis*, London, Macmillan.

——(1975), *Thinking About Thinking*, London, Fontana/Collins.

——(1976), *Sociology, Equality and Education*, London, Macmillan.

Gaita, Richmond (1991), *Good and Evil: An Absolute Conception*, London, Macmillan.

Gingell, John and Brandon, Edwin (2000), *In Defence of High Culture*, Oxford, Blackwell.

Good, T. L. and Brophy. J. E. (1975), *Looking in Classrooms*, New York, Harper & Row.

Goodman, Paul (1971), *Compulsory Miseducation*, Harmondsworth, Penguin.

Gowin, D. Bob (1981), *Educating*, Ithaca, Cornell University Press.

Graham, Keith (1977), *J. L. Austin: A Critique of Ordinary Language Philosophy*, Hassocks, Harvester.

Gray, John (2002), *Straw Dogs: Thoughts on Humans and Other Animals*, London, Granta.

Gregory, I. M. and Woods, R. G. (1971), 'Valuable in Itself' in *Educational Philosophy and Theory*, vol. 3.

Gribble James (1969), *Introduction to Philosophy of Education*, Boston, MA, Allyn & Bacon.

——(1983), *Literary Education: A Revaluation*, Cambridge, Cambridge University Press.

Hare, R. M. (1952), *The Language of Morals*, Oxford, Oxford University Press.

Hare, W. (1979), *Open-Mindedness and Education*, Montreal, McGill-Queen's University Press.

——(1985), *Controversies in Teaching*, London, Ontario, Althouse Press.

Hepburn, R. W. (1972), 'The Arts and Education of Feeling and Emotion' in R. F. Dearden, P. H. Hirst, and R. S. Peters (eds) *Education and the Development of Reason* London, Routledge & Kegan Paul.

Hirst, P. H. (1974), *Knowledge and the Curriculum*, London, Routledge & Kegan Paul.

——(ed.) (1983), *Educational Theory and its Foundation Disciplines*, London, Routledge & Kegan Paul.

Hirst, P. H. and Peters, R. S. (1970), *The Logic of Education*, London, Routledge & Kegan Paul.

Holt, John (1969), *How Children Fail*, Harmondsworth, Penguin.

Hospers, John (1970), *Human Conduct*, London, Hart-Davis.

Hudson, Liam (1967), *Contrary Imaginations*, Harmondsworth, Penguin.

Illich, Ivan (1973), *Deschooling Society*, Harmondsworth, Penguin.

International Encyclopedia of Education (1994), Oxford, Pergamon.

Jonathan, Ruth (1997), *Illusory Freedoms*, Oxford, Blackwell.

Kleinig, John (1982), *Philosophical Issues in Education*, London, Croom Helm.

Langford, G. and O'Connor, D. J. (1973), *New Essays in the Philosophy of Education*, London, Routledge & Kegan Paul.

Levinson, Meira (2000), *The Demands of Liberal Education*, Oxford, Oxford University Press.

Lister, Ian (ed.) (1975), *Deschooling*, Cambridge, Cambridge University Press.

Lloyd, D. I. (ed.) (1976), *Philosophy and the Teacher*, London, Routledge & Kegan Paul.

Lucas, C. J. (ed.) (1969), *What is Philosophy of Education?* London Collier-Macmillan.

Lyotard, J. (1984), *The Postmodern Condition*, Minneapolis, University of Minnesota Press.

Lytton, Hugh (1971), *Creativity and Education*, London, Routledge & Kegan Paul.

McPeck, John (1981), *Critical Thinking and Education*, Oxford, Martin Robertson.

Marshall, James (1981), *What is Education?* New Zealand, Dunmore Press.

Mitchell, B. (ed.) (1971), *Philosophy of Religion*, Oxford, Oxford University Press.

Murray, C. (2003), *Human Accomplishment*, New York, HarperCollins.

Neill, A. S. (1968), *Summerhill*, Harmondsworth, Penguin.

Noddings, Nel (1984), *Caring*, Berkeley, University of California Press.

Nowell-Smith, P. H. (1958), *Education in a University*, Leicester, Leicester University Press.

O'Connor, D. J. (1975), *An Introduction to Philosophy of Education*, London, Routledge & Kegan Paul.

O'Hear, Anthony (1981), *Education, Society and Human Nature*, London, Routledge & Kegan Paul.

Peters, R. S. (1966), *Ethics and Education*, London, Allen & Unwin.

——(ed.) (1967), *The Concept of Education*, London, Routledge & Kegan Paul.

——(1973), *Authority, Responsibility and Education*, 3rd edn, London Allen & Unwin.

——(ed.) (1976), *Role of the Head*, London, Routledge & Kegan Paul.

——(1977), *Education and The Education of Teachers*, London, Routledge & Kegan Paul.

Pinker, Steven (2002), *The Blank Slate*, New York, Viking.

Plato (1974), *The Republic* (trs. Desmond Lee) Harmondsworth, Penguin.

Postman, N. and Weingartner, C. (1971), *Teaching as a Subversive Activity*, Harmondsworth, Penguin.

Pring, Richard (1976), *Knowledge and Schooling*, London, Open Books.

Ravitch, Diane (2003), *The Language Police*, New York, Alfred A. Knopf.

Reid, L. A. (1962), *Philosophy and Education*, London, Heinemann.

——(1986), *Ways of Understanding and Education* London, Heinemann.

Ridley, Matt (2003), *Nature via Nurture*, London, HarperCollins.

Rubinstein, D. and Stoneman, C. (1970), *Education for Democracy*, Harmondsworth, Penguin.

Ryle, G. (1956), *The Revolution in Philosophy*, London, Macmillan.

Scheffler, I. (1973), *Reason and Teaching*, London, Routledge & Kegan Paul.

——(1985), *Of Human Potential*, Boston, Routledge & Kegan Paul.

Scriven, Michael (1976), *Reasoning*, New York, McGraw Hill.

Scruton, Roger (1999), 'Whatever happened to reason?', *City Journal*, vol. 9, no. 2.

Sealey, John (1985), *Religious Education: Philosophical Perspectives*, London, Allen & Unwin.

Searle, John (1984), *Minds, Brains and Science*, Cambridge, MA, Harvard University Press.

——(2004), *Mind: A Brief Introduction*, Oxford University Press.

Simpson, Douglas, J. and Jackson, Michael J. B. (1984), *The Teacher as Philosopher*, Toronto, Methuen.

Snook, I. (ed.) (1972), *Concepts of Indoctrination*, London, Routledge & Kegan Paul.

Sockett, Hugh (ed.) (1980), *Accountability in the English Educational System*, London, Hodder & Stoughton.

Sokel, Alan and Briemont, Jean (1998), *Intellectual Imposters*, London, Profile.

Stevenson, C. L. (1944), *Ethics and Language*, New Haven, Yale University Press.

Straughan, Roger (1982), *I Ought to But*, Windsor, NFER.

——(1983), *Can We Teach Children to be Good?* London, Allen & Unwin.

Straughan, Roger and Wilson, John (1983), *Philosophising about Education*, New York, Holt, Rinehart & Winston.

Strike, K. (1982), *Liberty and Education*, Oxford, Martin Robertson.

Strike, K. and Egan, K. (eds) (1978), *Ethics and Educational Policy*, London, Routledge & Kegan Paul.

Tarnas, Richard (1991), *The Passion of the Western Mind*, New York, Ballantine Books.

Tooley, James (2000), *Reclaiming Education*, London, Cassell.

Vivian, Frederick (1969), *Thinking Philosophically*, London, Chatto &Windus.

Waller, John (2002), *Einstein's Luck*, Oxford, Oxford University Press.

Warnock, Mary (1970), *Existentialism*, Oxford, Oxford University Press.

——(1977), *Schools of Thought*, London, Faber.

Wheen, Francis (2004), *How Mumbo-Jumbo Conquered the World*, London, Fourth Estate.

White, J. P. (1973), *Towards a Compulsory Curriculum*, London, Routledge & Kegan Paul.

——(1982), *The Aims of Education Restated*, London, Routledge & Kegan Paul.

White, Patricia (1983), *Beyond Domination*, London, Routledge & Kegan Paul.

Whitfield, R. (ed.) (1971), *Disciplines of the Curriculum*, New York, McGraw Hill.

Wilson, John (1963), *Thinking with Concepts*, Cambridge, Cambridge University Press.

——(1979), *Fantasy and Common Sense in Education*, Oxford, Martin Robertson.

——(1979), *Preface to the Philosophy of Education*, London, Routledge & Kegan Paul.

——(1986), *What Philosophy Can Do*, Basingstoke, Macmillan.

Wilson, P. S. (1969), 'Child-Centred Education' in *Proceedings of the Annual Conference*, Philosophy of Education Society of Great Britain, January, vol. 3.

——(1971), *Interest and Discipline in Education*, London, Routledge & Kegan Paul.

Winch, Christopher (1998), *The Philosophy of Human Learning*, London, Routledge.

Winch, Christopher and Gingell, John (2004), *Philosophy and Educational Policy*, London, Routledge.

Wisdom, J. (1963), *Problems of Mind and Matter*, Cambridge University Press.

Wittrock, Merlin C. (ed.) (1986), *Handbook of Research on Teaching*, 3rd edn, New York, Macmillan.

Wright, Nigel (1977), *Progress in Education*, London, Croom Helm.

Wringe, Colin (1981), *Children's Rights*, London, Routledge & Kegan Paul.

Young, J. Z. (1987), *Philosophy and the Brain*, Cambridge, Oxford University Press.

Index

Also by Robin Barrow

What Use is Educational Research? A Debate (with L. Foreman-Peck)
Plato: His Precursors, Educational Thought, and Legacy
Language, Intelligence and Thought
Utilitarianism: A Contemporary Statement
Understanding Skills: Thinking, Feeling and Caring
A Critical Dictionary of Educational Concepts (with G. Milburn)
Giving Teaching Back to Teachers
Language and Thought
Injustice, Inequality and Ethics
The Philosophy of Schooling
Radical Education
Plato's Apology
Happiness
The Canadian Curriculum
Moral Philosophy for Education
Plato, Utilitarianism and Education
Plato and Education
Athenian Democracy
Sparta
Greek and Roman Education
Common Sense and the Curriculum

Edited by Robin Barrow
Academic Ethics (with P. Keeney)
Beyond Liberal Education (with P. White)

Also by R.G. Woods
Education and its Disciplines (ed.)

CPSIA information can be obtained at www.ICGtesting.com
Printed in the USA
LVOW011403111111

254550LV00001B/1/P